ACcIdentaLLy in TraNSiT

Murray Laurence grew up in Sydney where he attended the University of Sydney for the study of psychology and government. His serious education began on a hot night in December 1968 when he arrived at a ramshackle airport in Jakarta. So began a long involvement with Indonesia and the Asian region, and a predilection for travel, always undertaken with one eye out for the unexpected. He has since wandered and worked throughout much of Europe, Asia and South America and now lives in Sydney with his wife and two children. His first book, *High Times in the Middle of Nowhere*, a collection of off-beat travel encounters, has just been re-released in a new paperback edition by UQP. Murray Laurence is professionally involved in the overseas marketing of Australian education, an occupation which takes him frequently to Asia and beyond.

Accidentally in Transit

The further misadventures of MURRAY LAURENCE compulsive traveller

Maps by Janet Laurence and Michael Snape

University of Queensland Press

First published 1991 by University of Queensland Press,
Box 42, St Lucia, Queensland 4067 Australia

© Murray Laurence 1991

This book is copyright. Apart from any fair dealing
for the purposes of private study, research, criticism
or review, as permitted under the Copyright Act, no
part may be reproduced by any process without written
permission. Enquiries should be made to the publisher.

Typeset by University of Queensland Press
Printed in Australia by The Book Printer, Victoria

Distributed in the USA and Canada by
International Specialized Book Services, Inc.,
5602 N.E. Hassalo Street, Portland, Oregon 97213-3640

Cataloguing in Publication Data
National Library of Australia

Laurence, Murray, 1948-
    Accidentally in transit.

    1. Laurence, Murray, 1948-   . Journeys. 2. Asia,
    Southeastern — Description and travel. 3. South
    America — Description and travel — 1981-   . I.
    Title.

910.4

ISBN 0 7022 2324 7

To Judith and Graham Laurence

Contents

Acknowledgments *ix*
Preface   *xi*

Wake up in transit   *1*
The one about the Spanish-speaking Italians who imagine that they're Englishmen living in Paris *(Buenos Aires, Argentina)*   *23*
High times near Paraguay *(The Iguassu Falls, Argentina)*   *39*
A matter concernin' a bicycle *(Castlebar, Ireland)*   *49*
Blame it on the bossa nova *(Rio de Janeiro, Brazil)*   *69*
Not quite into the heart of darkness *(Manaus, Brazil)*   *83*
On low beam in China *(China)*   *95*
Stopover in Salvador *(Salvador, Bahia, Brazil)*   *137*
Accidental Surfer *(Rio de Janeiro, Brazil)*   *157*
Side-tracked in Brazil *(Brazil)*   *172*
Tasmania in a hurry *(Tasmania, Australia)*   *203*

Acknowledgments

These pieces have been published in whole or in part in the following:
"The one about the Spanish-speaking Italians who imagine that they're Englishmen living in Paris" as "High Times in Buenos Aires" – *Times on Sunday*
"High times near Paraguay" as "Veils of Vapour" – *Flight Deck*
"Blame it on the bossa nova" as "Rio's Got Rhythm and Scanty Biquinis" – Good Weekend, *Sydney Morning Herald*
"Stopover in Salvador" as "Accidentally in Bahia" – Australian *Playboy*
"Tasmania in a hurry" – *Flight Deck*
"Not quite into the heart of darkness" as "Dateline: Manaus" – Good Weekend, *Sydney Morning Herald*

Extracts throughout the book are from: *Poems by C.P. Cavafy* translated by John Mavrogodato (Chatto and Windus, London, 1971); *Fodor's 89 Brazil* (Fodor's Travel Publications, New York, 1988); *Tieta*, Jorge Amado (Abacus, London, 1979); *The Beautiful Empire*, Zulfikar Ghose (Macmillan, London, 1975); *Beyond the Silver River*, Jimmy Burns (Bloomsbury, London, 1989); *Maíra*, Darcy Ribeiro (Aventura, New York, 1984); *Garôta de Ipanema*, Antonio Carlos Jobim and Vinicius de Moraesi; *Historic Malacca Pot-Pourri*, Robert Tan Sin Nyen (Malacca, 1990).

I would like to express my thanks for their support and assistance to the following: the University of Queensland Press and especially Craig Munro (who persevered with the view that my compulsive travelling was worth reading about) and Nicola Evans; Ivonne Correa and Shireen Win Pe who typed the manuscript; Eliot Taylor; the Australian missionaries in Montes Claros; Aerolineas Argentinas and Varig Brazilian Airlines; my family, Maureen, Daniel and Andrei, who with good humour put up with the travel and the writing; the map-makers, Janet Laurence and Michael Snape who may have been influenced by Flann O'Brien's de Selby ("Of all the many striking statements made by de Selby, I do not think that any of them can rival his assertion that 'a journey is an hallucination' "), and finally, the hundreds of Indians, Chinese, Australians, Arabs, Brazilians and others who, knowingly or not, populated my own journeys and stopovers.

Preface

Notes from the Departure Lounge

The use of travelling is to regulate imagination by reality, and instead of thinking how things may be, to see them as they are.

Samuel Johnson

After the publication of *High Times in the Middle of Nowhere*, I was interviewed by Sydney radio personality Margaret Throsby for the Qantas in-flight audio magazine. Here is an excerpt:

M.T.   Where wouldn't we find you, then?
M.L.   Well, I don't want to slander any country . . .
M.T.   No . . . on a list of fascination, for instance, one that might be a bit further down the list.
M.L.   Korea.
M.T.   Mmm
M.L.   Even though it's an Asian country and I'm very involved in Asia, it's a very . . . ah . . . it doesn't attract me . . . because there doesn't seem to be the type of . . . cultural diversity that you get in India or Indonesia, for example, or Brazil.
M.T.   Mmm. Did Brazil contain surprises for you?

Why, then, am I to be found here, sitting in the Cathay Pacific lounge at Seoul's Kimpo airport, awaiting a flight to Malaysia? I've just spent ten days in Seoul, my second visit within twelve months. And what have I made of the place, I wonder. Was my earlier, completely ill-informed opinion, to which Margaret Throsby responded "Mmm", at all valid?

Let's face it, Korea is an enigma. Between the Korean war and the Seoul Olympics in 1988 almost no-one took any notice of the country. In Australia it was known mainly as a source both of beautiful children for adoption and of secretive, hard-working immigrants. Galaxy class travel-writers like Jan Morris or Paul Theroux or Eric Newby never go there — or never write about it — and the only television coverage we have of the place is of the absurd theatrics of the peace talks at Panmunjom and of periodic riots — equally theatrical — staged by students and police.

But in the mid-eighties people began to notice that almost everything they bought was made in Korea. When the Australian government woke up to this they commissioned a report called *Australia and the Northeast Asian Ascendancy*. This report argued that Australia had until about the end of the century to attract more of those hard-working Koreans. After that they would be too rich to bother moving.

Leaving for Seoul a fortnight ago I bought some gifts at the airport for my Korean contacts. These included cigarette lighters embossed with pictures of Australian wildlife and coasters and ash-trays with images of the Opera House, Harbour Bridge — all the usual. The first man to whom I presented a cigarette lighter lit a cigarette (first things first) turned the lighter over and read, loudly, "Made in Korea". Fortunately he and the other lucky recipients of these trinkets thought that the compliment was intended.

So the Koreans have been creating their industrial nation on the quiet and now it's their turn to decide if they want or need to visit us: "Tourism's up 75% this year," enthused a visa officer, desperate for numbers, at the Australian embassy in Seoul. But more often they're choosing to go to Paris, New York or Los Angeles where there is a chance of them doing some shopping and not bringing home stuff they made in the first place.

This book is about travel I undertook in the late eighties early 1990s. In *High Times* I reported on interminable journeys across the Indian sub-continent in shambling, seething railway trains, on river-boat voyages into the heart of Borneo, on days and nights spent in starless hotels in Vientiane, Calcutta, Phuket, Samarinda and many places on and off the map in between. They were travels made whether or not they seemed like a good idea at the time, travels without guide books and usually without maps (indeed, the Sherpa Society in Kathmandu still uses a map drawn by me and some friends of a trekking route in East Nepal — or so I'm told).

In the foreword I wrote that "my travels and my writing about travel are a celebration of chance, purposelessness and movement." Further, I revealed, "I find that the travel is often more absorbing than the arrival. This is perhaps the secret of those tourists who never leave the bus."

Nowadays my travels are usually rushed, pre-planned strikes, always with a purpose and invariably involving journeys by aircraft and taxis. The trains and the river-boats (except, of course, the Pearl of the Orient dinner cruise in Hong Kong or the Meeting of the Waters tour on the Amazon) are sadly off my itinerary.

This visit to Korea has been typical. And while there may be people still travelling as I reported in *High Times* — I saw some recently in Jogjakarta — I suspect that most journeys are a bit like mine.

The world's departure lounges, 747s, customs halls and hotel lobbies are full of men in suits with names like Hartmut Krebs and Cha Jae Woo. There are Germans and Koreans selling components for nuclear power stations to Lybian and Saudi middlemen; Vietnamese men counter-trading shipments of nuclear waste for tonnes of slag-cement; Americans going to semi-conductor, high-carbon steel wire or injection moulding machine trade fairs; French businessmen selling high-speed trains, missiles and culture; chain-smoking Bangladeshis trying to interest Iranians in Indian-made laser printers and locomotives or Chinese-made atomising sprayers and medi socks; Koreans and Taiwanese with sales catalogues of everything from super-tankers to electric hoists and cigarette lighters; Australians in batik shirts or safari suits arranging meetings with Egyptian and Kuwaiti buyers of shiploads of live sheep or on their way to trade shows in Budapest or Winnipeg where they'll demonstrate lawn spiking machines and automatic sprinklers; and Pakistani generals off to report on the military situation in Manila (hem, hem).

Most of us, "des compagnons de Boeing ou de salles de transit" (to use Jean-Claude Guillebaud's phrase), sit against one another trying to avoid conversation or even recognition of a fellow species. But there is always the garrulous Polish trade official, the Pakistani military attaché or retired Australian hockey team manager who wants to turn your flight into an eight-hour monologue. Then there are the people who, for the time being, are Soviets — mostly Lithuanians, Latvians and other rattletrap Balts — embarked upon futile missions to sell coal, tractor exhausts or truck tyres to the world. If they don't speak English the blessing is only marginal: they brattle at the rest of their party, scattered around the smoking section of the plane like smouldering grey feedbags. If they do speak English, the entire cabin is rewarded with a live commentary on the movie, delivered with Baltic or Russian heartiness:

"Ha! Ha! Ha! Now man is gettink into hollow copta!"

"Ha! Ha! Inside is surprise! Womans mint guns machine."

"Ha! Ha! Her is tellink to man gettink into hollow copta: 'Gettink off trouser-pants!' "

Even Indians don't become this involved in the movies.

So if this is travel, is there anything at all to celebrate?

Well, as some of the stories in this book show, the chance and the purposelessness are still around, even, as I've recently discovered, when you're away on business in Korea.

The foreign businessman arrives in Seoul in the middle of a bleak, heartless winter. Who are these people, he wonders. They look like Asiatic Finns, remote northerners who've strayed across the 42nd parallel and down into this peninsular from Gory Byrranga or some other frozen tundra-land, delivering their own version of a Finno Ugric language in a succession of slight sneezing fits, living in their strange square buildings, decorated at night with their bright square writing. Most of them appear to be inexpressive men, dressed in dark blue poly suits and black overcoats, black slip-ons and white socks, driving their black Hyundai Sonatas and Excels or Daewoo Grandeurs through this wintry haze of cement dust and iced kerosine particles. The trees they drive past are *wrapped-up* in rope; the planter boxes are full of green and purple cabbages! What must *North* Korea be like, ponders the foreigner.

And then the taxi-driver breaks the ice. He offers his passenger a gulp from his bottle of Glenmorangie or Black Douglas and then opens the glove box to reveal a display of perfumes, cigarette lighters, aftershaves, world-time calculators, stationary, miniature bottles of alcohol and Nintendo games. Such enterprise, concludes the foreign businessman. Which is, after all, why he's here.

Once in his hotel the businessman phones his contacts. It is always a Mr Lee, Mr Kim, Mr Song, maybe a Mr Park. He is always the president of the company and is never in. The receptionists, using their softest voices, promise to pass on the message. Then the visitor waits in his room, or wanders about the austere lobby wondering about the tides of Korean men who flow in and out and about the Americans who are lucky enough to meet them, their stern voices hovering like shining sermons over the hubbub of the atrium and coffee shop.

When, finally, the visitor makes contact with Mr Lee (or Mr Kim or Mr Song) he is greeted with enthusiasm and with the words that frighten all foreigners to death (except maybe Japanese and Poles): "I HOPE YOU LIKE DRINKING!"

Business in Korea, the businessman soon discovers, consists mostly of going to *room-sarongs*, where you sit on heated floors around a low table and order as many bottles of beer as will fit on the table, as well as plates of *kim-chi*, fried fish and fruit. These are impatiently consumed and then you move on to another *room-sarong* where the beer is replaced by whisky. "I hope you like drinking!" the foreigner's hosts keep warning.

Final negotiations take place in a karaoke club, a Japanese entertainment that has spread vertically from Sapporo to Melbourne with astonishing speed.

Even here, life is chancy enough for the foreign businessman. There are few pastimes more alarming than being in a KOK club with several hundred crazy, dog-fed Korean men filling the black air with fire and garlic, and being forced to sing *You Are My Sunshine, Country Roads* or *Killing Me Softly*. Solo is horrifying enough, but with Mr Kim and the others swivelling savagely all around him, every line drenching the visitor in hot alcohol, it becomes a party to oblivion.

When not doing business in this way in Seoul your visitor spends a lot of time in taxis in horizon to horizon traffic jams. But there is a dramatic shortage of cabs and the streets, night and day, are full of aggressive men hurling abuse, folded umbrellas and themselves at Sonata after Sonata demanding to be taken somewhere. The drivers of these cars sit, immobile and unimpressed – not even lowering their windows – until, without a sign, the doors unlock and the chosen blue suits fall in.

This incomprehensible system for securing a taxi means that the foreign businessman often finishes up on the subway – particularly if his meetings conclude at about 6.30 pm when the streets of Seoul have about them the ambience of the running of the bulls in Pamplona.

Underground, by contrast, it's more of an English soccer riot quelled by sudden bouts of narcolepsy. The visitor is transported on a hurricane of limbs through the labyrinths beneath the streets, until he finds himself pushed through the doors of a waiting train. Here everyone abruptly falls asleep, the lucky ones jammed onto benches, most dangling from handles, their bodies compressed into crushed cylinders.

So here I am, eyes out for Yoksam, feeling like one of those rope-wrapped trees in a dense forest of overcoats. There has already been a fight on the platform between two groups of men who, in proposing to help me, had disagreed about which line I should take. The winners have bundled me into this train, squeezed themselves in somewhere and gone to sleep.

Looking at the sleeping faces around me, I keep thinking that I see people I know . . . Mr Kim, Miss Kwan, Mr Chung.

"Oh, is that you, Mr Kim?" or "Ah, Miss Kwan, what a surprise" . . . but the sleeper does not stir, and indeed is probably not my Mr Kim nor my Miss Kwan.

Then there is a voice: "I'm a Canadian and I can't stand this either." The voice coincides with finger-movements across the front of my trousers.

"Christ," I think, "a pickpocket who's got the wrong pocket."

I look around to identify the voice. I'm looking for . . . well, a Canadian who is awake.

The pickpocket is still busy with my trousers, but I can't move my own hands to intercept his.

Just as I conclude that there are no Canadians, awake or asleep, in the area of the car that I can see, the voice says:

"Mr Chang Soon, from Vancouver," and a face materialises like a spirit from the midst of the slumbering masses.

Mr Soon's hand wriggles away from where it had first made contact with me and up through the hot glomerations of wool to reveal itself in front of my eyes carrying a business card reading Prince World Song International, with Vancouver and Seoul addresses.

Saying again that he can't stand the crush, Mr Soon proceeds to harass me with a business opportunity: key-rings.

Prince World Song International, he explains, specialises in the manufacture of key-rings with an attached battery-operated beam. But the real feature — the unique Prince World Song International variation — are the designs that fit onto the back of the disc that holds the light. Nude girls, the Princess of Wales, American and Korean flags, the Taj Mahal, the Sydney Opera House, pandas, horses . . . Mr Soon struggles with a catalogue of these designs whilst I explain that I, too, don't like the crush, nor doing business within its grip. Mr Soon is not put off: I can buy 500 of these unique key rings — just specify the images that I want — at a special, introductory price; they'll be ready at my hotel within 24 hours . . .

"Listen," I interrupt. "I'm looking for Yoksam where I have to get off. That's all I'm interested in."

This gives Mr Soon another opening. He'll tell me when we're at Yoksam, and come with me to my hotel where we can talk business. Perhaps I'd be interested in a franchise arrangement . . . help him to develop a market for his products in Australia, find cheaper manufacturers in Thailand or Indonesia.

"By the way, I hope you like drinking," he warmly cautions.

"These people are half-cut," concludes the foreigner, preparing himself at breakfast for another hazardous day and night. But imagine North Korea, he thinks again, reading in the newspaper the North Korean Central News Agency's report on the visit by the South Korean president to Moscow:

SPLITTIST'S TRIP
We cannot regard Roh's forthcoming visit to the Soviet Union as anything other than a flunkyist, division seeking trip and part of the open anti-Pyongyang manoeuvres in essence. Roh's visit will result in doubling his indelible crimes against history and the nation and in perpetuating his isolation and destruction.

So, finally, what about Korea — the flunkyist south — and what I said to Margaret Throsby in that interview?

Well, clearly, I was wrong and the high times and the fascination are there as much as anywhere else; whether you notice them or not just depends on what you're looking for. For travellers like myself and the Mr Songs, Mr Krebs and Mr Moustaphas of the transit lounges, most of what happens is an irritant. One is the victim of everyone else's just being there. But by design or accident, I look at the bright or hazy edges, the sidelines and sideshows, for if it weren't for all those hard-case Koreans, dingy Russians and Pakistani windbags I'd have to be like those grizzled British journofantasists (as Salman Rushdie calls them) and take 6 months off to cycle through the Shia valleys of Lebanon, raft down the Mekong or wait for the last shrapnel-scarred 727 out of Kisangani or Luanda.

Malaccan Footnote

I have come to this torpid Malaysian city — for the first time in over 20 years — seeking some historical connections. After all, I've spent quite a lot of time over the past few years in Brazil, Goa and Portugal and here is a place whose name just resonates with the history of the Portuguese empires.

According to local character and historian Robert Tan Sin

Nyen, Malacca was founded by a Hindu Prince from Palembang in Sumatra in 1400. In the wake of Chinese, Indian and Arab traders, the Portuguese arrived in 1509.

This is how Tan in his book, *Historic Malacca Pot-pourri*, records their century:

> With trade, in particular spices, flourishing in Malacca . . . the first Portuguese to land in Malacca in 1509 was Admiral Dom Diego Lopez de Sequerah. He came with the intention of establishing trade relations, but the local traders did not welcome competition. Admiral Dom Diego Lopez de Sequerah's expedition was, therefore, a total failure and his ships were attacked and his entourage captured. Nonetheless Admiral Dom Diego Lopez de Sequerah managed to escape from Malacca and returned to Goa, India where he reported to the Portuguese authorities there of his very awful experiences. This resulted in the Portuguese conquering Malacca on 25th July 1511 under the command of Admiral Alfonso d'Alburquerque. Thus the Portuguese not only enjoyed the control of the spice trade in Malacca for 130 years, but they also brought Christianity to this region, that is Catholicism.
>
> The Dutch a far more formidable rival of the Portuguese, made their appearance in Malacca in 1640 . . .

So here is a real pot-pourri for the diligent traveller to explore, but . . . as I was coming down from Kuala Lumpur in a shared taxi, you see, there were these two enormous European men on the back seat. They were from Hungary and had been at a Mister Universe contest in Kuala Lumpur, and were now going to Malacca to meet some of their friends and some of the other contestants at the Ramada hotel. That's where I would be staying.

Later I see them at the pool. There are about a dozen Mr Universes sitting around like upended dump-trucks, a number of Ms Universes (a terrifying sight, those construction slab shoulders appearing out of small bikini tops) as well as a few wives and girlfriends. The sideshow *and* the freaks.

I am greeted by one of the Hungarians from the taxi and invited to join him and his wife at a table. We chat for a while and then Mr Universe challenges me to a race across the pool. Glad that it wasn't an arm wrestle that was proposed, I accept. We dive in and I beat him easily — leaving him waddling across the pool like a bloated toddler, his muscles sinking like leaky lilo rolls.

"He's not much of a Mr Universe in the pool," I declare to his wife (only joking, only joking).

She gets the joke. Watching him struggle to the surface and up the side of the pool, she laughs, a wanton Hungarian roar. "He's maybe not so much Mr Universe in bedroom, too," she replies, pointing accusingly in the direction of the sugar lump buried somewhere within his massive thighs.

How did this happen, I wonder. How did I become mixed-up in this stump-yard of Italian and Hungarian body builders when I should be out looking at other, wider universes and trying to pull from the shadows the spice-laden currents and gold-spun threads of time and geography?

My excuse, poor perhaps, is found in a recent *Economist* survey of travel and tourism. Betting that today most ordinary tourists would choose Disney over Dominica, the magazine concludes that, "When families say, as in one of the Walt Disney World theme parks they do say, 'We did France this morning, let's do Mexico', and move from one pavilion to another, travel will have finally been stripped of that sense of purpose that Dr Johnson thought was so important."

Seoul, Korea
Malacca, Malaysia
February and March 1991

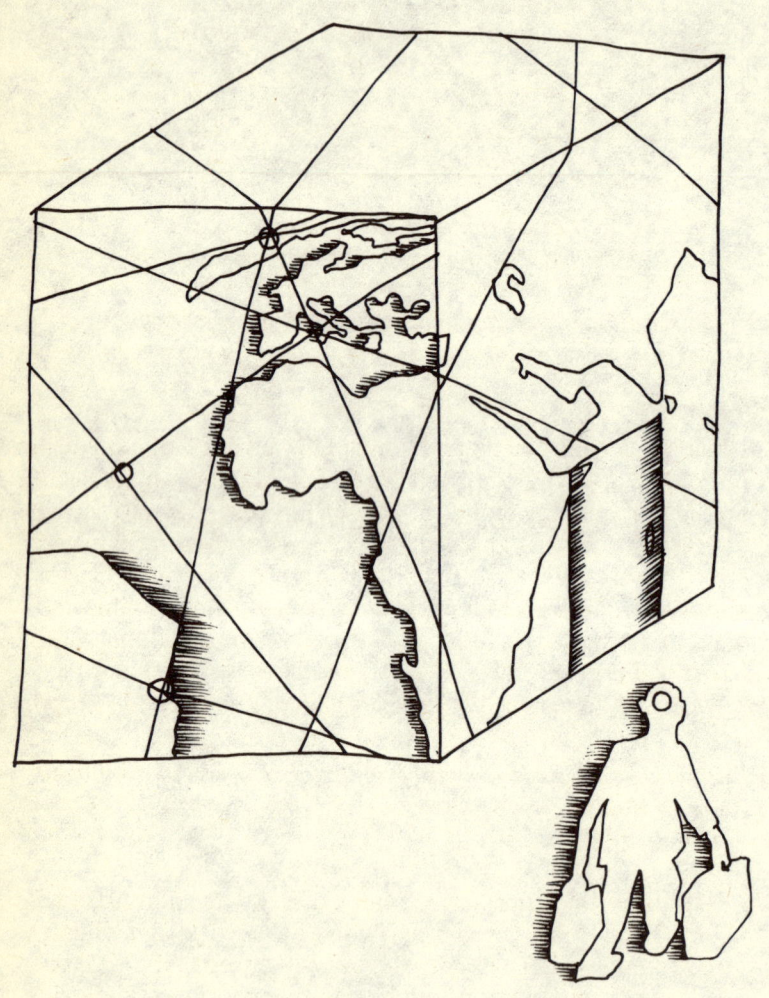

Wake up in transit

Setting out on the voyage to Ithaka
You must pray that the way be long,
Full of adventures and experiences.
The Laistrygonians, and the Kyklopes,
Angry Poseidon, — don't be afraid of them;
You will never find such things on your way,
If only your thoughts be high, and a select
Emotion touch your spirit and your body.
The Laistrygonians, the Kyklopes,
Poseidon raging — you will never meet them,
Unless you carry them with you in your soul,
If your soul does not raise them up before you.

C.P. Cavafy, *Ithaka*

During a recent Northern Hemisphere spring, an expedition of twenty-eight Swedes and seven Sherpas began an assault on the north-facing slopes of Mount Everest. Around the corner, twenty Americans and their Sherpas, eleven Spaniards, two Italians and ten Sherpas as well as twenty-three Czechoslovakian climbers, four Sherpas and an entire film crew were hurrying to the summit. The traffic was such that a British expedition retreated to Kathmandu to await a clear run.

Meanwhile, several Japanese students were roller-skating across Australia, another group was preparing to soar in a kite over the English channel and the Australian adventurer Tim Macartney-Snape had also set out to scale Everest — starting in the quagmire at the mouth of the Ganges, thousands of kilometres away to the south.

At about the same time, Stan Cottrel was running across China, Rick Hansen was crossing half the world in a wheelchair, Mohammed Abas Ali was walking from Abu Dhabi to Mecca and an unnamed Indonesian had set out to walk sideways across Java. As well, there were reports of an English bishop traversing the Sudan pushing a Chinese sailing wheelbarrow, and of course Indians continued to criss-cross their nation using many means of locomotion, including the famous Mount Abu three-step (prostration-walk-prostration) and the Bengal sideways roll.

Everywhere people seem to be embarking upon the most extraordinary and personal of journeys. And as the so-called Golden Age of travel retreats further into the sea-fog of memory, so these epic and eccentric attempts to find one more challenge, one more mode of transport that has not been tried before, one more void on the map, are becoming more numerous.

For most of us, however, the voids we fill in on the map are mere transit points and stopovers.

I first became aware of the possibility and meaning of being "in transit" when I landed at Bangkok airport on my first ever visit to Thailand about twenty-three years ago. As I was walking down the corridors towards customs, I noticed a group of people walking beside me behind a glass wall. They were Europeans and their most impressive feature was their clothing. They were dressed in thick pullovers, jackets and long boots. I had rarely seen people dressed like this and as they headed towards a room labelled "Transit" it struck me as astonishing that people could travel across the world, touch down in one country and, wearing the clothes of another hemisphere, await a flight to somewhere else.

Since then I have had a few transit stops myself. A couple of years ago I spent several days flying to South America. The first leg finished with a twenty-four hour stopover in Tahiti.

Arriving in Papeete late at night, I was greeted by a Tahitian band and dancers. The girls had what looked like brown flowerpots over their breasts, while the men had leaves and branches in their hair. All of them were so relaxed in their role that only their great, slowly shuffling feet kept them from toppling over backwards with drowsiness. Why had we been greeted in this way, I wondered.

Later, having checked into a hotel, I asked the receptionist about going down to the port for a look. He was so alarmed that I wanted to do this that he closed his hotel and drove me to town in his van. Normally I give foreign cities the benefit of the doubt and walk around at night quite freely, but this enormous Tahitian's worries really gave me the shivers, so instead of promenading I went straight to a *roulotte* — a fast food van — and ordered a pizza. Then, as I ate it, the proprietor, a thin *Marsaillais*, said he'll tell me a joke.

"All right, what's the joke?" I asked.

" 'Ere she is," he said, and then announced the following things.

"One: never eat anything bigger than your head." (He actually said: *"Un: never heat any sink big zen you ed"*, but I will avoid the phonetic transcription.)

"Two: never eat anything that looks like vomit."

"Three: never eat anything that's the colour of blood."

He roared.

"And?" I said.

"So," he shouted, "look at what you are eating!"

The next day I decided to take the ferry to the spectactular island of Moorea. Sitting around me were parties of American tourists whose conversation perfectly expressed the in-transit perspective.

"Humid here," one remarked.

"Was warm in San Francisco," someone responded.

"Hot in Honolulu," added another.

"Windy in Sydney."

"Shit in Melbourne."

"Dry in Canberra."

"Auckland . . . what was it in Auckland?"

Such observations kept them sufficiently preoccupied that they missed the vision of Moorea, looming out of the satiny spray of the Pacific like a jagged black hole in the world, until we were right under its very peaks.

On the return journey there was a lot of drinking going on. At the bar another man wanted to tell me a joke.

"The English got Australia," he chortled, "but the French got Paradise."

"But at least the English gave Australia up," I responded, bringing the jokes to an abrupt end.

And that — aside from a vision of women in the suburbs dressed in bikinis washing their cars, a sight that suggested Punchbowl rather than Paradise — was Tahiti. The next stop was Easter Island, or Rapa Nui as the Polynesians know it.

* * *

There is something both exhilarating and troubling about flying through a night and a dawn across a paralysing vastness of ocean, with nothing below except perhaps Pitcairn Island for a second, to emerge from the clouds heading towards a rocky island of only a few square kilometres. You marvel that the crew managed to find it. Even more, I marvelled at our landing. We were approaching the airstrip from the northwest, everyone peering through the windows for a glimpse of the island's famous *moai*, the monolithic stone heads. Seconds before touchdown, the jet, an elderly 707, swerved to the right and proceeded to circumnavigate the island, *below the level of the cliffheads*, to come in from the opposite direction. During this half circle, thoughts of the monoliths were banished as passengers contemplated the great rocks and surging surf not far below our under-carriage.

During this descent I had been unable to bring my seat-back forward.

"*Que pasa con ésto?*" (What's the matter with it?) a man behind me asked.

"Don't know. Seems to be broken," I replied.

"Buggered eh? Do you want me to stick the boot in?" he suddenly proposed. The broad Australian with a Spanish accent was a startling reminder that many of the passengers were Latin Americans from Australia, visiting their home countries.

Moments later we were deposited on one of the most isolated islands in all the world — yet one that we had all marvelled at through primary school, never imagining that our travels would ever take us to so baffling a place.

I stood at the utter western limits of Chile, over 3400 kilometres from Santiago, and tried to imagine how Chile came to be in possession of this island in the first place, and why she had advanced this far, but no further, into the Pacific. And I contemplated the little commented-upon fact that Chile and Australia, while not exactly neighbours, faced each other across the Pacific Ocean, and were each, at that time, trying to ensure that they were included in plans for the Asian-Pacific century.

The Rapa Nui stopover used to be about five hours. Then tours were available, taking sightseers to the principal monoliths. Lan Chile has brought the halt back to an hour, and now the tour operators stare at you glumly from behind their counters and try to sell you Easter Island heads on key rings, bottle-openers and paper-weights, even some suspended in snowstorms. One stall offered a thirty-minute tour, but was not clear as to what you would actually see.

My fellow passengers demonstrated the unsettling ambiguity of modern travel. There were Chileans dressed for Punta Arenas and Tierra del Fuego in fur-lined boots and jackets with hoods. Had they boarded the plane like that in Tahiti, I wondered, and what did they know about Santiago that the rest of us didn't? In particular that the Swedes didn't. They had been in Australia and were wearing shorts and tee-shirts bearing the words "g'day, mate" as they stalked about the terminal on handsome, fair legs without surprising anyone – including those dressed for Punta Arenas. As well there were tourists who had taken a week-long stopover on the island. They were wandering around with looks of blank agitation as they awaited our flight as if a week on Isla de Pascuas with its bewildering and imposing stones was no more enjoyable or interesting than a week at Burleigh Heads or the Kiama Blowhole.

The music playing in the terminal was of a variety that strikes you at about Samoa and does not leave you until the very western shores of the Americas. It is that Polynesian/Hawaiian wedding song sound which gives every singer the timbre of Tammy Wynette. But it does remind you that this place is Polynesian – yet another of its mysteries, and one which has preoccupied the Norwegian wanderer, Thor Hyerdahl, for decades.

The Chilean-Australian from the seat behind accompanied

me on the interminable Easter Island – Santiago sector. It was late afternoon when we first saw the distant outline of America, a haunting sight that eventually revealed itself as the lacerated horizon of the Andes.

"See what Chile's like?" my companion inquired unexpectedly.

"You mean mountainous?"

"No . . . well sort of. It's skinny. If it wasn't so skinny you couldn't see the mountains."

We came in very low over dry foothills and landed at an airport in a misty valley. Argentina was just over the darkening wall of the *cordillera*, not far beyond the runway's end, it seemed. And I was in Santiago, Chile, in transit again.

You do not know how to approach a country governed by a regime as shocking as Chile's was then, but normally you expect far worse than you see. Customs and immigration were surprisingly informal and staffed by far less surly persons than those who grace Sydney airport. We wandered about for a while, not knowing where to go, until a man dressed like an archaeology professor appeared.

"I am custom," he announced gravely.

I put my bag on his table and he went to unzip it.

"Any dead thing in there?" he asked. "Animal, bone, skin etc., etc.?"

"No, nothing dead," I responded, and he waved me through with a disappointed sigh.

"This is Chile," I kept reminding myself as the airport bus rattled through farmlands to the city. The temperature was spring-like, although the trees were still bare and the earth grey and hard. The people were dressed in luminous coloured pullovers and scarves with suit-jackets on top.

And then we entered a once illustrious and grand, but now decrepit, city centre, and there on Avenida Bernardo O'Higgins, grinning at the world, was Australia's own monolith, Paul Hogan, floodlit above queues and queues waiting for *Cocodrilo Dundee*.

Once settled into a hotel, I bought a ticket for a "Santiago by Night" tour and when the bus came I was its only passenger.

My recollections of Santiago by night are of groups of men standing in complicated knots on street corners arguing passionately, of lovers snatching little kisses and caresses in shop doorways, at bus stops and in parks, and of a lonely meal in a once busy steakhouse while the bus driver smoked furiously at the bar and a folk group played me poignant Andean laments.

The next morning the lovers were at it again, or still at it. I climbed Santa Lucia hill which dominates the centre of the city, clothed in mad Italianate stairways, plazas and ornamental gardens, and found distracted men smoking alone and clusters of teenage school students who were doing one of two things. Either they were doing their homework with great concentration under trees, or they were sitting with a partner, hands clasped, staring dreamily at the mountains of ice and snow soaring through the haze on the other side of town.

If it was cool to mild in Santiago, it was hot and wet in Panama City. My Varig flight from Rio to Los Angeles was due to make a stop in Panama. What was Panama, I wondered. Was it a country? A city? A canal? A hat? It was a place I had never thought about before — in those days, prior to America's nasty scuffle with Pineapple Head Noriega — and, like the rambunctious Republican reptile, P.J. O'Rourke, I let myself off with the excuse that "damn it, we can't be expected to stay up to speed on every one of these Third World pissing contests". Then I asked a flight attendant, who sat beside me for the landing, what she knew about the place. Duty-free shopping, she replied, was what Panama meant to her.

Duty-free shopping! You cross the unimaginable vastness of the Amazon rainforest, the high cloud-lands of Colombia, and come out of the skies on to the thinnest part of the Americas to walk into a humid hall of duty-free shops.

Perhaps I could get a Panama hat, I thought. But Panama

hats, I learnt (as everyone else does), are made in Ecuador and there were none in this airport. There were more stores than passengers, so perhaps I could have bought a CD player for the bargain of the year.

But I kept thinking about how strange it was for all these Japanese, Taiwanese and French-made goods to be shipped across the globe to a place that, as Paul Theroux has said, "scarcely existed before the canal was dug", to be displayed before restless transiting passengers who do not buy because they think they are going to get what they want cheaper down the line in Miami or Los Angeles.

But at least we could all say we'd been to Panama.

* * *

In late 1989 I had the opportunity to enjoy an accidental transit in Vienna. I was actually heading for Athens but learned, in the midst of a flight from Bangkok, that Athens airport — always disagreeable — was closed by a strike. ("Athens is strict" was the Thai inflight announcement). We were told that we would carry on to Vienna, the flight's destination, and go to Athens later that day on the plane's return to Bangkok.

So at 5 o'clock on a November morning we were causing some unanticipated bother at Vienna airport. The Austrians were delighted, as were the Thai passengers — most of whom had been headed for Austria, rather than Greece (you have to be from a country richer than Thailand to have any appreciation at all for the dilapidated, Mediterranean disorder of Greece).

But the rest of us — mostly Australians of great variety — had wanted to go to Athens. There were Greeks, Lebanese and Turks from the suburbs of Sydney and Melbourne going to their homelands for Christmas, and Jews en route to Israel. There were young, female backpackers, who'd picked the wrong season to go to the Greek Islands, but who would be met anyway — when they finally reached Spetsai, Corfu or Mykonos — by the usual packs of predatory spivs. And there was a group of Queensland mining executives, with flecks of paper napkin and food clinging to their polyester suits, who were on their way to conclude a coal-supply deal in Ankara.

Together we milled around awaiting our orders. After about an hour we were asked to pass through Austrian immigration and were told that we would be accommodated in an airport hotel for seven hours.

Most Western European immigration procedures are fast and efficient — often the staff just wave you through when they've glanced at the front of your passport to see what country you are from. As long as you avoid any queue containing Indians, Bangladeshis or Africans, you're through in seconds. But that morning in Vienna passage was slow. There was only one officer on duty, there were a few people who would normally require visas for Austria which they didn't have and there was one unfortunate couple from Sydney whose story we all heard as we waited behind them.

The man was Iraqi-born, travelling on an Australian passport, so he was admissible, but his hapless wife was Chinese and still travelling on a passport of the People's Republic. There was no way that the immigration officer was going to admit her — even for our seven-hour transit.

"But she don't live in China anymore," pleaded the husband. "She live in fuckin' Miranda." He tried to show the officer every stamp in his wife's passport, desperately looking for evidence of something, and turning to seek support from people behind him in the queue. A few Arabic speakers grumbled at him and each other; the rest of us just waited for the couple to get out of our way — which they did finally when they were sent back with an escort to the transit lounge.

"See . . . Miranda," the man was saying. "That's in Sydney . . . Sydney, Australia . . ."

Once assembled at the Novotel across the road from the airport, our transiting group was given a choice: we could take a four-hour tour of Vienna, or we could go to our rooms and sleep for the rest of the morning. Such is the mind-narrowing impact of travel, none of us volunteered for the tour, preferring the fake Bavarian snugness of the Novotel to the wintry charms of central Europe's most romantic and wonderful city.

* * *

Anyone in the world who goes anywhere sooner or later transits in Frankfurt. At the conclusion of that trip which took me to Athens, Milan, Lisbon and Madrid, I flew into Frankfurt to await a flight to Singapore. Around me streamed the populations of nations, making the airport a high-tech global version of Calcutta's Howrah railway station.

Unshaven rag-heads in stained-crotch jellabas from every state, fiefdom and kasbah of the Middle East and North Africa and blacks dressed in anything from brilliant flapping robes to filmy green suits and platform shoes, representing every tribe, guerilla-army, secessional group, fleadom and half-stuffed nation in Africa, hustled and squabbled, smoking and spitting as they proceeded to spill across the very ramparts of Western Europe.

Families with pale, helpless looking teenagers from the high-rise outskirts of Paris, Zurich, Hamburg and Munich guarded their hand-luggage — eyes out on the rag-heads — and waited nervously for their Christmas charters to Tunis or Casablanca, the very places where half this riff-raff had emerged from, or to Bangkok (their minds no doubt full of beautiful images of the Far East: all that sun, those coconut palms fanning tiny islands, magical gold, emerald and sapphire temples, lyrical wooden houses with carved balconies overlooking shimmering, translucent seas; what will they make of the City of Angels when they wake up tomorrow morning, I wondered).

Groups of Taiwanese globe-trotters — the men, ridiculous in their floppy pork-pie hats, swigging cognac and whisky from milk cartons; the wives, tiny and prickly between their perms and Reeboks; all of them towered over by their own 11-year-old sons and daughters — clustered tightly together amidst all this foreign ratbaggery.

A black American woman with two small children was sitting beside me. She was agitated and kept glancing at her watch and at some notes on a piece of paper. After a while she asked me if I spoke English. I owned up and then she asked where I thought she should wait for her husband, here or somewhere else. I said that I needed more information before I could advise her, so she explained that she had arrived several hours earlier from the United States and that her husband was a serviceman based "someplace like Salzburg, Stuffgarth or Salzberry", and he was coming here to Frankfurt to meet her.

"Well, I think you should go through immigration and customs," I said. "You're still in international transit here."

The woman looked up in the direction that I pointed and a sign caught her attention. It read "Domestic Arrivals."

"Yo!" she shouted. "That's it. *Domestic arrivals!* Am I dumb or what? Where else for meeting husbands and wives?" And she thanked me, gathered up her poor, exhausted children, and rushed off in the direction indicated by the sign.

* * *

One of the ever-present hazards of transits and stopovers is the possibility that your luggage will have its own stopover somewhere else. Once I arrived in Buenos Aires to find that only one of five pieces of luggage had accompanied me — a tube containing posters. I went to the appropriate office and completed all the necessary forms, giving the name of my hotel and the date and number of my flight to Santiago — in two days' time. I felt that all of this was an elaborate piece of bureaucratic theatre, put on to keep me hoping until I reached Santiago, where I would again give my hotel and flight details and so on until I had forgotten about whatever it was that had caused so much bother in the first place.

An Australian who had sat beside me in the plane and who wanted to share a taxi to the city confirmed this feeling, telling me that I was *rooted*.

"Even if your bags turn up," he announced knowingly, "the cunts'll rifle through 'em."

This man was a representative of a chemical company in Newcastle and made frequent trips to Brazil to buy products too lethal to be made in Australia. His view of South America was one created by his chemical shopping agenda. It was, I gathered, a fairly horrid business through which he met and mixed with horrid types. Like most travelling suits, he saw little, did little and thought about little outside his trade; but he did have a well developed, philosophical approach to taxis.

As he waited for me to finish at the lost luggage counter he had passed the time arguing with taxi drivers about the fare to Buenos Aires, paring away their miserable margins, setting them up against each other, and calling them all "macho cunts".

"Taxi drivers," he hypothesised when we were finally seated in a wrecked Ford with the man who had won the tender, "are the country in miniature. Look at those bastards at the airport. Desperate, aggressive, macho dickheads. That's Argentina. Seen 'em in India? All rags and bones. Red fangs wobblin' in their dirty gobs. They're about to cark it, their cars are half-carked and India's already carked it."

"And Australia?" I asked gingerly.

"Sydney," he declared. "Lazy mongrels, jabberin' in every language under the sun except English. Couldn't find Sydney Harbour if they were pissin' in it."

"See?" he went on as if the great and complex truths of his theory needed further elaboration. "You just take a dekko at the taxi drivers and you know what the country'll be like."

You could take a dekko at the chemical buyers too, I thought, but decided not to widen the parameters of our discourse with this observation. This was a man who had told me that he had two dogs, a male called Pol Pot and a bitch called Crumpet, and I wasn't sure how much more we had in common beyond our need to reach Buenos Aires in safety. Fortunately our hotels were at opposite ends of the city centre and the last I saw of him was when we parted at the Sheraton.

The next morning I went shopping for new clothes and a toothbrush and found that the day was, unexpectedly, a public holiday and the shops were closed. The inauguration of the new president, Carlos Menem, had been brought forward because of the economic abyss into which the nation had found itself tumbling.

I telephoned the business contact with whom I had a meeting that day; he wanted to keep the appointment so I strolled towards his office on Avenida de Mayo. Along the way, crowds were gathering, many holding the flags of Argentina and its provinces, as well as placards bearing Peronist slogans.

Carlos Klein is an old, German-born Argentine who owns a small but profitable business placing students in schools and colleges abroad, mostly in America and Britain. As I stepped from the antique elevator on to the fifth floor, I found Dr Klein in his usual summery mood.

"It's an utter catastrophe," was his greeting. "Utterly, utterly hopeless."

Naturally I thought that Dr Klein was referring to the political and economic climate, expressing his lack of faith in the ability of Menem and the Peronists to restore Argentina to its former virility (a faith that was being demonstrated so touchingly by the swelling crowds on the streets below us).

"Yes," I replied in agreement, hoping he would continue.

"Your country has rejected *another* student. It's a catastrophe."

So that was the dreadful news: the niggardly approach of Australia's consular officials to the matter of student visas — a gripe that accompanies me around the world and with which I have great sympathy. Still, given the ruins of the once great country that Menem was about to inherit, I did find Klein's sepulchral gloom a little misplaced.

Then I told Klein about my luggage. He was shuffling about the office in his slippers holding a coffee pot, searching for a power point out of which electricity might be persuaded to come.

He stopped, the pot shaking, and he closed his eyes.

"Awful, awful, awful," he intoned.

Mr Klein was so upset that I expected him to give me the very slippers from his feet to atone for the truly ghastly inconvenience which faced me in his country.

I decided not to tell him any more hard luck stories and to cheer him up suggested that we go out to his balcony to watch the presidential parade which was passing up Avenida de Mayo to the Casa Rosada. "Oh," Klein muttered. "That. Forget about it. It's not worth worrying about."

Here was a man who had, for his own reasons, decided to abandon the great cares and trials of the world, instead to concentrate on, to embody even, all the small fears and aggravations that beset us.

While I went on to the balcony to watch, Dr Klein spent the time trying to telephone the airport about my lost bags. I could hear him dialling and dialling on his old bakelite phones, groaning, hanging up with a thud and trying again with another machine. Looking at the buildings opposite, I could see why he was having such difficulty (other than the fact that it was a holiday). Every office wall was thick with dirty festoons of wiring; it hung in huge tangled webs into which birds flew and never returned and from which telephone calls rarely emerged. Phone calls to New York or Vancouver or Paris were carried simply by satellite; to the next building, the next street or home to the suburbs they ran, or didn't run, through these wires.

I had stepped on to the balcony just in time to see Carlos Menem's slow motorcade. Horsemen from the presidential guard preceded and flanked the cars; the crowds were roaring in excitement; so many country people, and the poor from the *barrios*, their dreams smouldering again, and yet again focused on just one man.

Then he came, standing in an open car, one hand on the windshield, waving to his admirers, to the cohorts of the hopeful: Carlos Menem, the outsider from La Rioja, whose Bee Gees haircut and Beatles suit made him an oddball amongst statesmen – a cross somehow between a middle-aged Latin heart-throb ("Touch me, *ees so eesi*") and a dope-smoking Anglican hipster.

Just as I glanced over the balcony, he looked up at me. We made eye contact and then he waved at me. I had never been waved at before by any president or president-elect, or indeed by any prime minister, duke, politician or box-office heart-throb (Lord De L'Isle had once spoken to me when he was Governor-General and I was a schoolboy cadet: "What's that badge for private?" he had wanted to know) and, momentarily, I was flustered.

And then I waved back and won a smile from Argentina's new president.

Dr Klein was still at his arrangement of antique telephones, trying to connect with anyone in the Republic who would pick up a receiver. He stared at me, defeated, when I returned to the office, beaming after my brush with fame.

"Yes, yes," he said impatiently when I told him my story. "But whatever is the poor man going to do about the telephones?"

Nothing, I expect.

But back now to the story of my luggage.

The morning after my meeting with Dr Klein I was able to buy underclothes and shirts, Dr Klein's ambient despondency having convinced me that my bags were gone forever. What I didn't know or believe was that as soon as I had reported them missing in Buenos Aires, an extraordinary international operation had begun.

I arrived in Santiago with my tube of posters at about midday on the following day and went to the lost luggage office. There, to my amazement, the clerk had a file on my belongings — with the information on the dimensions and appearance of my bags that I had supplied in Buenos Aires and, more wonderful, the news that they had been located in . . . *Bombay* (where else?) and would be arriving in Santiago, Chile, on an Eastern Airlines flight from Los Angeles via Miami and Lima the next day.

Incredulous at the precision that was being demonstrated here, I asked the girl where my bags had been after Bombay.

"They've had quite a nice trip," she replied. "From Bombay they went to Amsterdam, and after that, direct to Los Angeles. It's here in the file, even the flight numbers."

"I won't laugh about Indian incompetence again," I promised. "Or even Argentinian." (I carefully didn't say *South American*.)

"Or Chilean," she added, overlooking my discretion. "You won't even have to come here to collect them. We'll deliver them to your hotel — the Galerias, isn't it?"

Did this girl know my inside leg measurement, I wondered, or the fact that I like short blacks with no sugar and always ask for a non-smoking aisle seat near the front when flying?

Well, maybe she didn't know all of that, but she was dead right about my luggage. Twenty-four hours later I returned to my hotel room to find three bags and a box neatly lined up on the floor. Someone had even dusted them, to remove traces of their long journeys and unanticipated stopovers.

And, despite these stopovers in Bombay and elsewhere, no one had rifled through them.

* * *

One place on the planet where bags are never rifled, where you will never need to threaten taxi drivers, and where, inevitably, you will spend some time in transit, is Singapore.

At midnight, Singapore's Changi Airtropolis looks like an Australian shopping centre — a super, state-of-the-art Warringah Mall or Roselands. It seethes with Australian families, couples and businesspeople (although "seethes" is not quite the word for the movement of Australians, no matter how many there are) awaiting their flights and shopping for everything that they forgot in Singapore, left at home or just discovered that they needed. At other times the character of Changi changes: it becomes English, European, North American, Middle Eastern and Southeast Asian, depending upon the source of arriving flights and destination of departures.

But whatever time of day or night you are there, you can't escape the Indians. (I know I promised not to laugh at their incompetence again, but this is different.) There are just so many of them and they are always going to or coming from every place connected to Singapore by the fine isobars of flight.

Indians have perfected the psychology of being in transit. They wait for longer, in larger numbers, with greater discomfort and with less apparent reward than any other people (their flights usually turn out to be delayed or cancelled).

However, their waiting is no more or less than life; they might be at home waiting for television transmission to resume, or at Eden Gardens in Calcutta waiting for Pakistan or Australia to be all out, or in any government office waiting for service.

In fact, travel, cricket and public service (indeed any form of service) are said to correspond with the Hindu concept of eternity, integral bits of the great wheel of existence, turning with it through its endless gyre. ("When the train which is not coming doesn't come, all matters will be clear," is how a train conductor on the Jodphur Night Mail, sometime in 1973, explained it, or as Sri Aurobindo says: "An eternal instant is the cause of the years.")

But as the wheel of fortune revolves ("they must enter into the last finite if they want to reach the last infinite," says Sri Aurobindo), the messy business of reincarnation and transmogrification can't be avoided.

This might be why those great conglomerations of people and luggage that you see waiting in places like Changi are blurred at the centre: those misshapen, hastily tied black sacks started this voyage as grandmother and great aunt; those old fellows heaped untidily as they sleep become the carry-on suit bags that father has just bought from some Pakistani-descended thief in Johore Baru.

And while they await the turn of the wheel, and indeed their boarding calls, they are often joined by Indian airline crews, the pilots accompanied by their bossy, overfed wives, all of them stranded together in eternal transit.

As the rest of the world rejoices in minimalism and miniaturisation — in hi-fi, computers, videos and other electronic gadgetry — Indians (who, after all, invented the miniature as an art form) are marvelling at size. They travel with crates of electronic machinery that would have satisfied the audience at an early Who concert. Clearly the traders at Raffles City and on Nathan Road — half of them Indian anyway — are "thinking with their customers", as good salesmen should, and are off-loading entire warehouses of 1960s and 1970s sound gear upon every Indian family that happens by. (This applies to the airline crews as well; in my experience only Aeroflot and the unfortunate Tarom crews burden themselves with greater quantities of boxed hardware than their Indian counterparts.)

This is just one of the reasons why my firmest rule when travelling is — as I've mentioned earlier — to never stand in any line for customs or immigration that contains Indians (for this read Indians, Pakistanis, Bangladeshis, Sri Lankans).

It is a rule, I have discovered, which is shared by other frequent travellers, some of whom add their own riders or amendments. For example, many include under the generic term "Indian" Fijian, Malaysian, Singaporean, British or Trinidadian Indians, which I think is a bit unfair. Similarly, others widen the list to take in Africans and Filipinos — all of whom have been known to aggravate immigration and customs officers. A frequently observed corollary is that any queue in which you find yourself after a flight of twenty hours or more will be found to contain Indians et al.

Everything that Indians buy, they want to transport as hand luggage when it should be sent by P&O or the Flying Tigers. The reason for this is that everyone knows what happens to unaccompanied goods when they reach shipping and air-freight terminals on the subcontinent (my suitcases being happy exceptions). And a result is that most airlines quietly place Indians at the back of the plane. It's true! Wander down and have a look! They're always there, with only the occasional Taiwanese businessman asleep with his fifth glass of cognac sliding about the tray in front of him or a dejected, lowly ranked Sudanese diplomat trapped in their midst.

Even here, life seems like a sort of stopover, with their boxes and luggage piled around them, the women mixing tiffin in tins with their fingers — one arm holding the baby and a hand keeping the sari out of their eyes and the tiffin tins — and the men sitting on the armrests, their own hot winds, bearing the tang of *aloo chat* and *mutter paneer*, circulating amongst them, arguing and adjusting the arses of their pyjama pants or Gwalior suitings and watching that foreigners don't make off with their possessions (including grandmother, or whoever it is in the bags).

But what the Indians are seeking in their states of transit, an Iranian in France has already achieved. This man has been *in transit* at Paris' Charles de Gaulle airport for almost eight years!

Arriving at airports like Charles de Gaulle, or Orly, or Frankfurt, or Athens, you might think that all those Arabs, Persians, Kurds and Turks have been there for months, such is their littery, pyretic appearance. In fact, these new golden hordes receive reinforcements every quarter hour or so. But the gentleman at Charles de Gaulle arrived some time in 1984, was refused entry to France, as a refugee or anything else, and since then has supposedly been trying to find an airline that will cart him away — to anywhere except Iran. It is said that he will accept asylum in Chad, even, or Togo, if offered it. But I doubt it. Like a character from Samuel Beckett's *Endgame*, he has found his own kingdom come under the white neon at Charles de Gaulle, and has no need to ever go anywhere else, for there, in a day and a night, the whole world surges by him.

* * *

4 March, 1991. Qantas Flight 32 lifts off from Changi and, roaring at the breathless, crystal night, spirals across the Straits of Malacca before settling on a southerly track over the Java Sea. The captain outlines our route, which is also illustrated in front of us on a video screen: across the western Timor Sea, crossing the Australian coast over the Kimberley, Alice Springs, the Simpson Desert, Bourke, the Great Dividing Range and Sydney. We're currently climbing through 20 000 feet to our initial cruising altitude of 32 000 feet; when we've burnt more fuel we'll climb to 41 000. Our ground speed is 850 kilometres per hour; the weather en route is expected to be calm, although we are likely to encounter periods of turbulence over northern Australia; the outside air

temperature is . . . I yawn through most of this and fall asleep before dinner.

Hours later I wake up when passengers on the left side of the aircraft begin opening their window shades to watch the fierce dawn ignite the Australian desert.

The man beside me, noticing that I have stirred, has decided that it is time to talk. He is Japanese, perhaps a university student. His first question, which he has probably been saving all night, is from right outside my orbit.

This is it: "Do you like the funky chicken?"

"I'm sorry . . . do I what?"

"The funky chicken. Do you like it?"

The funky chicken, I wonder. What the hell is it and do I like it?

"Sorry — was that something on the menu or what?" I ask in reply.

"The funky chicken. It's not a dinner. It's a dance. Do you know it?"

"No I don't, I'm afraid," I respond, absolutely sure of my ground.

"Oh." The young man looks troubled.

"Why did you ask me that?" I inquire.

"Well, while I'm in Australia I want to learn to ride a skateboard . . ."

"Yes?"

"And learn to do the funky chicken."

"Of course," I nod, warming to the theme. "Will you learn them together?"

"Can you do that?" the man asks. "Do the funky chicken on a skateboard?"

"For all I know. Why don't you give it a try. You might be the first."

"Yes. That would be great," he enthuses. "Then I might try to skateboard around Australia."

"Or funky chicken," I propose, indicating the terrifying yellow hell stretching away to the horizon beyond the windows.

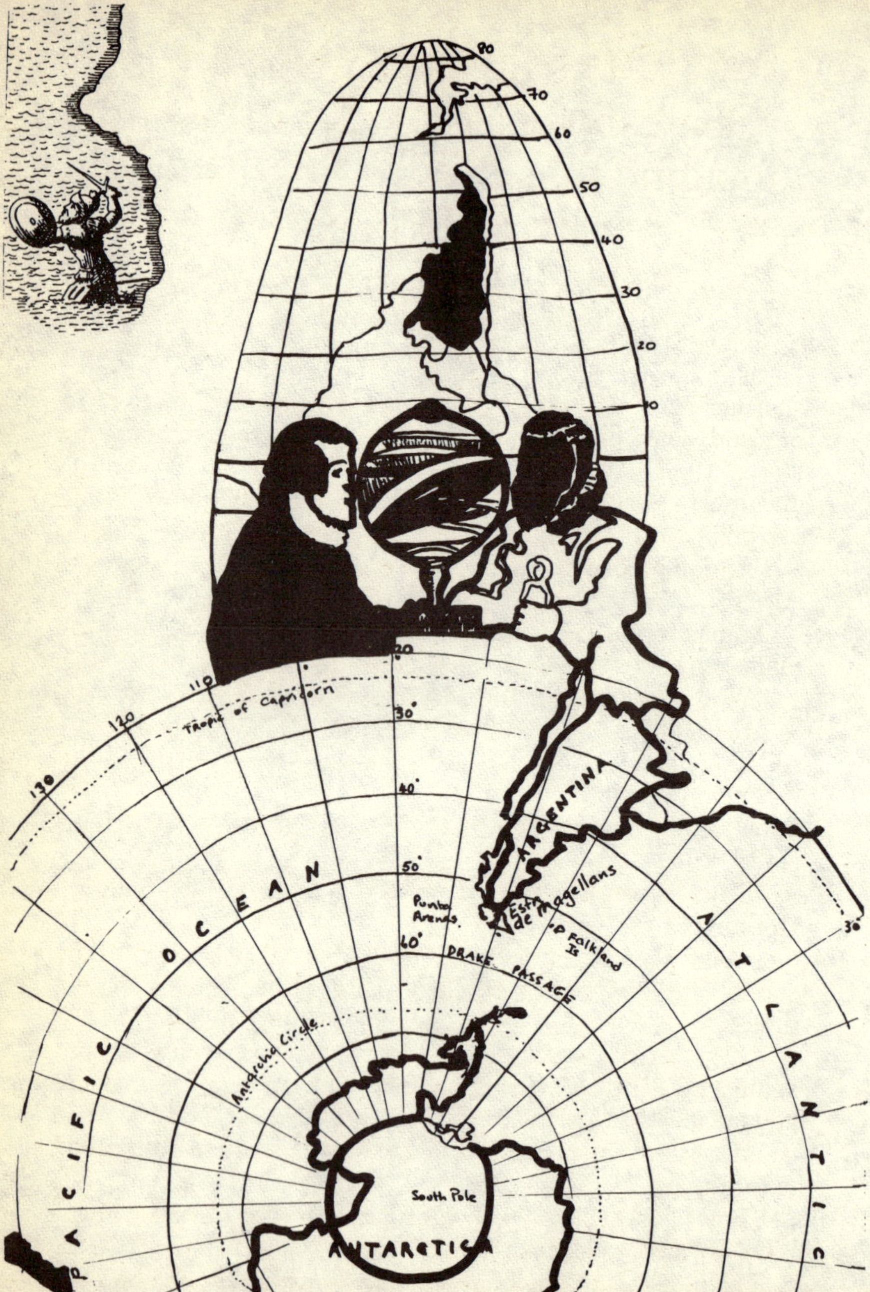
Tropic of Capricorn
ARGENTINA
PACIFIC OCEAN
ATLANTIC
Punta Arenas
Estr. de Magellans
Falkland Is
DRAKE PASSAGE
Antarctic Circle
South Pole
ANTARCTICA
NEW ZEALAND

The one about the Spanish-speaking Italians who imagine that they're Englishmen living in Paris

(Buenos Aires, Argentina)

I was in the transit bar at Auckland's International Airport sharing a table with an English couple who were going to Disneyland. They had flat heads and were broadcasting at me in stereo, the husband about his cousins — first, second, third and fourth — who were dispersed all over the shop, from Haringay to Harare and Halifax, the wife about Disneyland.

I interrupted with the news that I was going to Buenos Aires.

Transmission ceased for a moment while they tried to make sense of what I had said.

"Wot's that?" asked the man after the pause.

I thought that he said "what's that?" meaning "pardon?" so I announced again that I was going to Buenos Aires.

"Yeh, but wot is it . . . I mean is it a country, or is it, you know, a fun place . . . the likes of Disneyland or Alligatorland?"

"Take 'is cousin," the woman began, "the one wot lives in Horlando . . ."

"Buenos Aires," I declared, interrupting the prattle, "the capital of Argentina. I suppose it's a fun place. At least sometimes."

"Argentina!" exclaimed the man, the word splattering against his dentures. He began thinking hard. And then, "Oh, you mean Bew Nose Hairs!"

"'E's got a cousin out there, 'e has," the woman attempted to inform us.

"Bew Nose Hairs!" repeated her husband, interjecting. "'Ow the hell you gunna get there?"

The news that you could fly from Auckland in one hop to

the Argentine capital really threw them. They had lived in New Zealand for twenty-five years and had never imagined that Argentina was closer to their world than Disneyland and not some remote, invisible domain on the dark side of the planet.

Eleven hours later, as our Aerolineas Argentinas 747 emerged from the long night of the day before, it was my turn to feel astonished, watching the great continent of South America looming below me in black reefs beneath breakers of boiling cloud.

The jet swept into a loop above the immense swamp of the Río de la Plata which in 1516 the hapless Juan Diaz de Solís had imagined to be a passage to the fabled Indies, and which later Jorge Luis Borges declared to be a river of "dreamery and mud" — and we arrived.

On the airport bus ("half-built expressways, like inner Sydney or outer Bangkok, jammed, crumbling tenement houses" say my notes, showing how quickly I got down to work), a young Australian investment broker in the seat beside me was discovering his own version of the New World. Brazil and Argentina, he said, had to be the countries of the future: Argentina for its resources, Brazil for its huge, youthful population. Invest in the local K-Marts and Big Ws he advised, promising a passage to a land every bit as fabled as the dreams of Juan Diaz de Solís. Introducing literature to caution him, I observed that, despite Martin del Barco Centenera's poem "La Argentina," from which the nation takes its name, there never was much silver in Argentina.

My first impressions of Buenos Aires were of fur coats, people smoking furiously and magnificent boulevards. Together these give the city the appearance of Paris. Although not completely unexpected, this was nevertheless striking, for Buenos Aires is no mini-Paris like, say, Vientiane, but a colossus of 11 million people, the world's second largest Spanish-speaking city and home to one-third of the population of Argentina.

I checked in at the Hotel Colón and raced out to the street in a state of excitement. Was I in Paris? Or Barcelona? Or

Milan? I was reminded of all these places in turn and at once. And who were these people dashing about in cashmere, fur and silk? They dressed like Frenchmen and women, moved like Italians and spoke Spanish — the aspirated Italian mush of Argentine Spanish.

I had arranged to meet my new mate and investment adviser for dinner and at about nine o'clock I went to his hotel. There we asked the receptionist how we might best find the area known as La Boca, Buenos Aires' original Italian quarter. The receptionist was alarmed that we wanted to go there.

"That is not a very funny place," he warned and suggested that we try a restaurant on Esmeralda. The restaurants in La Boca, he continued, were not very fantastic. As well, the men were all *carteristas* (pickpockets) and the women all prostitutes.

This advice contrasted somewhat with that given in *South America on $25 a Day*: "La Boca is lined with neighbourhood bars and restaurants. Late at night these are crowded with area residents and other Porteños (Buenos Aireans) who dance and sing until 4 or 5 in the morning." However, we took it and resolved to try La Boca on some other occasion.

At half-past 9 we entered the Italian restaurant he had suggested. Middle-aged waiters in stiff white jackets were standing about gloomily, and at the centre of the room a woman was idly making pasta with a complicated and noisy piece of machinery. They all stared as we entered. There were no other guests.

We sat down and ordered. Initially we suspected that we had been guided to a very poor restaurant, but when our meal arrived we realised that this was not the case. Porteños, we were learning, eat late, and it was not until about 11, as we were preparing to go, that customers started rushing in, mostly older couples, beautifully dressed, amazingly animated and very hungry.

By now the streets of central Buenos Aires were congested and the bars, pizzerias, restaurants and cafes were alive. And it was only Wednesday night. I was reminded of a story told to me by an Argentinian in Sydney. When he first came to

Australia and was living in Wollongong, he and his wife wanted a night out – to go to a restaurant and then a show. They had great difficulty, he said, in finding a babysitter who would come at midnight. When eventually they did secure one – willing to take on a second job that night – they went out and drove around glumly in darkness, finding no bar, no restaurant, no show, nothing at all. They were at least three hours too late for everything.

When do these people *sleep?* That is the question that worries most visitors – except perhaps the Spanish who are similarly hyperactive as dawn approaches. When I returned to the Colón at midnight, the receptionist asked me where I wanted to go now.

"To bed," I replied. I had, after all, been awake for thirty-one hours.

"You are not very glad of our city?" he inquired, clicking his tongue. "No one in Buenos Aires goes to bed at this time."

"I've noticed," I replied, "but no one else out there has flown all night and arrived here an hour before leaving home."

That was the sort of brain-teaser that caused hotel receptionists in remote cities to grind their teeth together and wonder, so I left him in this state and went upstairs to my room.

Next morning I joined a city tour, part of an Aerolineas Argentinas stopover package. Our guide was Lily, a chain-smoking veteran in a long fur coat who took advantage of the heavy unseasonal rain to hurtle us around the necessary sights so that we could spend more time smoking in cafes and at her friends' wool and leather shops.

Our tour party consisted of a Peruvian family from Maroubra Junction, Sydney, an English couple from Melbourne (the wife had in fact spent her childhood in Argentina on an *estancia* near the Río Colorado), an immensely fat Chilean, also from Sydney, and myself. Lily tangoed easily in English and Spanish and provided all sorts of information about the city, the nation, the people and the continent, as well as offering comparisons with Australia where necessary.

As we rode towards Plaza de la República, she observed

that 95 per cent of the population of Argentina (which totals more than 30 million) were European.

"We have almost no coloured people," she announced to the bus. "No Asians, no Indians, no blacks." I'm not sure whether this was intended to be taken as a point in Argentina's favour, or as a simple statement of fact, but it is true that in the metropolitan area the only Indians you see are Andean buskers outside the cinemas on Lavalle, and I'm sure I did not see an Asian face. Later I asked Lily about immigration and she said that it consisted mainly of people from neighbouring countries, particularly Uruguay and Paraguay, although there was a modest intake of business immigrants from Korea. "Today it's mostly emigration," she lamented, "to North America and Australia."

The Plaza de la República has as its centre piece an 80 metre-high obelisk which celebrates the 400th anniversary of the founding of the city in 1536, and around the square are the coats of arms of the twenty-two provinces of the republic. Situated in the centre of the vast Avenida 9 de Julio − said to be the world's widest street − it is an extremely impressive sight of the sort that republics do best. It is reminiscent of the Place de la Concorde in Paris and, indeed, were it not for the generations of Falcon Futuras and Ford Cortinas grinding around the plaza on bald tyres (giving a road level impression of Marrickville or Canterbury or some other inner Sydney speedway) you could be in that distant and beautiful city.

No time for contemplation, however. Lily, sticking two fingers around the cigarette in her mouth, whistled us back to our coach and we joined the stream of disintegrating Mercedes buses honking down the Diagonal Norte to the Plaza de Mayo, a delightful, shady park overlooked by the Casa Rosada − the Presidential Palace then occupied by Raúl Alfonsín, the democratic hope of Argentina as she emerged from the long madness of the "dirty war".

The sight of the pink palace, the grand public buildings towering over the square and the San Martín Cathedral drew forth a moment of contemplation from Lily herself.

"Such a rich country," she mused, "and always so broke."

"Argentina's not alone there," I put in, but Lily would have none of it and, like others I met, couldn't believe that Australia's foreign debt was greater than that of Argentina, that our currency was then cheaper than the Austral, Argentina's chimerical inflation fighter, or that Australia was as ravelled in the net of *yanqui*, British and Japanese "imperialism" as any South American country.

Our next stop was the Plaza San Martín, named after José de San Martín, the liberator of Argentina. Now I was reminded of Neuilly in Paris, with the beautifully landscaped park, its trees still bare, and the streets of elegant nineteenth-century apartments, many placed behind high walls, and each hiding a small, exquisite garden. Around the plaza are sophisticated *confiterias* and cafes, as well as expensive designer-label shops, all frequented by smart women who park their Renaults and Peugeots with a Parisian's pure disdain for the regulations and for the finish on other people's cars.

As we reached La Boca, Lily alerted us to the houses which "look like they were built for pygmies". In this area — a world away from Plaza San Martín, although only ten minutes by bus — the houses are packed tight, only two or three storeys high, and often made of bright sheets of corrugated iron. One street, Caminito, has been preserved as a monument to the Italian working-class artisans of La Boca; it is traffic free and local artwork in the form of murals and brilliant ceramic tiles decorates the walls of the houses. Lily disappeared into a cafe, leaving us to wander about. One of the Peruvians whispered to me that La Boca looked like an *Indian* town, not at all like Maroubra Junction, so we strolled over to look at the real La Boca — the mouth of the Riachuelo River emptying into the Río de la Plata. Here there were clapped-out steamers being demolished by the poison tide and neat little ships loading for Colonia del Sacramento and Montevideo on the Uruguayan side of the estuary.

When Lily emerged coughing from her cafe, we resumed our journey to the National Congress. In front of the Parliament, on a great square, is a lovely, baroque sculpture, dedicated to the Congress of 1816 which was of importance in

Argentina's struggle for independence. The monument has seen generations of demonstrations and each, it seems, has left its graffiti. The most recent of these took up both sides of the family law controversy then before the Parliament: NO DIVORCIO and AHORA DIVORCIO. In a sense it was a measure of the great achievement of Argentina since Alfonsín became president in 1983 that the nation could now debate the relatively trendy issue of divorce after the decade of incandescent horror which preceded him.

Now it was time for shopping. At a leather "factory" on Reconquista, the Englishman from our bus, browsing through leather jackets, sought the help of an attendant.

"Por favor," he began, *"Cuanto . . ."*

"Oh, come on, stop all of that," chided the attendant in an accent that had perhaps been iced over in Bournemouth or Brighton. "This is Buenos Aires, you know, not La Paz or Quito. Now, what do you want?"

Meanwhile the Chilean was looking for a pair of leather trousers. Lily wanted a sale – this was, after all, her "friend's factory" – and this man's terrific volume was not going to prevent it. A few attempts were made to heap him into the largest sizes – the results of which I preferred not to watch – and then, in conference, it was decided that they would manufacture a pair for him that afternoon.

A few of us bought jackets and handbags and then departed for Lily's other friend's sweater "factory". Here an entire jumbo load of Americans had created havoc amongst the knitwear, buying eight or ten sweaters each and leaving the place in ruins.

When we reached our hotel, Lily gave me the address of another sweater factory where an even better friend of hers could be found. She arranged night tours for some of us, and transport to the airport for others. She even arranged to pick up and deliver the leather strides – if that is the word for the parachute flares that had been ordered – to the Chilean that evening.

A night or two later I strolled up Calle Florida – surely one of the world's most beautiful and enticing shopping streets, not least because of some of the beautiful and enticing shoppers — to the establishment recommended by Lily.

A lapse of memory caused me to tell the manager that "Alice" had sent me.

"Miss Alice?"

"Yes, the tour guide."

"Ah. Is fat, no?"

"Yeah. A bit. Smokes a lot."

"Si . . . Alice. Esmoking." He was looking at me in ambiguous wonder.

"Yes. She said you'd give me a good price for sweaters and a good rate on the dollar."

"Ah. *Si.* For my friend Alice, especial rate."

I chose a couple of pullovers which were labelled "cachemir" (and which my wife Maureen later discovered were made of lambswool and alpaca) and then entered very detailed negotiations over the exchange of one hundred or so dollars. What we agreed on was a price for Alice's clients only and as I walked out of the shop I felt pleased with myself and my good sense in using contacts.

And then I remembered that my tour guide's name had been Lily.

Flicking through the Buenos Aires telephone directory in search of an acquaintance, I got diverted, for the book is an index of the waves of immigration that created Argentina. Aside from the millions of Italian and Spanish surnames, there are pages and pages of German, Polish and Russian ones (Argentina has the world's fourth largest Jewish population). My friend's name is Irish and, other than his, there were scores of Kellys, Fitzgeralds and O'Briens. There are many more Laurences in Buenos Aires than in Sydney, and as many Murrays. Who was María de la Mercedes Laurence, I wondered. Perhaps we shared the same great-great-grandfather, James Lister Laurence, who was born in Caracas and fought with Simón Bolivar in the liberation of three republics.

What about Asian surnames? There was not one Chan, Chen or Nguyen — of which there are fifteen columns in the Sydney directory — but the world's most common surname,

Wong, was there: Lopez V. Wong. I would like to meet Señor Wong, I thought, curious about the details of his particular, lonely exile.

The economic histories of Argentina and Australia are in many respects identical, both being antipodean southlands dependent upon immigration for their population and commodity exports for their wealth. The Argentine economy began to decay sooner than ours; when Australia boomed in the years between 1950 and 1975 — the great decades of immigration when Australia's programs began to open to the world — Argentina was already stagflating and closing the gates.

It is said that the essential Argentine fear is to be thought of as an "Indian" nation, or as a *Latin* American nation, for to be Argentinian is to be European in the way that no other South American can be. V. S. Naipaul has written that: "To be European in Argentina was to be colonial — to claim the achievement and authority of Europe as one's own." This remark, of course, could be as easily applied to Australia, for what we have gained through our very diverse recent immigration we have partly lost by remaining colonial in a profound sense. What San Martíns have Australians to be proud of?

But this *Europeanness* has alienated Argentines from their own continent. Their neighbours party all night on jokes about them; I heard this one from a Brazilian: "What is an Argentinian? An Englishman who didn't come out right." And this from a Chilean: "If you want to make a lot of money, buy an Argentinian for what he's worth, and sell him for what he thinks he's worth."

And people everywhere — even Argentines themselves — tell and retell the old saw about the Argentine identity crisis. This is how Perez Celis, peripatetic *porteño* artist, puts it: "The Argentine has a distinctive trait which makes him very easily identifiable: He is an Italian who speaks Spanish and thinks he is English."

But what if they are bluffing? Jimmy Burns, in *Beyond The Silver River,* declares that: "The longer I lived in Buenos

Aires, the more I came to realise how much of 'Argentinismo' was bluff."

The bluff must stop somewhere though, and right now Argentina was discovering that an imagined specialness, together with decades of government as appalling as only Spanish-speaking Italian-Englishmen could produce, had resulted in a calamitous economic situation. And what infuriated the *porteños* most about this was the influx of Bolivian, Peruvian and Paraguayan tourists. Brazilians had been bad enough, but Bolivians and all the rest, shopping on Calle Florida, picking up bags of what they thought were bargains, the only real fashions this side of Milano, in fur, leather and wool and taking them back to their Indian camps or wherever they lived. This was unimaginably serious.

One night, at the Casa Rosada Club, I joined a party of Mexicans, Spaniards and Cuban Americans for a show which was to be a distillation of popular Argentinian folklore. Three principal elements were presented: the music and dance of the Andean Indians, the songs of the *gauchos* from the great plains, and the tango, from the immigrant working-class heart and fringes of Buenos Aires. All were performed with brilliance and the acute passion that has come from the fusing of Italian and Spanish spirits in this tormented and desolate land. The *gaucho* crew presented songs and dances that echoed the tense rhythms of southern Spain, augmented with astonishing sessions with their *boleadoras*, which whirred and cracked around their heads like detonators.

But the tango is perhaps the quintessential Argentinian creation. It is a dance which is at once insolent and sly, sharp and precise and, although totally without the bouncy rhythms of, say, a Brazilian samba, is immensely sexy in a sullen, cynical way.

A Cuban from New York let me know that the tango was now back in style in America.

"The tango says you can be sexy at any age," she explained, "so it's caught on with the yuppies." And, indeed, the performers on stage, seated with their accordians or at the piano, or slithering around in their white suits and pork pie hats, were "any age". And with every move I saw illustrated that line from a Borges story about "a man from the suburbs of Buenos Aires, a wistful compadrito with no other virtue than an infatuation with courage". A *compadrito*, of course, was the archetypal *porteño* of the thirties: a hustler, gambler, womaniser, lover of the tango, drinker and family man; a multi-function sort of fellow that the yuppies of New York would find difficult to emulate today.

But in focusing on the urgent sexuality of the tango, New Yorkers probably miss its real truth: its utter, profound sadness. Enrique Santos Discepolo described the tango as "a sad thought that is danced", for it is a dance that contains all the dreams, the longings, the broken hearts and the nostalgia for homelands that are lost forever . . . the other side of life in the New World.

On Esmeralda one night a would-be *compadrito* attracted my attention as he hissed at me from his ramshackle Fairmont taxi. (Buenos Aires low-lifers didn't all disappear with the thirties.) Would I like to see the show at Rugatinos? Sure! It was only midnight, and half the night people of Buenos Aires had not yet appeared.

When we reached Rugatinos, the driver, whose name was Eduardo, locked up his car and said he'd come in with me. Perhaps we could have a drink together. Strange taxi-driver, I thought.

Inside, the club was half filled with older men and younger women and a tango was underway on-stage, the poignant songs echoing oddly in this plush environment. As Eduardo and I sat down, we were immediately joined by two bar-girls and the pressure was on me to buy everyone a drink. Champagne was suggested and I ordered a bottle, insisting on Argentinian, not an imported brand.

We drank, watched the show and chatted — without anyone understanding me very much — and then it was time for another bottle. Fine, I said, but asked for the bill for the first one before ordering a second.

A waiter arrived and handed me a docket which read "A160".

He's forgotten the decimal point, I thought, and wondered where it should go. One austral sixty would be a ridiculous price for champagne (one Australian dollar was then equivalent to about one austral), and so the price must be sixteen, I concluded.

"Dieciseis australes?" I asked the water.

"Ah . . . non . . . Ciento sesenta australes," he corrected.

"A hundred and sixty?"

Eduardo and the girls were fidgeting and the former was rapidly drinking his glass in case this was to be his last drink.

I told the waiter that a hundred and thirty American dollars was an astonishing price to pay for a bottle of local champagne, and that anyway, I had only sixty australs in my pocket.

He invited me to speak to the manager and as I squeezed past him, Eduardo gazed at me sadly, a failed *compadrito* with his two bar floozies, fingering their empty champagne glasses.

The manager was a man with a lugubrious face and thick framed spectacles. There was something about him in his tuxedo that reminded me of my neighbour's black Valiant charger. Without looking up, he waved me to a seat, listened impassively to the waiter and continued stuffing money into envelopes. I tried to speak and his hand moved heavily my way in a gesture which suggested that I shut up.

Just then another man entered the office and introduced himself as the club's choreographer, saying that he had been sent as an interpreter.

I told him what had happened and how no one had shown me a menu or indicated in advance what a round of drinks would cost. I said that I would be happy to hand over the sixty australs and that I would then leave.

The manager did not at first react in any perceptible way as this was relayed to him, and then, after a minute or two, he moved a hand to a drawer and took out a deck of cards.

"Uh oh!" I thought, recalling an incident in the Philippines once where a pack of cards had almost cost me twenty thousand dollars.

The manager explained that the choreographer would shuffle the cards and split the pack. We would each pick a card and the highest card would win. If I won, I would pay up the sixty australs that I had and my debt — one hundred australs — would be cleared. If the club won, I would be sent back to my hotel to collect more money or my credit card. Hey, this is a weird manager, I thought. Very weird.

The deck was split, we drew our cards and I won. The manager, his features as still as sediment, put out his hand for my sixty australs and then shooed us out of his office, asking the choreographer to make sure that I was given a complimentary drink and that I stayed for the rest of the show. As I said, very weird.

Eduardo and the girls had vanished. The choreographer sat me down and, over a drink, began talking. He liked very much the Englishmen, he said. In fact he liked very much England, too. You couldn't say that too loudly in Argentina, but he couldn't help it. Anyway his wife was English. Did I want to see her strip?

"Not necessarily," I replied.

"You must. She's in the next act."

"Oh, well. If you insist."

"You like very much English girls, too?" he asked, after a pause.

"I'm not English, I'm Australian."

"Ah. I like very much Australians, too."

But especially, the choreographer declared, he liked the English language. It was so precise.

"For example, Yorkshire Pudding. That's two words. What's that in Spanish? I'll tell you. It's *especie de panecillo hecho con pasta de hojuelas, cocido al horno, donde se dora y forma una corteza en el exterior.* Now you see why the Englishmen beat Argentina. We have too many words."

That was one angle, I supposed, and perhaps one that had not yet occurred to the historians.

After the performance, I went out to the street and began walking back to my hotel. And there, just emerging from his

Fairmont, was Eduardo, hurrying another gringo in for the late, late show.

Ten days later I flew south on the return trip to Australia. Our jet stopped at Río Gallegos to take on extra fuel for the long westbound journey into the bellows of the roaring forties. Río Gallegos is a town 52 degrees south of the Equator, on the same latitude as the Malvinas or Falklands – almost 400 kilometres away into the bitter Atlantic. We spent a freezing hour in the terminal wandering from the restaurant which offered a dish consisting of "egg yocks" to the souvenir shop (penguins, Harrington's jam and faded pennants proclaiming *Las Malvinas son Argentinas*). At the tourist office I asked what there was to do in Rio Gallegos. Well first, I was told, there was the British Club, and then there was ping-pong, pony-trekking and an activity called *"paseo en sulky"*.

An Aerolineas Argentinas jet was loading for Ushuaia, on the Argentinian side of Tierra del Fuego, and the southernmost city in the world. All the passengers, it seemed, were either flat-featured Indians who moved with the economy of men brought into a world of ceaseless winds, or flame-haired Irishmen with eyes like melting ice.

We took off and flew south-west over the tip of Patagonia and the glacier land of wind and frost that is Antarctic Chile. Across Punta Arenas and the iceberg bound Straits of Magellan, and into a pure air as blue as washed sapphire. A year before I had stood on the beach in the Philippines where Ferdinand Magellan was killed. Here now were the straits he discovered on the way to his death – a passage from the Old World via the New into the Pacific and the hallucinatory wealth of the Orient. Our aircraft, climbing to cruising altitude, intersected Magellan's path and slipped down the globe to the Antarctic latitudes, and as we tracked across the icy void of the world's loneliest air route, a troupe of teenage Brazilian acrobats kept the entire cabin entertained until landfall in New Zealand.

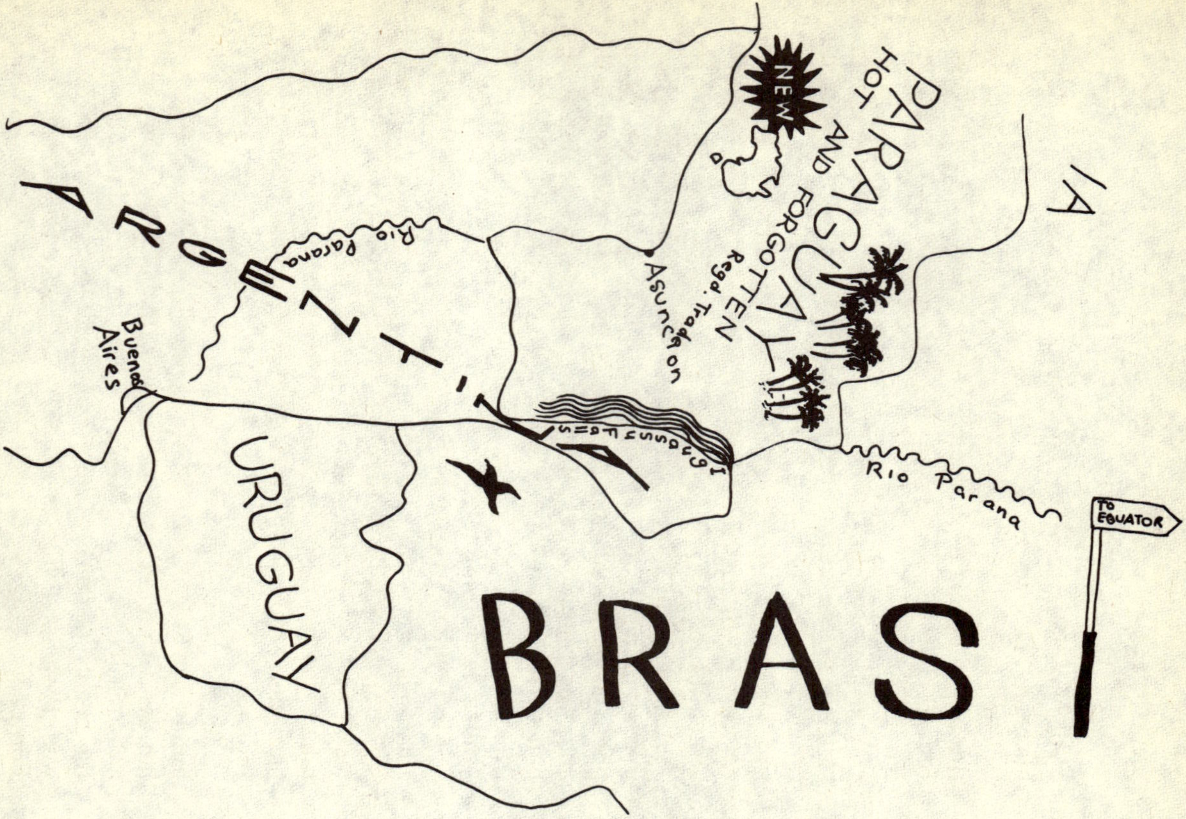

High times near Paraguay

(The Iguassu Falls, Argentina)

"Todo ha sido destruido," lamented the taxi driver, shaking his head. *"Destruido."*

What had been destroyed, I wondered, as we zoomed through the jungle on our way to the Hotel Internacional Iguazú. The falls? The hotel? The national park? The economy of Argentina?

You could see the Iguassu falls from both the Argentinian side and the Brazilian side, continued the driver, glaring alternately at the jungle and at me. But the view from Argentina was terrible. Everything was destroyed; you couldn't walk on the paths or bridges anymore – the river had engulfed the lot.

A photograph hanging in a plastic bag from the sun-visor in front of me identified the driver as Hector Carriego. In the photo he had a wild, undernourished look, his yellowing teeth and eyes jumping out of haggard flesh. But beside me, as he banged his limbs at the bits of his old Cortina and dialled aggressively with his steering wheel, he seemed robust enough; "full of beans" might be an apt description.

For US$40, Hector went on, he would drive me to the Brazilian side where the falls were much better. And you could stand in the middle of them, on an island in a raincoat, the water streaming down around you, and have your picture taken. The jungle in Brazil was richer too. There were jaguars, deer, tapir. Here in Argentina? Nothing. *Nada.* A few Indians, that's all.

As we pulled into the hotel driveway, Hector thrust a lumpy, well-fingered book of photographs and maps into my lap. He distracted me from pictures taken in Argentina with a dismissive wave and a sort of nasal grunt, and pointed out the beauty of the Brazilian shots. And then of course there was Paraguay. For an extra $35 he would take me to Paraguay and back.

Did I want to visit Paraguay, I pondered. The country

where William Lane had founded a "New Australia" in the 1890s and which was recently described in the *Guardian* as "hot and forgotten" was only a few kilometres from here. And if I missed this chance, would I ever see Paraguay again?

"Paraguay es lindo," insisted Hector. Paraguay is beautiful.

I didn't respond.

Well then if I didn't want to go to Paraguay tomorrow, what about tonight? Hector produced from his glovebox a brochure headed "Paraguay by Night". For about $30 I could sample the night life in Asuncion, illustrated with unambiguous honesty in the brochure, and sleep safely in my hotel in Argentina.

Paraguay by night would certainly be good for a story, I felt. But I resisted — last night in Florianopolis had been steamy enough — and arranged to meet him at about nine the next morning. I said that I would think about whether we would go to Brazil, Paraguay or indeed anywhere.

My room in the Hotel Iguazú was on the second floor and had stunning views of the falls. Why go back to Brazil, when only a few hundred metres from my room the entire Iguassu river was tumbling over a precipice with the roar of a free-falling ocean? I sat on my balcony and watched. Cataracts of spray were soaring skywards like inverted rain-squalls. As they rose, they formed clouds which drifted rapidly away to the horizon, providing instant demonstrations of the water-cycle. Meanwhile, about a kilometre to my left, on the other side of the river, was the beautiful and vast republic of Brazil, stretching away to the equator through a haze of rainbows and humming-birds.

The Río Iguazú takes its name from the Guaraní Indian word for "great river". The falls are located some 23 kilometres upstream from the Iguazú's confluence with the Río Paraná. Here are the statistics for those who want them: the water falls about 82 metres across a great curving front of about 3 kilometres. The flow at the height of the wet season (November to March) is over 12 750 cubic metres per second;

when I was there (October) it was a relatively scant 1750 cubic metres per second.

The Guaíra falls in Brazil were once the greatest on earth. In the early 1980s, a joint Brazilian and Paraguayan venture inundated the Paraná river and falls at Itaipú, producing the world's most powerful hydro-electric plant, an ecological catastrophe *and* a massive acceleration in Brazil's foreign indebtedness, all at the same time. This is recorded on a notice at Iguassu listing the most significant of the world's waterfalls. *"Destruidos por los hombres"* is the short sharp footnote to the details on the Guaíra falls. The fact that *los hombres* were not Argentines helped, no doubt, in having the matter listed.

The hotel was full and there were streams of visitors walking down the paths for a closer look at the action. I strolled out into an afternoon which had a juicy feel to it, surprising in these supposedly dry months, and followed the crowds into a mini-rainforest. On both sides of the border the waterfalls are located within extensive national parks and, aside from a few hotels, there is almost no intrusion. The paths and bridges are carefully constructed and do not detract from the splendid surroundings.

Brilliant red butterflies were soaring and diving like birds; the birds themselves were darting and sipping at the orchids like butterflies; lizards dashed about, while above us towered evergreen trees hung with nets of lianas.

I walked through veils of vapour to the end of the path. In front of me the catwalk had indeed been destroyed as promised by Hector. All that remained were a few crumbling concrete piles and torn steel handrails; the rest had been swallowed whole. But for me and the crowds huddled at the end there was no disappointment, only relief, perhaps, at having to proceed no further. Below our feet, the great river seemed to stall at the lip of the abyss before rolling like a honey tide to the whirlpools below. Amidst all this, tiny swallows, adapted to a life of eternal cataclysm, pirouetted between nests tucked into holes in the basalt beneath the surge.

Later I followed a treacherous path which led to the lower

ground. There, in an area of calm, a boatman was taking people over to the Isla San Martín which, according to my brochure, is "furnished with adequate installations". On my boat was an Indonesian couple. Upon establishing that I was from Australia, the man became ecstatic.

"Indonesia and Australia like this!" he shouted, putting his two digit fingers side by side. His pleasure was not shared by everyone in the boat. Most just stared, not appreciating this communion of wanderers from the other side of the planet.

We never did see those adequate installations, however. As our boat puttered towards the island, its driver chose to sail it beneath a mini waterfall, a sort of drizzling branch line compared with the main event nearby. Unfortunately the drizzle was sufficient to alarm a passenger, filling her mind perhaps with haunting visions of Jesuit fathers, martyred by Guaraní savages, plunging over the falls on floating crosses.

The woman began shrieking and gabbling at the boatman and at the rest of us, and reaching out for the vines and branches growing from the green, wet rocks above us. The boatman, astonished, and wondering about the nature of this particular phobia, decided to abandon the crossing and, muttering violently, puttered us back to the beach that we had started from.

My brochure also indicated that "in that vast forest it will not be uncommon to have a glimpse of a jaguar, charming flatfooted foxes, or the noisy ramblings of tapirs and peccaries. The shadow of deer among the boisterous monkeys and birds. A feathered coming and going of bright colours..." proving that Hector was wrong at least about the wildlife on the Argentine side. Not having time to venture further into the forest, however, I returned to my hotel.

A holiday in Iguassu is not all waterfalls and jungle. Back in the hotel, I read the noticeboard, where a variety of exciting activities was proposed: "TENIS, SCRABEL, GYMJAZZ, BOGGLE, ROMPECABEZAS ETC". As well there was a disco, a sauna and a swimming pool, where, I read, "All the vibrant landscape of the Misiones jungle will join you in a perfect dive."

Misiones is this sub-tropical province of Argentina, so named because it was first explored and settled in the seventeenth and eighteenth centuries by Jesuit missionaries whose story was told in the 1988 film *The Mission*.

The landscape is indeed vibrant and, I thought, as I lazed in the hotel pool amidst chubby adolescents from Montevideo and Buenos Aires, I would have liked the time to explore properly this very historical corner of the country.

That evening I debated whether I should visit Paraguay or Brazil in the morning.

To be honest, Paraguay held a certain attraction. Hot and forgotten it might be, but it *was* the country that had been chosen by eccentric Australian socialists for the establishment of a "communistic utopia". There in the hotel, I had no way of finding out where the Río Tebicuary – the site of New Australia – or Paso Cosme – the site for a second attempt – were. No one at the reception had much interest in Paraguay. I might have been inquiring about Upper Volta or the United Arab Emirates, so vague were their replies.

It is difficult to imagine what could have been going on in the mind of William Lane when he left Australia with his 200-odd fellow utopianists and sailed for Paraguay in 1893. Clearly, many of his companions had similar trouble reading his mind and intentions. The colony soon disintegrated into feuding factions – Lane's despotism and unyielding teetotalism being at the centre of many of these feuds – and ultimately Lane led the puritans away, pledging "straightness and mateship", to a new start at Paso Cosme.

A British diplomat who visited Cosme soon afterwards concluded that the settlers were destined to become "a peculiar people, like Cromwell's Ironsides". William Lane, who was probably peculiar even before he left Australia, gave up in 1899 and returned, disillusioned and deeply in debt.

Gavin Souter, the author of *A Peculiar People*, observed that in addition to William Lane's tendency towards personal dictatorship, the characteristics which ensured the decline of the settlements were racial prejudice, which prevented intermarriage with the Guaraní, and isolation from population centres and transport, which hastened economic collapse.

Today New Australia and Paso Cosme still exist as small agricultural communities. New Australia is now known as Colonia Stroessner, after the father of the late president of Paraguay. There are supposed to be a couple of hundred people claiming to be Australian-Paraguayans, and a number of nineteenth-century Australian linguistic and cultural attributes which have stayed on as local peculiarities.

All of this would have given a journey into Paraguay the edge over Brazil. But we're talking about three hours here. At noon on the second day I had a plane to catch.

After dinner, having failed to find the Boggle, Scrabel or Rompecabezas, I sauntered into the disco which was located in a cavern beneath the swimming pool. There I found the same adolescents dancing to American music ("Come on, it's not half as bad as it sounds," reassured the barman when I winced at the noise) whilst their parents supervised them from lounges in dim corners.

And at the bar I met Dr Alexandria Kirshenblatt-Kingscott. I know that's her name because she presented me with a business card within a minute of my taking a seat. The card read:

Dr Alexandria Kirshenblatt-Kingscott MA, D.Phil, Phd
Professor of Folklore
World College
Professor of Performance Studies
Chairman, Department of Performance Arts
Purchase Institute, New York
Visiting Chair, Ethno-Arts,
Winooski College, Vermont

Seeing that, I decided not to give her my card.

Dr Kirshenblatt-Kingscott, was, as you may have guessed, an American. She was an untidy 50-year-old, all loose grey-blonde hair, ethno-Indian-Peruvian-Baluchi clothes, shawls and bags and creased notebooks shut into a fat filofax.

As I sipped a beer and sought ways of escape, she ranted at me about (I think) a nest of fascists she had unearthed somewhere in the Andes or on the Mato Grosso or beyond the Pampas, or was it in Patagonia or near Lake Atacama? And about the naive painters of Salvador or Cochabamba and about the corn-straw crafts of the Lake Titicaca Indians and . . .

"Speaking of colonies . . ." I suddenly interrupted.

She screeched to a halt, her silence coinciding with a brief lull in the music.

I went on: "I've been tracking down the remnants of an attempt to create a socialist utopia in Paraguay."

The filofax flew open and she burrowed into her bag, drawing out a pen.

"Yes? How? Where? When? Who? Wow!" She was dazed at the implications of this discovery.

I began by telling her that the colony was established by a man who had once written a book called *Workingman's Paradise*. As I told her what I knew of New Australia and Cosme, Dr Kirshenblatt-Kingscott took detailed notes, staring at me in ecstatic wonder from time to time.

At the end of my telling, I excused myself and left. And as I returned to my room, I realised that Dr Kirshenblatt-Kingscott had been so busy collecting the bits of information that I had on the settlements – these nests of socialists – that she had not considered for a second that I had not been to Río Tebicuary and researched the find like a true anthropologist myself. No doubt she would. In a day or two, when she had finished whatever she was doing amongst the Guaraní leftovers around Iguassu, she would cross the border into Paraguay and strike out on another mission.

That's the sort of traveller I'd like to be, I thought. Someone with a purpose.

The next morning, when Hector arrived, I told him that I'd decided to skip Paraguay. "Take me to Brazil," I said. With this he smiled. He didn't want to go to Paraguay anyway. Paraguay was *"un país patético"* (a pathetic country).

We drove through the forest to the border. Hector didn't stop at the Argentine post and at the Brazilian one he simply accelerated past the frontier guards who were energetically taking other visitors' cars apart.

"*Son locos,*" Hector remarked, tapping his temple.

"Who?" I inquired. "The guards?"

"No, the people who stop."

We raced along country roads, overtaking tour bus after tour bus.

"Yesterday you told me there were no bus tours," I chided.

Hector spat out of his window. The tours were for cripples, he said. For people like me there were no tours.

He dropped me near the Hotel das Cataratas and directed me to a path descending through white and mauve flowering trees. I followed the course of the river upstream to an opening beside the falls from where a catwalk led to a viewing platform pitched adjacent to the awesome Garganta do Diabo (Devil's Throat). I hired a raincoat and marched out with the squawking crowds – past the poor sodden man with a polaroid pleading for grins – to the lookout. Here, a holocaust of water and noise gave an impression of what life must be like on a raft during a typhoon, as half the water of Brazil, it seemed, plunged recklessly away to Paraguay. And this was the dry season.

"*Impresionante,* no?" asked Hector when I returned to his car.

"*Impresionante,* yes," I responded.

That afternoon, as my Aerolineas Argentinas jet lifted off through flocks of spiralling hawks, I watched the falls receding to jets of steam rising from the featureless jungle. And then we were away, crossing the flat rich plains of Uruguay, heading towards the great city of Buenos Aires.

Note: *Iguassu* is spelt *Iguazú* in Spanish, *Iguassu* in English and *Iguaçu* in Portugese.

ATLANTIC OCEAN
Glencolumbkille
Blue Stack Mts.
Donegal
FERMANAGH
Benbulbin
Drumcliff
Sligo
Ballyscadare
Ballycastle
Killala
Bunny-connellon
Toberscanavan
Mullanys Cross
Attymass
Ballyfarnan
Achill Is.
MAY
Knockbreaga
Curry
Doocastle
Roosky
Castlebar
Clew Bay
Kilmeena
Kilmovee
Belfast 140 miles
Elphin
Knock
Mayo
Knappagh
Creggenhaun
Castleplunket
Dublin 110 miles
Roos
CONNEMARA
Joyce's Country
Maam
Kilmaine
Kilconly
Cork 140 miles
Clifden
Lough
Moycullen
Menlough
Galway
Bally foran
REP
C
IRE
Cappataggle
Kelly's Gro
Kilreekill
Kiltormer
Laurencetown
Kilchreest
Kiltartan
Gort
Ballyboy
Killinaboy
Ballinruan
Feakle

A matter concernin' a bicycle

Castlebar, Ireland

"This is an uncommonly complex matter. A pancake of a puzzle."

The man had stopped his car when he saw me with my bicycle perched upside down beside the road investigating its ventral mechanisms.

The puzzle referred to was the problem of fitting the bike and me into his Ford Escort for a ride into Castlebar, where, the man advised me, I would be sure to get the machine fixed.

I was cycling around the shores of Clew Bay somewhere past Knockbreaga when my gear system began to come apart. The bike wobbled to a halt beside the hedges and so began my attempts to restore its workings.

It was as bright a morning as you would ever see in Ireland with an ethereal August sun illuminating the edges of high, fast-moving lumps of cloud. The fields beyond the straggly fuchsia hedges were patched with moving areas of brilliant light dotted with miniature men cutting and bagging peat, and whistling.

The man introduced himself as Danny Quigley — one of the Quigleys of Pontoon. He had thin, stalky hands with which he struggled with the pieces of bicycle that would not fit through the car door.

"A complete pancake," he muttered in frustration. "A worrisome wonder."

I told him not to be concerned about me, that I would push the bicycle to Castlebar; I had no plans at all for the day and it wasn't yet 10.

Quigley was sweating and breathing heavily. He was wearing the heavy black suit with the stained cream shirt underneath — buttoned at the neck but with no tie — that serves most men in the Irish countryside. As he mumbled and shoved he suddenly had an idea. He would tow me.

From his boot he produced a 4 metre-long rope which he

tied around the rear bumper bar. I was to hold the other end as he drove into Castlebar.

We set off, Mr Quigley driving with intricate care and patience for the first dozen or so kilometres. He would slow for bumps and bends so completely that I cruised past his window; on hills the Escort moved fitfully, making it very difficult for me to hang on to the rope.

Then, after about half an hour, as we were going over a particularly rough stretch of road, Quigley suddenly accelerated. The rope jerked out of my hand and the car and Mr Quigley rattled off at twice the speed in the direction of Castlebar. I shouted, but he didn't hear or notice. He had apparently forgotten completely what he was doing; either that, or he had tired of having a bicycle and a man in tow.

I pushed the bike the remaining few kilometres. Castlebar was at the bottom of a long hill, so I was able to freewheel into town. Once there I began asking where I would find a bicycle shop.

"That would be Gormley's," explained the first woman I asked.

"Now to get there, you go down to Kilgallon's. Opposite — I mean on this side, not the other two sides — is Carroll's the paper shop. Down the next lane, O'Connell it is if I'm not mistaken, which is in between Carroll's and Glesson's . . ."

"Look, thank you," I interrupted. "Would you just point me in the direction of Kilgallon's first."

She looked at me with a look that might have been astonishment.

"Kilgallon's is it? For sure it's just past the other side of Bridget McLaverty's tea rooms. But if it's concernin' a bicycle, it's Gormley's you're after, with Jams Gormley himself your man. And watch out for the mouth of him when you find him. He's a desperate man for the talkin', a desperate man altogether."

I thanked her and set off in the approximate direction of Bridget McLaverty's tea rooms. I did eventually find the bicycle shop. It had a sign reading "J. GORMLEY" above the door, and outside, leaning against the walls and window, were about six decrepit, heavy-framed bicycles of the sort that country people all over the world ride.

I parked my own bike in the doorway. It looked insubstantial and untrustworthy beside the country-men's bikes, I thought, as I entered the shop.

Inside there was just one bicycle on display, and a lot of boxes on which old men sat smoking and growling gruffly about bicycles.

"Is it a matter concernin' a bicycle?" one of them asked. He stood up. A tall, heavily-built man in his 50s, with thick untidy hair, he was wearing an oily black serge suit. In one hand he held a bit of a cigarette and a pair of pliers; in the other a number of bicycle bells. I assumed that he was Gormley.

"It is," I replied, pointing to my Peugeot. I felt insubstantial myself in here, and ludicrous in my Spandex shorts and yellow Santana Moda tee-shirt.

"Nice wee lass," he replied. "French girl."

He went across and patted my Peugeot on the saddle in the way a man might pat a small child on the head or a dog between the ears . . . or, it suddenly seemed, a French girl on the bottom.

Gormley wanted to know where I'd come from that morning and how I'd found myself in Castlebar. I told him that I'd left Keel on Achill Island before 8, hoping to reach Connemara that night, but had broken down somewhere near Loch Feeagh. I explained that I was unable to fix the gears and that a man had towed me part of the way to Castlebar but had abandoned me without warning and disappeared. Gormley and the other men still sitting on the boxes were nodding knowingly — as if this were a regular event.

"Would that have been Dennis O'Meara?" Gormley asked, unexpectedly.

"O'Meara? No . . . Actually I can't remember his name." As if it mattered anyway.

"Peter Mulrooney?"

"No, not that name."

"Ned Plunkett?" another man asked.

"Not Ned Plunkett."

"Stumpy Finnucane, then?"

"Definitely not."

"Not Stumpy? Then it must have been Joseph. Joseph Finnucane."

"It wasn't any sort of Finnucane."

There was silence in the room. Just the sound of men breathing and the slight creak of boxes being sat upon.

"This fella, who towed and then untowed you and the lass," said Gormley after a while, "would he have been a fella from Kilmeena?"

"I don't know where he came from," I replied.

"Did he not tell you?"

"I think he may have, but . . ."

"Knappagh?" Gormley interrupted.

"No . . . I . . ."

"Perhaps he was from Cushcamcarragh or Ballycroy?"

"I don't think so."

"Then it must have been Cloghjordan, Moyvoughly or Cloonfad."

"None of those names rings a bell."

"What about Screggan, Doocastle, Knockalinda or Mallaranny?"

"Sorry."

"Horseleap, Ballynacarrigy, Kiltamagh or Crockets Town?" offered one of the old men.

"Definitely none of those."

"Ballinafad, Knockcroghery or Aucloggeen?"

"Absolutely not."

"Sixmile Bridge or Attymass?"

"No . . . Yes!" I suddenly answered. "The *bridge* . . . he said something to do with a bridge."

There was silence again as the men concentrated on gathering to their thoughts all the towns whose names contained the word "bridge". I was thinking more clearly now myself.

"*Pontoon*," I confidently declared after a moment. "He said he was from Pontoon."

"By the powers!" Gormley shouted, amidst the muttering of the men, "then for sure it was Joseph O'Conroy."

"Nope."

"Joseph Malloy?"

"Not him either. It wasn't any Joseph at all."

"Jose Carlos Oliveira De Freitas?" Gormley proposed wildly.

"No chance whatsoever."

"Horrie O'Rourke?"

"No."

"Horrie Fox, then?"

"It wasn't Horrie O'Rourke, or Horrie Fox, or Horrie anything. I think his first name was Danny," I said, remembering.

"Danny O'Leary," concluded Gormley, "or his cousin Danny Lynch."

"Neither of them."

"Neither?" asked Gormley, astounded.

"Look, this is not really helping to get my bike fixed," I reasoned.

"Were he driving a Ford Cortina?" a man asked, ignoring my remark.

"An Escort."

"An Escort?"

"Not a Cortina?"

"Or an Anglia?"

"Surely it was a Vauxhall Viva, then?"

"It was definitely, positively, undoubtedly an Escort," I stated.

"Then it were Danny Quigley," Gormley declared, a dirty smile coming to his face.

The men mumbled and nodded, satisfied.

"He was in here this very today morning," Gormley went on.

"He was here?" I asked, astounded.

"He surely was. But could he remember what it was he came in for? Not Danny Quigley. An inductive but forgetful sort of fella he is. Has four brothers. He's older than Gerry, but younger than Mick, Kevin and Davey."

"A contagious family," a voice from the boxes said. "Mrs Quigley had a nice green Raleigh. It were stolen from a Ballina bus stop."

"It were not," someone corrected, speaking through waves of black smoke. "It were in Bunnyconnellan that the bicycle were stolen. She were going to take the bus to Inishcrone to see a certain party name of Malloy."

This is all fine and dandy, I was thinking, but I couldn't help wondering whether anyone was going to attend to my Peugeot.

"What do you think of the toe cages?" Gormley asked, pointing his pipe, which had replaced the cigarettes, at my pedals.

"Fine," I answered.

"They're a menace in the traffic," one of the men declared.

"But they're your man for the hills," another said.

"But they're no use at all if your crank's not working," I suggested, smiling hopefully and helpfully.

"Your ten-speed crank's your man for the hills too," remarked Gormley, taking up my theme.

"But an unmentionable bother in the town," added one of the men.

Gormley tilted his head to think further about the matter of gears.

While he was doing this, I said again that gears were no use at all if they were not working.

"That's an inescapable point of view," agreed Gormley. "Would you say that the ten-speed's a power for the roundabouts?" he went on, ignoring the meaning in the first part of his sentence.

"Definitely," remarked one of the men on my behalf. He added, "I see you haven't a dynamo for the lights."

"I haven't any lights at all."

"The toe cages, the ten-speed and no lights at all," the man observed. "You'd be a worry at the give-way signs on a dark night, you surely would."

"Without a dynamo," theorised Gormley from behind his steaming pipe, "you've only got half a bicycle. Like Jimmy and Brendon Doughtery of Aghleam on the other side of Blacksod Bay. They share a girlie without a dynamo, and they have no lights at all for the black nights. A fine day it is altogether when you cannot go out at night for the want of a dynamo to power the lights."

These men with their intricate knowledge of the bicycles and cycling habits of half the people in the ancient kingdom of Connaught seemed to inhabit a world of bicycles and bicycle lore, just as cattlemen seem to think only of cattle and pilots only of aircraft.

Lured a little into their way of thinking, I began to wonder whether my French "girl", being French and therefore Cartesian, was becoming irritated with all this fanciful Irish blather, and would have liked straightforward scientific answers to straightforward questions.

"Can you fix my gears?" I said, suddenly and loudly, taking up my girl's thoughts.

The smoke seemed to clear with the surprise of my question.

"That would be the ten-speed crank and the Athena derailleurs you're talking about, would it not?" hypothesised an unfazed Gormley.

"It would."

"Let me tell you they're ten and eleven of the most worrying matters in here at the moment," Gormley reassured. By now the bicycle bells that he had been tinkering with earlier had both been fitted to the handlebars of the solid, silent Raleigh on display near the window and he was doing something detailed and inscrutable with a small electric motor.

A man shifted his bottom on a creaking box. "A worry at the lights," he said, going back to our earlier topic of discussion.

"They should be unauthorised by the Garda, like battery-powered wheelchairs and Belgian-made tractors."

Only one other man took up this theme.

"They say it is a queer and unflavoured land. Flat and circumstantial."

I certainly had no idea what he was talking about and perhaps no one else did either, for they sat there in silence, darkly smoking, watching Gormley and occasionally holding something for him.

"They say that all kinds of accidents and half the deaths in County Mayo are due to the complications of gears, Belgian-built tractors and thoughtless farmers," announced Gormley, without looking up from his work.

"Then there's the drop handlebars," put in one of the men, warming up again.

"The drop handlebars are no benefit at all for the spine, and have they not done terrible things for the Germans and Italians, who, I hear, are fond of cycling with their heads lower than the seats of their trousers," Gormley said.

"The Italians are an arbitrary race, without rhyme or reason," the man who had expressed views on Belgium declared.

Here was an interesting seam to be mined.

"A turbulent and excited race, overly fond of fireworks and politics," continued another.

"Who make meagre and inconstinuent bicycles that are divils for the speed but would not carry the daughter of a Roscommon farmer as far as the market-town of Ballinaboy."

Suddenly we were all aware of a presence in the doorway. The theorising ended as we watched a sinewy man glide a bicycle deftly past my Peugeot and prop it up against the wall.

He was dressed a bit like myself in clashing cycling gear, so he was clearly not a local. His bike was a custom-made Bianchi, a super-light machine with modified racing handlebars containing aerodynamic arm-rests and dual-control gear-shifting levers; the saddle was extremely high — although he was not a tall man — and his pedals were not the worrisome toe cages, but shark teeth.

As I observed all of this, I realised that new material, sufficient to fill an afternoon with hypothesis and speculation, had just been wheeled in, and I resigned myself to not leaving Castlebar that day.

The old men on their boxes blew geysers of smoke and coughed as they assessed the newcomers.

"It's himself," Gormley said after a while, "with two legs as handy as each other and a provocative pair of wheels as well."

The man had not yet said anything, but was carefully removing his gloves, his Giro Air Attack helmet and Kona sunglasses.

Who was he? An arbitrary Italian? An inconstituent Frenchman? A German? A lightweight American?

"Fine day," he finally said.

So he was a Scot – or perhaps an Ulsterman.

"A fine day for taking a pretty colleen down to the Knocklofty roundabout," Gormley elaborated.

Everyone cleared their throats and mumbled a response.

"Well then, is it a matter concernin' a bicycle?" Gormley went on.

"Aye, it is that."

"Then you'd better sit down," I dared to observe, pointing to a spare box. The man walked over. His shoes were stunning, like a pair of Spandex socks in a range of flamboyant colours, and they had a rivetting effect on the old men.

"You're an Australian, then, and she's French," he noted, winking and inclining his head towards my bicycle. His tone was lascivious, and I half expected him to add "say no more".

"And you're Scottish and she's Italian," I answered, almost at home by now with the principles at work in this part of the world.

He winked again.

"Passed a lass on the road this morning," the man said, not to me, but to everyone in the room. "Name of Schwinn. Loaded down with a mechanical looking fellow and excess-baggage."

"American?" asked Gormley, "or even foreigntner?"

"American. Put together by the clever lads in the clever

city of Chicago, in the state of Illinois. We'd all stayed together last night in the youth hostel in Glencolumbkille. There were Italian, French, American, English, even Japanese bints everywhere. One lovely, bright little Shimano 400 EX, I think, seventeen-speed, hyperglide . . . gorgeous she were."

I was sitting there thinking miserably about my Peugeot when I realised with a start that this man must have ridden that morning from Donegal. I had stayed at the same hostel in Glencolumbkille four nights ago and had taken three days to reach Clew Bay.

He had cycled, then, through the dark Blue Stack Mountains, skirting the wet corners of County Fermanagh, and under the shadow of Ben Bulben, down to Drumcliff and Sligo, before entering the green, rocky turmoil of County Mayo. All in less than a day.

"Quite a ride," I put in, as the other men dreamt of Japanese hubs and cog clusters.

"She's made of ultra-light matter," he replied, as if his own efforts had had nothing to do with him being here in Castlebar by afternoon-tea time.

"She nipped up Slieve Gamp and across the bogs like a fox. My own thrashing pinions could barely thrash sufficient."

I guessed that the American from Chicago and her load had probably stopped for pancakes and jam in Sligo and would not have gone much further that day.

Gormley and the old men were listening to this talk out of the corners of their ears and surveying the Scotsman's bike with the corners of their eyes. I sensed that my Peugeot, too, was eyeing off the Bianchi, possibly concluding that she was a typically Italian show-off. A liar, too, perhaps.

"You are the two most unexpected gentlemen I have ever had in this shop together," Mr Gormley suddenly revealed, "and them's two of the most surprising girls."

"Like the reciprocal joke," another man offered, "about the Scotsman, the Australian, and the Italian and the French girls."

"But even more unexpected are the brakes," Gormley went on, ignoring the putative joke. He pointed the stem of his pipe to the Bianchi handlebars. "Are they not a terror in the wet and a menace to the limbs?"

The bicycle had Sattui finger-touch brake extensions.

"They are not," the Scot replied, "anything but the essence of safety."

I looked at my watch. It was half-past two. I had been here almost four hours, passively smoking and passively participating in a discussion of the most absurd matters I had ever heard discussed in any place at all, and nobody had made even the slightest move to examine my bicycle.

"What's wrong with yours?" I asked the Scot, hoping to refocus minds on the purpose of our being there.

"What do you mean, what's wrong with mine?" he asked. "My what?"

"Your bicycle."

"My bicycle?"

"Yes."

"There's nothing wrong with her," he answered defensively. "Who said anything about anything being wrong with anything or anybody or any bicycle?"

"I thought you might have come in for repairs," I reasoned bravely.

"Or a part," someone added helpfully from a dark corner.

"Or a new tyre," someone else said.

"Or a set of sturdy brake pads."

"Or a replacement hub, or bottom brackets."

Gormley moved in to settle the matter.

"He's here for a chat, he is, and to introduce us to his new girlie. For he's a handy boyo altogether for the girls and the talk, Tommy is."

"Aye, Jimmy. She's only a week between my knees and will not be needing a check-up between here and Christmas day."

Tommy? Jimmy? The two men — although a normal word of friendship had not passed between them — obviously knew one another.

"So, you've been here before?" I inquired.

"Tommy's as pleasant and regular a customer as ever you seen," answered Gormley for him, "and he's an awful terror for the girlies as you will see reciprocally if you allow your eyes to visit the fine surprise he's brought in here this Tuesday day."

The Scot proceeded to explain to me that he had retired when he turned 60 – this astonished me, for he had the agility of someone thirty years younger – and spent his time slipping around Scotland, Ireland and England with lassies – mostly from the continent. The "lassies" were, I now understood, bicycles, like the flighty Italian he had arrived with today, but they seemed to have as engaging an effect on him as their human counterparts might have had on other men (me, for instance).

"Mother can't stand me around the house," he went on. "Tommy McManus," he began, mimicing a hectoring, tired woman, and he reproduced a lecture, delivered often it seemed, to a man who had his head, his hands and his house full of bicycles. There were bicycles and bicycle bits, apparently, in every room, being matched and married, separated and re-matched, retired and retrieved, made-up, painted, oiled, examined, prodded, stroked, fondled and ridden, flirted with, danced with, escorted and even slept with, without cease, and so, to give Mrs McManus a break, he frequently pedalled away with a friendly lass, or an aristocratic head-turner or even a country girl, put together in his own kitchen in Inverness with a wheel from Coventry, a frame from Birmingham, handlebars from Glasgow and perhaps an Irish saddle.

And when he was off and away, McManus explained, he often enough called in here with James Gormley of Castlebar for a few minutes' talk and a pint of plain at the end of the day.

"But if you're here often," I inquired, "why did he – Mr Gormley – say that you were unexpected, or something?"

"Jimmy Gormley's not an ordinary fellow," McManus replied. "He's a speciality sort of fellow with some specialised views on life and bicycles. You know," he continued without a break and turning to Gormley, "this yesterday morning I saw two English girls cycling off the Stranraer ferry at Larne ... I moved my eyes to examine their parts and they were from Coventry — but they were with two particularly worrisome boyos."

The point of this story eluded me — it went on and on (with me wondering: "He thinks Gormley's got a particular view on life?") its conclusion being something about ruin and rot being brought to the moral standards of the province of Ulster.

"It should be banned and unauthorised," someone mumbled in response, "if not by the Customs then by the Constabulary of the Royal Ulstermen."

"It is unexpected to have Tommy McManus here at the same high noonday time as yourself," said Gormley, working actively and intimately with a tiny screwdriver at a series of tiny screws. He was responding to the question that I had put in some time before McManus's discourse on the matter and manners of the English bicycles.

"The Royal Ulstermen and the Constabulary of the Royal Kingdom could nip it in the bud handy enough," went on a voice, hopelessly stuck on the subject.

"I thought that someone said something earlier about Italian bikes being too ... thin ... or whatever," I declared, thinking, what the heck, you can say anything you like in here.

"By the jappers, they are thin alright!" pronounced one of the old men with authority, pointing a boot at the Scotsman's flyer.

"And couldn't carry a bag of turf the breadth of the barren Burren," continued another voice.

"Did she not just cycle here with all the powers of the roarin' O'Conors of Ballintober Castle?" roared Gormley himself, coming unexpectedly to the defence of the Italians. "She'd be away over Ballyfinnegal Hill and restin' in the hedges before the likes of thems outside would be at Kilgallon's corner."

The sky, so distant and radiant that morning, had darkened and sagged, the clouds rushing in from the Atlantic and building up in impending bulges above the town.

"The rain hasn't started rainin' yet," said Gormley, observing.

"Are you for the road or for stoppin' in Castlebar?" he asked me.

He had connected several wires with dozens of tiny bulbs attached, like Christmas lights, to a transformer and one of the other men, the first to shift himself from a box, was trying to lift the Raleigh in the window on to a tripod, so that both its wheels were off the floor. All this activity was taking place without any instructions being given, as if everyone else knew the designs that Gormley had in his mind.

"Well . . . I had hoped to be on my way," I replied, "but with the rain coming and . . . THERE'S STILL THE MATTER OF MY BICYCLE . . . ITS GEARS." I said this very carefully and clearly.

"Gears?" interrupted McManus.

"Yes, there's something wrong with them which I can't fix and I've been here all day wondering if we were ever going to get around to the subject."

In a world where men were men and bicycles were girls and Irishmen were full of blarney, my Peugeot by now would have been acutely irritated by everything, and in particular, by the attentions that everyone had lavished on the Bianchi.

And Gormley had in train something for the Raleigh that would only add insult to injury.

Whilst McManus told me that this was the last place he'd have come to have gears fixed, Gormley and the man with the tripod were decorating the shop bike with the tiny lights, running them around her wheels and frame, and putting rosettes of lights on her pedals.

"So what do you suggest?" I asked McManus.

"I suggest I take a look at the technicalities of the lady and report back," he replied, and wandered over to the Peugeot.

As the rain — which had now begun raining — swept in thin, rapid sheets across the street, McManus knelt beside my bike and in the dim light seemed to caress and squeeze its parts as he examined the nature of the trouble.

"The Italian will be near as eaten up with the jealousy," a voice warned from the smoky gloom, "if you are putting your hands too close to her intricate matters."

Gormley rummaged about in a box and produced a contraption with a handle, something like a small grindstone on a stand.

"It's her birthday," he said to himself (whose, I wondered, the grindstone's? Mrs Gormley's?) "and this will really take her to the fair."

McManus was by now expertly executing repairs to my cranks and cogs without any obvious threat to the morals of the shop or the republic. He took no notice of Gormley's filamentary fiddlings; the latter had run wires about the floor, connecting the bicycle to a transformer to the grindstone-like machine and to the little electric motor. There was as yet no visible result of all this activity, but two or three men were now off their boxes, the glow of their cigarettes moving about in the dark as they followed unannounced instructions connecting unseen items with unseen other items.

Gormley flicked a switch and a triangle of green and white fairy lights twinkled to life around the frame of the Raleigh. We all commented upon how lovely the bike looked, but Gormley was still working on something else and took no obvious interest.

A few minutes later, the electric motor started up and the bicycle's wheels began spinning, throwing out a sparkle and then a whirl of red lights.

"Now is that not a wonderous thing altogether?" declared a satisfied Gormley. "And will it not worry the fairy people from here to Knock-na-Feadala?"

It was certainly a surprising and beautiful vision, made more striking by the sheer blackness of the room and of the street outside.

We all sat, silently transfixed. Only McManus ignored the show and kept working on the Peugeot, whispering to himself — or to the bicycle — from time to time.

Our reveries of fairy lights and bicycles were broken, however, by a light being turned on in a room adjacent to the rear of the shop. There was the sound of kitchen articles being moved and of water running.

"JAMS!" A human woman's voice suddenly engulfed the world. "Are you ready for your tea?" An arm reached in from the kitchen and turned on the shop lights, effectively extinguishing the display in the window.

"By the divil!" the woman spluttered when she saw that there were at least eight idle men in the room and two saucy *continental* racing bikes.

All the men — except McManus — stood up and greeted Mrs Gormley in a humble, desultory way. She was a stout, firm-faced woman who looked from one to the other moving her lips silently and derisively. She had the appearance of someone who had done the shopping and other heavy duties, and was now looking in to see what her husband had done with his day.

"With this lot in here and himself over there," she declared to Gormley, nodding her head in the direction of McManus, "I have no doubt that you've been enjoying all kinds of recreations and diversions, no doubt at all."

"And I suppose you're here concernin' a bicycle," she went on, looking at me. She laughed. "Sure your head's cut. It's not only meself but the whole of the county knows that Jams Gormley's a great man altogether for the gab and a great man for the tricky inquiries. But he's an awful man for the no-workin'."

"Now, Mrs Gormley." It was Tommy McManus, standing up from his labours with my bike.

"And didn't I know that you'd be here," she responded. "The lord of the bicycles, himself, and dressed up like something from Romper Room."

Gormley had no defence at all and stood through the gales of his wife's anger and ridicule, concentrating on another electrical riddle.

There was silence as Mrs Gormley looked mockingly from

one to the other of us with her broad arms folded. She then turned and went back into the kitchen.

The men stoked up their pipes or re-lit the cigarettes that they had hurriedly crumpled. Someone turned off the main lights and the Raleigh glowed again in the window. Life resumed as before and the interruption was immediately forgotten.

I went over to examine McManus's Bianchi. "Mind," he growled softly from behind the spokes of my Peugeot. His bicycle was indeed lovely, painted in an iradescent red and black, with matt black working parts . . . as fine an athlete as you would ever see. And wasn't there an alluring and provocative glint about her . . . ?

I stopped myself.

This was ridiculous. The Bianchi was a splendidly designed and engineered bike, and nothing more.

"There," announced McManus, standing up and wiping oil from his hands. "She's ready to take you to Galway by supper time. Mind if I join you?"

"I . . . I . . ." I'd had no intention of riding to Galway that evening (it was at least 80 kilometres away) and in any case, had the bike been fixed earlier, I would have headed westwards to Clifden in Connemara, rather than south to Galway.

"Thanks but I think I'll stay in Castlebar tonight," I said.

Gormley looked up holding a hatful of winking lights.

"That's grand news all round," he declared, the winking reflecting on his face. "Sure it's a dirty night out there altogether and no place for a couple of foreigntners" (meaning me and my bicycle). "And you Tommy, are you for stayin' too?"

"I am," replied McManus, having reassessed. Gormley put down the hat with all the lights in it flicking and blinking and rubbed his big hands together.

"By the cripes, then, men," he announced cheerily, "it'll be a brave night of porter and volubility!"

"MRS GORMLEY," he shouted at the kitchen, "TOMMY McMANUS AND THE FOREIGNT GENTLE-

MAN AND THE FOREIGNT LASSIES WILL BE STOPPIN' OVER."

It was no use protesting that I would be as happy to cycle away to a bed and breakfast. The night was arranged.

McManus placed the Bianchi and the Peugeot carefully in the rear of the shop, well away from the window where the Raleigh was now flashing prettily.

The old men helped Gormley put away bits of wire, tools and electrical appliances, and straightened their boxes.

"We've earned the right to open our mouths around a jar or two, tonight," Gormley enthused, "but first you two had better get off them circus clothes."

McManus and I were shown upstairs to our bedrooms by a grumbling, but now not unfriendly, Mrs Gormley. It appeared that bed and breakfast was also part of the family business — perhaps the only profitable part, I mused.

We changed into clothes more suitable for the pub and went down to join Gormley. Some of the other men had switched on their dynamos, put on their bicycle clips and cycled away to their own homes. The remaining three joined us, first wheeling their ancestral bikes into the shop.

Six of us walked outside and ducked across the road into a bar. Its front window was decorated with two empty bottles of Guinness, one full bottle of Bushmills, two walking sticks and a poster advertising "Philomea Begley and The Rambling Boys". The gold lettering above the doorway read simply "FINNEGANS".

Inside, the bar was small, gloomy and smoke-filled. Three or four groups of stubbly men in overcoats sat around tables, black pints in front of them, whilst others leant at the bar, arguing and disclaiming.

The publican greeted Gormley.

"That's a fancy show in your shop, sure it is," he said warmly.

"It's for the lass's birthday," explained Gormley abstrusely.

As the drink orders were being taken, I said that I'd like a whiskey to start with, perhaps a Jameson, I noted, eyeing a bottle behind the bar.

"Jameson?" Gormley accused. "Them's a Presbyterian crowd, and cold and hard with it. You'll take a Bush."

Bushmills it was — a drop of the hard, as Gormley put it when he ordered — and Guinness for the others.

McManus knew a few of the patrons and went over to talk to a man who was robustly roaring and drinking at the other end of the bar. He brought him back a few minutes later and introduced him to me as Constable Heaney.

"I hear you like a bit of the bicycle," Heaney bellowed. "Like a bit myself, I do, from time to time."

McManus explained that Constable Heaney knew more about bikes than even Jimmy Gormley himself, and declaring that we would have a lot to talk about — because Heaney had an utterly queer and particular attitude to things — went away to the bar to order another round.

"And what brings you to Castlebar?" Heaney asked between great mouthfuls of porter. "A matter concernin' a bicycle, I'll have no doubt, no doubt at all."

Santos-Dumont
CENTRO
MARINA (da GLORIA)
Flamengo Bch.
BOTAFOGO BAY
BOTAFOGO
CHARLES LE CORBUSIER
URCA
Pao de Acucar
ATLANTIC OCEAN
COPACABANA
Rio de Janeiro

Blame it on the bossa nova

(Rio de Janeiro, Brazil)

Rhythm, grace, beauty, the exotic, everything comes to the minds of good and bad people

— from the *Golden Rio* program

The sight of jets of flame spurting gracefully from the engines of an aircraft as it taxies for take-off on a dark, mercury-splashed runway is impressive. Particularly when you are in the aircraft.

I watch, rivetted, as the green and scarlet fires, arching from each of the engines in turn, illuminate the fuselage of our Aero Peru 707. They don't interfere with take-off, however, and within minutes the old ship is climbing uncertainly towards Cerro Aconcagua and the jagged, snowy peaks of the Andes, shrouded now in a black mist.

Two hours into the journey, the captain comes in from the flight deck, leans across a row of seats and appears to gaze at something on or beyond the wings. More flames, perhaps? He goes back to his post and a few minutes later his co-pilot appears and proceeds to study the night-view through the same window. By now a crowd has gathered, everyone offering advice, no doubt, in the usual way. Maybe we're lost, I think, but since by now we would be crossing the flat acres of Paraguay, with no more mountains in the way, it doesn't really matter. Or perhaps they've discovered a clutch of condors nesting on the wing. These and other silly thoughts come to me as I try to keep my eyes and mind firmly on my even sillier book, Isabel Allende's *The House of the Spirits*.

By 8 o'clock we have begun a turbulent descent through the constellations of cloud hovering above the Tropic of Capricorn. The lightning, when it strikes, is almost expected after the fires at take-off and the in-flight worry over the wings. The strike lifts the plane and sends a crack like a disintegrating timber bridge to every corner of its body and everybody inside.

There is immediate pandemonium and prayer, but in seconds we are back on the bitumen (as pilots like to say) and winging in on finals through clear, still air.

The 707, losing height rapidly, glides past the glare of a city, skirts a small aerodrome and touches down at an airport in Guanabara Bay like an elderly wandering albatross after an interminable flight across the raging heavens.

Muchas gracias y buenas noches, Aero Peru.

Hello Rio de Janeiro.

Immigration procedures are surprisingly speedy — for a country famed worldwide for its clotted and overwheening bureaucracy — and in a couple of minutes I find myself standing at a welcome desk for tourists.

The attendant, a girl who demonstrates fluency in at least English, Spanish, French and Portuguese in the short time I am in front of her, gives me a stern warning about carrying my passport, travellers cheques and other valuables about Rio.

She offers me a mock passport, which I am instructed to carry, leaving the real one locked up in the hotel, a map of the city, a list of hotels and their prices, and a curious language disc which later I will fail to master. Finally she advises me to change money only in *recognised foreign exchange establishments*. Even as she speaks, a large black man is beside me, rocking on his air-cushioned Nikes and counting cruzados.

"Change money?" he asks as soon as the girl has finished. "Fifty dollars, nine hundred cruzados."

I have no way of knowing whether this is a steal for him or me, but the girl who just then had issued her warning winks, so I accept. In any case he turns out to be the porter who she has assigned to carry my bags to the taxi, so I'm somehow ensnared.

My taxi moves through fast traffic pouring into tunnels. After the chill nights of Santiago, I feel the intoxication of being back in the tropics. This is my weather, I think, and I am in a country that I have wanted to visit since I first opened my National Geographic Encyclopedia when I was 6 years old. In that book the pages depicting The Ancient Roman

Forum, Princes Street in the Historic Scottish Capital or even Windmills on the Flat Dutch Lowlands remained undisturbed, whilst those showing Sugarloaf Mountain, The Mouth of the Amazon River Nearly Three Miles Wide and São Paulo's Skyline much like Chicago's had me endlessly transfixed, marvelling at this extraordinary place.

My first book, *High Times in the Middle of Nowhere*, described me in its subtitle as a "compulsive traveller", yet I had never crossed the Pacific to the Americas. Asia and Europe had been my beat, and it was not until Aerolineas Argentinas introduced its transpolar service out of Auckland to Buenos Aires that the continents suddenly seemed closer. Most maps of the world put Europe and Africa in the centre, with the American continents to the left and Australia and Southeast Asia to the right, so exaggerating the yawning nothingness of ocean in between. And the airlines of South America – like those of Asia and Australia – fly north, to North America and Europe. There are few horizontal routes following the latitudes of the south. Yet look at the latitudes: Sydney and Buenos Aires on about 35 degrees south, Rockhampton and Rio de Janeiro on the Tropic of Capricorn. The Argentine airline has shown that Auckland is as close to Buenos Aires – eleven hours – as Buenos Aires is to Paris, or Rio is to London, and closer than either Buenos Aires or Rio are to Los Angeles.

At the Hotel Martinique the clerk at the reception desk welcomes me and then observes, with an air of surprise:

"You have booked a very small home."

"First point," I ask, "don't you mean *room*?"

"Yes. *Home*. And it is very small."

"I didn't book a very small home at all. I booked a single *room*."

The clerk pretends to study a sheaf of telexes, adjusting his glasses and frowning.

I quickly surmise that the only vacant room is this particularly small one so I tell him that I'll take it and worry about a change in the morning.

The room to which I am assigned is indeed small. It reminds me of those boxes in which the staff sleep — or live — in Indian hotels, and I suspect this is its purpose here in the Martinique.

At midnight, having settled in to this little home, I walk almost the full length of the beach at Copacabana.

The wide footpaths — constructed of elaborately patterned ceramic tiles — on either side of Avenida Atlântica are teeming as if a major public event is about to commence. There is no event however, just the warm South Atlantic trades, the dazzle of lights and the breezy buzz of cafés and restaurants drawing the crowds. At a café I order a beer and, trying to ignore the vendors of string puppets, 2 metre-long bouncing balloons, tee-shirts, hot nuts and luminous tops, sit astonished at finding myself in this fabled place. The sound coming from inside is the tangy voice of Gal Costa singing *Olhos Do Coraçãs* and at this point I can only agree with the inhabitants of Rio — the Cariocas — who refer to their city as *cidade maravilhosa* (the marvellous city). Mediating thus, it takes me some time to realise that a small boy is beside me yelling "Sit, sit, sit!" and pointing to my shoes.

He is a shoe-shine boy and what he's pointing at is not marvellous at all. It is a roll of dog shit which has lodged itself on top of my shoe, right on the little leather frills. The boy immediately gets to work — removing the turd, wrapping it neatly in paper and slipping it into his box, and then points to a figure scratched on to a card. it reads "100 000". A hundred thousand is not a hundred thousand, but a hundred. Or is it? Perhaps it's a thousand or ten. You have to ignore the zeros, the girl at the welcome desk had told me, but how many? I pull a bundle of notes from my pocket — as thick as a prayer book — and start fingering through them. But even if a hundred thousand is a hundred, I think, is that five dollars, or ten, or two? It depends where you change your money, and whether you're talking about cruzeiros or cruzados. Each can be the other, but assumes a different value. The boy's eyes light upon a 100 000 cruzeiro note. I give up and hand it to him, and as he dashes away, beaming, with his turd in a box, I know that I've fallen victim to my first little *cambalacho*.

Returning to the Martinique, I discover a further problem with my new home. The key won't unlock the door.

The clerk sends me away to the lounge to watch television whilst he and the porter go up and down the lift trying every key in the building and (just in case) the keys belonging to the taxi-drivers, money-changers, security guards and out-of-work drummers loitering in the hotel doorway.

During this time I discover that Brazilian television, at least on first viewing and at two in the morning, is rather like French TV, consisting mainly of well-dressed, grey-haired men discussing matters endlessly and ponderously, with frequent cuts to undressed girls selling everything from houses in pretentious, fortified estates to holidays in Disney World and toddlers' wading pools.

Finally the locksmiths complete their task and I am sent up to my room. There I find that they have resorted to the screwdriver and hammer, leaving the jamb and part of the door in splinters and the door creaking softly in the wake of the fan.

In the morning a new receptionist is flabbergasted when he learns firstly that I have been sleeping in the "home" that is reserved for other purposes (specifically the manager's after-lunch liaisons), and secondly that I have broken the door down. I deal with these matters swiftly, change rooms and then prepare for a day's sightseeing.

Consulting *South America on $25 a Day*, I decide to visit the 400-year-old Gloria church first. In the taxi I try out my new language disc.

"Eu desejo..." (I wish), I stutter, spinning the disc and searching for a conclusion.

"Sim?" (Yes), asks the driver, peering at me and my device.

"Eu..." The outer disc lands on a phrase. *"Minha roupa"*, I declare.

The man gapes at me and at my little linguistic roulette wheel. I have just said that I desire my washing. I try again.

"Eu... Gloria, église," I blurt, resorting to French.

The driver shouts something and as his Volkswagen bats off into the traffic moving north along the coast, I quietly pocket my disc and resolve to use my copy of *Conversational Brazilian Portuguese: The Easy Method* in future.

A few minutes later the driver drops me at a marina on a bay just past Flamengo beach. My map shows it as the Marina da Gloria, so at least part of my message was understood. I decide to take a look around and walk into a scene that could easily be at Kirribilli or Ruschcutters Bay — with blond yachting types dressed in navy and red swaggering about, and the flags of all the countries which were then competing for the America's Cup in Fremantle, Western Australia, flying overhead.

Later I do find the church — one of many still standing which echo the Portuguese founding of this city in 1567 — and then get lost amongst the steep hills and dense pockets of equatorial bush around it, emerging hours later somewhere on the avenues of towering queen palms in Flamengo Park. Rio is a city of hills, much more than Sydney is. They rise suddenly and steeply from the water, or just a few hundred metres from the beaches, giving the city a dramatic and eccentric quality, and making navigation quite haphazard.

For lunch I follow the advice of the guidebook and drop in at Rio's in Parque do Flamengo. This restaurant is listed under their "Big Splurge" section, but with chicken and fish dishes for about three or four dollars, I feel that it's an affordable splurge. The day is a lively 30 degrees, I am seated at the bayside under an umbrella, the utter glassy beauty of Flamengo beach to my left and *Pão de Açucar* (Sugarloaf) looming above me, and I cannot imagine that I would rather be anywhere else.

A waiter approaches.

"Você bebe vinho, não é?" (You drink wine, do you not?) I announce, reading from my phrasebook.

He stares, perplexed.

"Bebem vinho no Rio?" (They drink wine in Rio?) I continue.

The waiter quickly tires of this idiocy and produces a menu which provides an English translation.

I order chicken. The menu also offers "Drinks: Wine or

Bear". I order a bear and sit back to consider my Easy Method book. There is scarcely a phrase in it with which I could have communicated with the waiter. Except perhaps this: *"Você não compreende o garçon?"* (Don't you understand the waiter?).

The rest of the book provides assistance with the sorts of encounters that tourists face every day in Brazil:

"Sir, I want you to make me a linen suit."

or "He is a professor, and his watch is fast."

and this, "Mary isn't a student, she is having her nails done."

or this, "Fortunately it isn't snowing. When it snows the temperature goes way down."

Late in the afternoon, since it isn't snowing, I set out to walk back to Copacabana. I skirt Botafogo Bay and head towards Urca where the cable-cars for Sugarloaf depart. Coastal Rio is truly a narrow strip of high-density housing. Across the avenues from the beaches there are continuous walls of apartment blocks, eight to fifteen stories high. Only three or four rows are crammed in before the hills take off, and these, where they are not too steep, are also covered in dwellings, the brick and timber *favelas* of the poor.

In 1936, Charles Le Corbusier was brought to Brazil as an architectural consultant. With Lucio Costa and Oscar Niemeyer, amongst others, Le Corbusier gave birth to an imaginative and uniquely Brazilian architecture which is apparent today in the bold, bright style of Rio de Janeiro. According to the biographer of Oscar Niemeyer, "The two decades that followed Le Corbusier's visit were imbued with the most ardent architectural optimism, a kind of creative lust which permeated Brazil's architects, clients, public administrators and the man in the street." Of course, in the business heart of Rio, Centro, located between Santos-Dumont airport and Gloria beach, there are nineteenth-century public buildings in the grand style of the European colonial era. These are set upon broad avenues, several of which, like Rio Branco, have footpaths illustrated with fantastic mosaic designs.

From Urca you take two connecting cable-cars to reach the 396 metre-high peak of Sugarloaf, a solid tower of granite which stands at the entrance to Guanabara Bay — Rio's South Head. At the first landing point, on top of Morro da Urca at 230 metres, there is a collection of shops and restaurants, and my attention is drawn to a sign which invites you to:

"COME LIVE AGAIN THE SPLENDOR OF A CARNIVAL PARADE. THE CHOREOGRAPHY OF THE MASTER OF CEREMONIES AND THE STANDARD BEARER. THE ART OF THE HOOFERS AND THE RHYTHM SECTION. SPECTACULAR MULATAS. LUXURY NUMBERS. DON'T LOSE THIS SPECTACLE IN GORGEOUS TECHNICOLOR".

The view of the Atlantic side of Rio from Sugarloaf is dazzling, and you can see how the first Portuguese navigators, when they saw the entrance to Baía de Guanabara, which is only a little wider than the Sydney Heads, assumed that it was the mouth of a river, and so named it Rio de Janeiro, as it was 1 January 1502. On board this ship was the peculiar Italian scholar, Amerigo Vespucci, who later wrote, "I have found, in these southern lands, a continent . . . One can, with good reason, name it the New World." As I am contemplating these words which contain within them the awesome recognition of what had been found, a storm spins in from nowhere and closes us off from the shining city in a damp cowl. The Brazilian tourists at the summit can't believe it. One group has small drums and tambourines, and to defy the skies they begin playing. *Kutatung, kutatung, kutatung* . . . the familiar base thump of a samba vibrates through the air and soon half the people on our island in the clouds are gathered near the coffee shop, moving instinctively to this, the fundamental rhythm of Brazil.

A day or two later I look up an old friend who runs an inbound travel agency and he invites me to join a night tour to the samba school display halfway up the peak at Urca. I board a coach full of Americans, Mexicans and Argentinians with a guide who translates each of his Portuguese sentences into Spanish, French and German — a time-wasting flatulence, given the composition of our tour. In any case, the Americans, all participants in a medical conference, spend the bus and cable-car ride hawing at one another about that day's papers on endocrinology, whilst the Hispanics gas between gulps of hot smoke about whatever urgent matters occupy their attention.

After dinner in a restaurant which offers magnificent views of the city under lights, we move to Concha Verde for the show, which I realise is to be the very one offering luxury numbers, hoofers, etc. The program given to us reveals that samba is:

> authentically Brazilian music with its roots in Ancient Africa that has acquired new life in Brazil, melding the influences of the negro, the white race and the Indians . . . Don't be backward in joining in the samba. Even if you cannot yet match the voluptuous sway and sensuality of the mulatas, the nimbleness of the chorus dancers, and the style of the Master of Ceremonies, why not try out a few steps: loosen up your body and let the heady rhythm pervade your senses.

Suddenly there is a group of drummers dressed in white on the floor, hammering out a beat that reaches your stomach. There are singers, women of all ages dressed in the rococo nonsense of carnival costumes and, yes, mulattas, sensuous beauties in jewelled trifles.

These are members of the famed Beija Flor samba school — about two dozen of the 3000 or so who belong — which has achieved star rating in carnival after carnival. If you can't be in Brazil for these pre-lenten celebrations, then the Beija Flor show at Urca is perhaps the next best thing, a tiny sample of the extravagant frenzy that overtakes Rio for a week or so each year.

The show is designed to involve the audience, and after various members of the group have demonstrated their skills — either with their instruments or their bodies — particular members of the audience are invited to participate. Hilarious scenes follow as stiff-kneed foreigners wriggle pathetically or batter away at a drum or tambourine. One of the mulatta dancers selects an antique man who might be a retired water metre-inspector for a little rhythmic togetherness. He has the time of his life — old legs emuing this way and that, brown cardigan flared, lips pouting, as his partner, probably 20 years old and dressed in nothing but dental floss and stars, lures him around in a slippery samba bounce. I fear for his heart but he survives and is given an ovation by the crowd.

Now, speaking frankly, it was not only the lure of São Paulo's skyline or Sugarloaf Mountain that brought me to Rio. There was also this:

> Tall and tanned,
> And young and lovely,
> The girl from Ipanema goes walking,
> And when she passes,
> Each one she passes
> Goes aah . . .

So here I am, seated on the terrace of the bar called Garôta de Ipanema (Girl from Ipanema), where the song — and the bossa nova — were created. I am surrounded by perhaps two dozen other men, all tourists, looking for, hoping for, waiting for the same thing. I feel rather like an American undergraduate in Dublin, clutching his copy of *Ulysses* as he eyes the pint of black porter wobbling on the bar before him. Or a seeker of the quintessential Parisian experience, buying a second-hand copy of Henry Miller's *Tropic of Capricorn* or Jean-Paul Satre's *Iron in the Soul* at Shakespeare's and taking it up the road to the Deux Magots to read until twilight at a table on the Boulevard St Germain.

My notes from the terrace read:

> Brazil's most famous song, however often or wherever it is heard, still carries with it the soft rhythms of the night breezes in Rio. To visit Ipanema is to visit a sort of shrine, a Latin Merseyside perhaps, where the bossa nova was created. The poetry of Vinicius de Moraes, the compositions of Antonio Carlos Jobim and the voice of João Gilberto came together in *this bar*, producing one of the world's major departures in popular music.

Did I really write that about a shrine? A *Latin Merseyside?*

Maybe I lifted it in a sideways swipe from one of the other seekers' tables.

Anyway, whatever we were seeking, whatever we were waiting for, whatever we were writing, the song goes on:

> Ah, but I watch her so sadly,
> How can I tell her I love her?
> Yes I would give my heart gladly,
> But each day when she walks to the sea,
> She looks straight ahead not at me . . .

And so it was.

* * *

At the Scala nightclub, the Golden Rio show is an attempt to put on stage some of the significant elements that are part of the diverse cultures of Brazil. It is an incredible show, fast-paced, expertly designed and brilliantly performed. I went on a Tuesday night to the early — 11.30 p.m. — show in an auditorium full of excited Brazilians, French and Argentinians.

In a noisy gale of colour and music we saw all the following (and more): *The Story of the Dolls' Vendor* (according to the Scala brochure; "he dreams of the day when his dolls will come to life"); *The Gafieira* (described in the brochure as being, "where all lovers of samba and maxixe meet; maxixe is a very special warm kind of dance to be danced cheek to cheek, very close together and very coluptuously. Fights arise sometimes but they always cools down, and everybody is happy again."); *Casa Grade e Senzala* (a depiction of love between a Portuguese girl and a negro slave: "it is a nightmare of the past when there was segregation specially towards the negroes"); *Mulatas* ("In Rio and this immense Brazil, the very sexy mulatas are the great attraction of the night. Exuberant and lustful bodies; exilerating bodies with special hot movements and different ways, appeal to the mind. Rhythm, grace, beauty, the exotic, everything comes to the minds of good and bad people. That's it."); *High Praise to Bahia* (the state of Brazil "that is full of odd beliefs, faith, voodoos, and all the black magic from Africa"); *Bossa Nova* ("this new rhythm took its inspiration from the ondulating walk of our bathing beauties and the loveliness of our girls and their scanty biquinis"); *A full samba percussion display* ("the drumming of the samba schools is the traditional rhythm of Brazil. It is violent and feverish and it gets into your nerves . . . that's why this country dances and sings eternally — Amen"); and *Carnival* ("four days of joy and sensuality where all the races and ranks of society take part").

For about $20 I watched all this in a show that demonstrated, in a highly professional way, the almost transcendental hold that their own popular culture has upon Brazilians. One of the great achievements of Brazil is that it is the world's most successful multi-racial society, and this is partly due to the fact that the whole nation celebrates the African origins of much that is today considered Brazilian.

The show ends and I walk out into the streets of Ipanema. From the south comes the percussion of the Atlantic surf. To the north, beneath the stars, are the silent citadels of the Carioca Serra; and there, a few degrees further north, standing nearly two kilometres high, is Corcovado, holding aloft the great floodlit statue of Christ, the ultimate redeemer and protector, watching with infinite patience the endless frenzy of the little Circean strip of Brazil that is Rio.

"O êsse Brasil lindo e trigueiro . . ." (This is Brazil, beautiful and golden), sang the amazing Watusi at the conclusion of Golden Rio.

'Land of samba and tambourine, Brazil for me, for me Brazil."

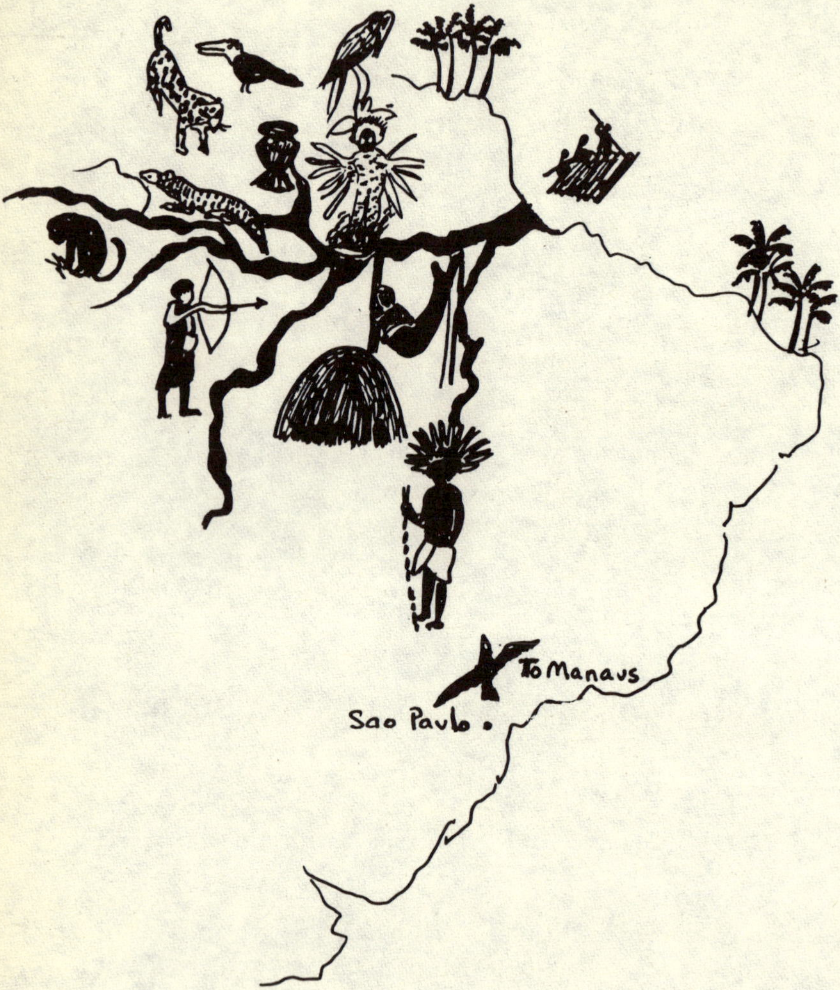
To Manaus
Sao Paulo

Not quite into the heart of darkness

(Manaus, Brazil)

"Welcome to Singapore!"
Singapore?

The man in the seat beside me was flicking his fingers at the scene on the ground as our aircraft broke through the clouds and rolled unevenly on cushions of hot air during our descent to Manaus.

Below us the great milky stream of the Solimões River, emerging from a tunnel of jungle, headed to its confluence with the Rio Negro — so forming the Amazon, which, even here, 1600 kilometres from the Atlantic, is 8 kilometres wide.

I must admit I was excited. It was the sort of chilling excitement (all too rare today) which you feel when you are about to see one of the world's great icons — a place with a riveting power that you have wanted to visit ever since childhood.

But *Singapore*? At first I thought that my neighbour was referring to the tropical location. Brazilians have a vision of Asia — particularly of Singapore — as being a delightful and exotic garden, lying tantalisingly beyond the farthest horizon.

"Televisions, videos, laptops, hi-fi," he went on after a while. "Brazil's Singapore."

Of course. Manaus was a duty-free city and most of the Brazilians on the plane were not coming here to see the jungle, or any of Manaus's architectural curiosities, but to stock up on the sophisticated goods which were imported and assembled in Manaus and which could be "exported" to the rest of Brazil tax-free.

We were at the end of a four-hour flight from São Paulo, a bit further than the distance between Sydney and Alice Springs. Like a journey across Australia, we had flown for hours over an apparent nothingness once we left the immense mass of São Paulo — a city of sixteen million people — behind.

For two hours we crossed the Mato Grosso, flat grasslands which eventually gave way to jungle. Crossing the state of Amazonas at 850 kilometres an hour, it was easy to be lulled into believing that it was not in danger — there was so much of it down there, a green wilderness of four million square kilometres, half the size of Australia divided only by thick, aimless-looking rivers. Where were the destructive fires? The sixty-one football fields of forest being cut down by the minute? The desolate, leached grazing lands with their skinny, cankerous cattle?

This, of course, was the view, traditional and widespread in Brazil, that has permitted and unleashed so much devastation: the *Amazon is endless, it is not in danger.*

Brazil has always needed extravagant visions. (And why not — it is in so many ways an extravagant country?) So right now the nation was reacting angrily to the developed world in general, and to Sting in particular, with their claims that if the present rate of burning and logging continued, by 2020 the Amazon would be no more than garden scraps, its dazzling conucopia of almost everything — plant life, animal life, reptile life, fish life, insect life, bird life (unfortunately you couldn't really use the term "dazzling" to describe the region's human life) — wantonly destroyed.

In the big cities, the media were carrying the debate, the Brazilian side often retreating into a nationalistic sulk: you did it to your wild areas; don't tell us what we can or can't do with ours.

But there *was* a Brazilian opposition — in fact there were many points of view which coalesced after the murder of the rubber tappers' leader and hero, Chico Mendes, and which were receiving serious coverage.

"See it while it's still there!" was yet another point of view. This is the one that some cynical denizens of places like Rio de Janeiro represented. There are tour operators capitalising on the anxieties of Europeans and Americans about the Amazon. And they are pouring in — from Copenhagen and Amsterdam, Rome and Paris, New York and Toronto. (To be fair, a lot of the Europeans are here not only for a chance to see the last of the rainforests but . . . to sunbathe; yes, there are many strange sights in Amazonia, but few stranger than that of wintry-skinned Europeans lying on an artificial beach beside this rushing river, this river full of pirarucu, tucanaré, capybara, crocodiles and of course, pirana, with their "cruelly armed jaws").

Our aircraft landed and taxied to the terminal. Tourists and duty-free shopping have made Manaus airport one of the busiest in the country, yet the sight of 747 and DC-10 freighters from Japan and Taiwan and wide-bodied jets from all over Brazil and from Surinam, Venezuela, Colombia and Peru was incongruous in this truly remote place.

I checked in at the Hotel Da Vinci and then went straight to the historical city centre. "Manaus is a legend," began my guidebook, and I wanted to see it all. If you have seen the Werner Herzog film *Fitzcarraldo*, you will recall the wonderful, opulent, extravagant opera house rising above a nineteenth-century boom-town setting. That is Manaus.

The city was a fantastic creation, materialising during the turn-of-the-century rubber boom and taking off to become one of the world's richest cities – so rich, the tour guides never tire of telling you, that even the average rich sent their laundry away to Lisbon and their children to school in Switzerland.

Craftsmen and artists from Italy and France and engineers from England (it would never have worked the other way round) built the Teatro Amazonas (opera house), the floating docks and Customs House, the municipal markets (modelled on Les Halles in Paris) and many churches and squares.

But it was all so brief. This flashy Babylon, where, according to one source, "at private parties in the luxurious villas and palaces of the rubber kings, naked girls took showers in iced Cordon Rouge", like all Babylons, quite simply collapsed in about 1910 when the British sneaked off to Malaya with rubber tree seeds.

Unfortunately, during my visit, the most precious remnant

of all this wonder — the opera house — was undergoing restoration, and was boarded up. But the sight of it, beyond the mosaics of Praça São Sebastião and illuminated by the late afternoon sun, was compensation for not seeing the frescoes and treasures inside.

Today Manaus is a ramshackle sort of place, historically rich, and expanding rapidly again. But it is a twentieth-century expansion of concrete and trucks, duty-free shops and tee-shirt factories. And there are always newer boom towns in Brazil, like Boa Vista in the country's extreme north, or the golden mountain town of Beiradão on the Jari river.

Later I dropped into the Beija Flor handicraft shop. Here there were excited groups of Italians buying 3 metre-long blow guns and poisonous darts. You could try out these items, aiming at a straw and cork doll perched on the counter. This was a crowded shop — lots of customers, a good ratio of staff and tumbling heaps of handicrafts all over the place. The sight of Italian girls, who had trouble holding the blow pipe up to their mouths, pointing haphazardly at the doll was terrifying. But they had enough puff to shoot the darts . . . zing . . . into the target (or, more precisely, into the boxes, walls, floor, bundles of feathers and wooden artefacts all around it).

I had an interesting chat with one of the salesgirls. She was Indian, as were most of the staff, and she whispered to me that *everything* — handicrafts, blow guns, bones and feathers — was cheaper at the market. Why tell me this, I asked. Surely you get a commission on sales here?

"Well, yes, 2 per cent in fact. But I get more if I send people to the Dinossauro shop in the market. Just tell them Acadia sent you."

Our conversation went on. She told me that a lot of tourists thought she was Japanese. Did I?

"No," I replied. "But I can tell you why they *think* you're Japanese." I explained how the Indians of the Americas had migrated from Asia via the Bering Straits during the last Ice Age and had spread throughout the two continents, and I used a receipt book to draw a map and illustrate the closeness of America and North Asia. So her ancestors were Asian . . . just like the Japanese.

This was astonishing. This girl, whose parents had come from a tribal area about 400 kilometres away, who was nevertheless well educated, spoke English fluently and mixed with foreigners, had never heard of such a thing and was inclined to disbelieve me. My further teachings were interrupted, however, by her supervisor, who glared at us, flourishing his teeth.

In response to this, I aimed a blow gun at him when his back was turned, causing panic amongst the sales staff who thought that I really was going to bring him down as casually as their parents might have shot a howler monkey or three-toed sloth.

Next day I took a "Meeting of the Waters" tour. At the docks — where the most astonishing sight is the ocean-going cargo ships, 1600 kilometres from the sea — we boarded a river boat and set off for a seven-hour exploration of the surrounding waterways.

The tourists with me were about 50 per cent Brazilian, 20 per cent Argentinian and the rest mostly Italian or French. There was another Australian, a loud-mouthed girl who had taken to the Brazilian habit of going about in tiny bikini top — to ill-effect. She reminded me of those silly Australians and Americans who dress up in saris when in India.

As we motored towards the convergence of the two rivers, the tour guide yammered effortlessly and endlessly at us in Portuguese, English and Spanish. When he discovered the large numbers of Italians and French aboard, he added their languages so that each sentence, such as "even the not-so-rich would send their laundry to Lisbon", had to be repeated four times, filling the air for seven hours.

At one point he was interrupted by a sudden and furious thunderstorm, which caused everyone to run around in panic. I had already located the life jackets and had positioned myself near the stern of the boat — standard practice when taking ferries on any body of water that lies between the two tropics. The storm passed, rushing away to the north to Guyana and Surinam, and the guide picked up the threads of his spiel, only, like a tape that's been reversed for a few moments, he began several sentences back, and repeated, without hesitation or variation, what he had said before. Something about the millionaires of Manaus lighting their cigars with the equivalent of $200 notes.

At the "meeting of the waters" our boat wallowed long enough for us to take far too many pictures of this natural oddity where the yellowish Rio Solimões and the black Rio Negro course side by side for about 18 kilometres before merging. My own photographs show a rippling sea of muddy water and a lot of people leaning over the bows to snap it.

Next we docked at a floating handicraft bazaar with about six other tour boats. The crush was fantastic, and the colourful handicrafts better value than in town. But there was a certain feeling of unease or sorrow here . . . just beyond the boards of the bazaar, a rickety bridge led into the swamps towards a couple of huts sinking into the mud and hyacinths, tiny clearings and then black forest.

Later we disembarked at a great floating warehouse on Lago Janaurii.

"In Manaus in the old days," sniggered an Argentine wit, "this warehouse would have been a *whorehouse*" — a quite clever observation that was lost on most of us as we struggled to board motorised canoes for a closer-to-the-water trip into the infinite puzzle of narrow passages at the great river's edges.

We had to wear life jackets and the sight was quite comical, as dozens of canoes loaded with awkward bodies zipped about this bewildering labyrinth. One would appear in front on a tiny waterway crossing ours, and then disappear. Another would be glimpsed through the trees and lianas, an orange flash, before it too disappeared into a green hole. There were accidents as canoes in line ploughed into creepers and spiky palms or intersected at the wrong place and moment.

And there were refreshment stops. At these, jungle children appeared in dugout canoes from the depths of the watery forest, with coolite boxes full of beer, soft drinks and coconuts and, for entertainment, sloths, snakes, monkeys and alligators on strings.

The Italians in particular — with their video cameras hard at work — became over-excited at the sight of all this wildlife. Despite this, most of the animals (taking their cue from the sloth) slept through it all.

Only the alligator was working. He was on a 4-metre string and had to swim about between the boats, his little boy keeper earning about one cruzado per photo.

Refreshed, we headed up a tangled, snaky reach of river, the torpid waters frothing under our outboard motors as we sought our promised "mystery surprise".

I was in the first canoe, and as we emerged from dank undergrowth into daylight and on to a broad lake, I detected the surprise: a group of Indians lolling beside the banks of the river in jeans and tee-shirts. I must have seen them a millisecond before they saw us; by the time I realised what I had seen they had vanished.

We docked and, like clumsy sailors in our life jackets, clambered ashore, the French amongst us intoxicated with ethnographic fantasies.

A minute or two later the Indians ran out of their little huts, their tee-shirts gone, their muscular arms and legs decorated with leather bands and feathers, and their jeans replaced by tightly rolled pieces of black cloth. Some adjusted their head decorations as they ran or hastily smeared on slashes of body and face paint.

And then they abruptly stopped running a few metres in front of us and stood around ceremoniously as tribal people do and as they should have been doing when we appeared from the sweating caverns of the forest. Only the children gave the game away, as they darted amongst us carrying trays of souvenirs, drinks and food.

We, in our turn, darted amongst them, cameras running hot, unable to believe our luck in finding ourselves right in the middle of an Indian village. The French and Italians were everywhere. They looked inside the huts, examined the cooking equipment beside the fires, photographed their canoes, took close-ups of the body paint and feathers, asked to see spears, knives and poison darts, and tirelessly debated their findings as if at a Levi-Strauss tutorial.

Our guide jabbered feverishly, explaining the world of the Indian in five languages. The Indians themselves, knowing a thing or two about other worlds, listened impassively, taking the occasional cigarette from a tourist and keeping an eye on their offsprings' commerce.

And then, the mystery over, we drifted away one by one to our canoes.

On the way back to Lake January, we scoffed beer and chattered excitedly about our jungle adventure. The Italians and Argentinians, forgetting the global issues, merrily tossed their beer cans overboard, leaving them to eddy forever on some oozy pond or insignificant creek, here in the middle of nowhere.

By now the Brazilians were bored with all this endless wet darkness. But when we reached the place where our boat was moored, a buffet lunch had appeared – fish, beans, bananas, beer, *guaraná*, even *farofa*, all the favourites – and their mood lifted.

The return trip was a party. Whether it was because we had been somewhere distant and were returning to civilisation (Manaus!) or just the music by samba king Martinho da Vila, everyone had a good old time.

All the while a video played – the story of our voyage which had been recorded quietly but continuously by an extraordinarily agile one-legged cameraman throughout the day. We all frolicked famously on the screen for a moment, with the most frolicsome being the Australian girl who, having detected that the camera was pointing her way, began making some fondly remembered but unlovely Australian gestures and squawking greetings to Val and Gary at home.

The arrival of the video camera has happened almost without my noticing. From being a "tool" advocated by ridiculous groups of people such as resource activists and squatters' collectives, it has become an unavoidable feature of an idle day's tourism. The practice of someone filming the tour group and everything that it does, and then offering the unedited epic for sale, means that, should you buy it, you can never delete from memory your fellow voyagers: the Australian girl in her tight red bra cavorting with the Uruguayan priest; the Argentinian being knocked out of the canoe *twice* by wads of leaves and creepers and them galloping hysterically back through the shallows, away from the *cocodrilos* that were supposedly lurking; the Brazilian families from the big cities in Rio Grande do Sul, Santa Catarina and São Paulo, as alien to this place as the rest of us, and only relaxing when the rice and beans were on the table; and the Italians, dressed in tropical Armani and Nazareno Gabrielli for a day in the wilderness, filming each other and filming me and filming the one-legged filmer as he hopped about filming those who, with their own video cams, would soon send him hopping into oblivion.

That night I had to telephone Australia. At the Da Vinci hotel I'd had trouble ringing for a taxi in the morning (the desk clerk banging wildly and vainly at the machine) but now I was able to call Chippendale direct from my room. This, of course, is what the world is like. A friend in Buenos Aires tells me that when he wants to get a message to his mother in another suburb he resorts to calling a third party in New York to deliver it.

The Amazonas telephone directory is a reminder, however, of where Manaus really is, and just how isolated you might be a few kilometres from the town, despite the jets and satellites flying overhead. There are ten pages of illustrated first-aid instructions, including how to deal with bites and attacks from a horrifying army of creatures, and how to handle a *parto súbito*, sudden childbirth.

It was hard not to be impressed with all this, and I began to look at the faces and hands of the young men and women — this is a city of very young people — with a new interest. They were the faces of Indians, backlanders and migrants, people whose struggle against poverty is almost heroic as they move back and forth between the cities and forest, the boom towns and the newest frontier.

The rest of us simply boarded our jets. Well, not *simply*. Because Manaus is a duty-free port, there are customs formalities to make sure that Brazilian citizens are taking no more than US$1200 worth of goods back home. There was also the problem of the blow guns — one blow gun per Italian — which presented security problems on aircraft. All Brazilian airports are models of good design and efficiency (better than most in Australia), but Manaus at peak hour is chaos as people with trolleys laden with high-tech communications systems or low-tech armaments compete for the attentions of drop-dead customs officers.

Four hours later I was in Brasília undergoing a tour of the night sights with aspiring politician Vinícius Cortes.

"Isn't that beautiful?" he said of the imposing, floodlit Congress buildings. "I bet they don't have anything *that* extravagant in Manaus."

* * *

Two months after my visit to Manaus, the annual torching of Amazonia began, as settlers and farmers — most of them impoverished — attacked virgin forest in a desperate and misguided search for new, more fertile lands. As an area of 32 000 square kilometres — about half the size of Tasmania — blazed, smoke haze darkened the skies for weeks, causing the frequent closure of airports in Manaus and Pôrto Velho and the crash of an airliner, which ran out of fuel as the pilots, disoriented by smoke and poor visibility, allowed it to drift far off course.

There is a chance, however, that the 1989 fires might have been the last great burn. The new government of Fernando Collor is not referring to international outrage as a foreign threat to Brazilian sovereignty, as its predecessor did, and the responsible minister, José Lutzenberger, is a credible environmentalist.

Their mission is to prove to Brazilians that the rainforest standing has greater value — even in monetary terms — than the rainforest felled.

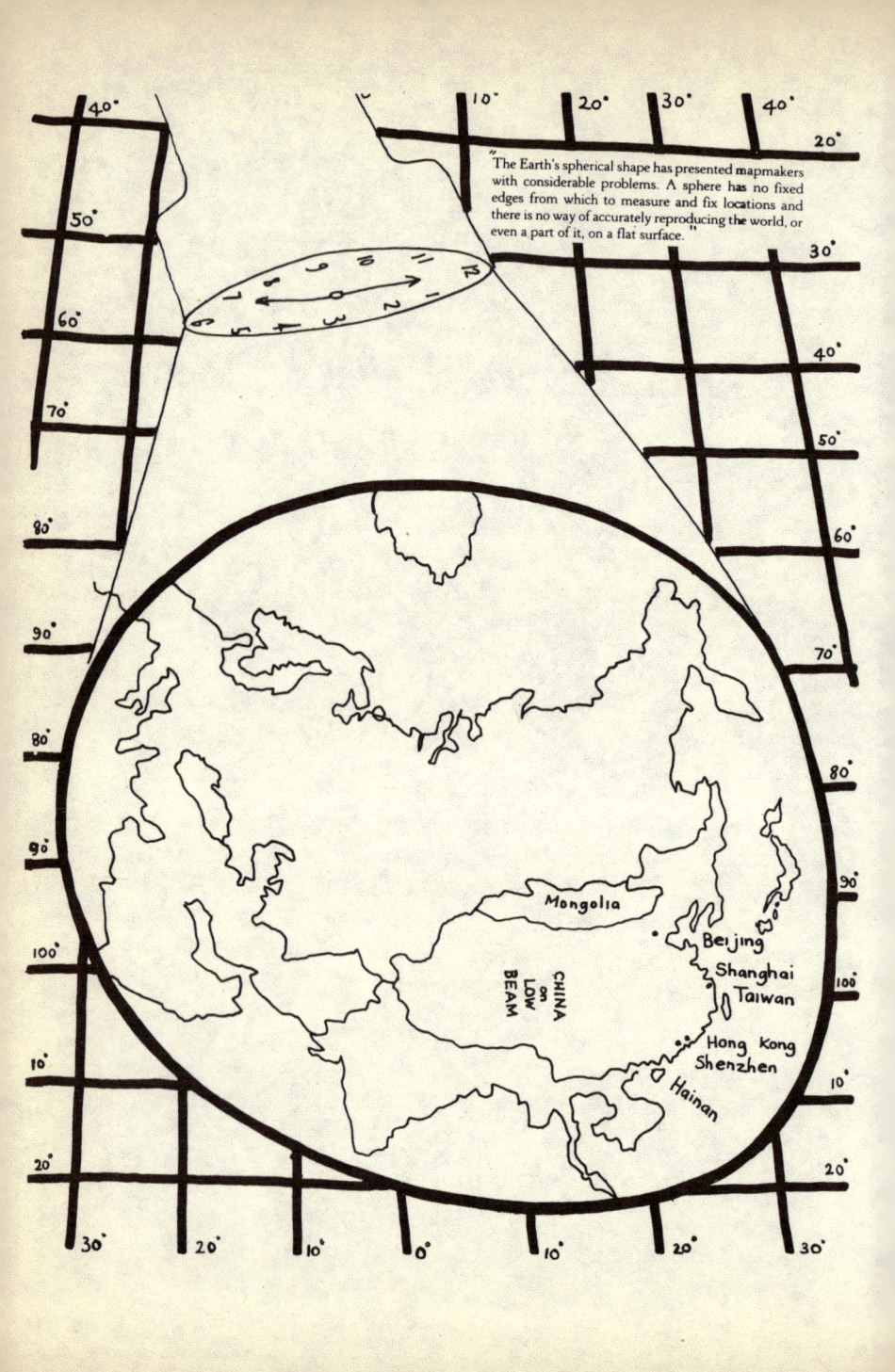

"The Earth's spherical shape has presented mapmakers with considerable problems. A sphere has no fixed edges from which to measure and fix locations and there is no way of accurately reproducing the world, or even a part of it, on a flat surface."

CHINA on LOW BEAM

Mongolia
Beijing
Shanghai
Taiwan
Hong Kong
Shenzhen
Hainan

On low beam in China

(China)

Doctor Beam Ng's office in Kowloon would be familiar to anyone who knows the back-rooms or even the front-rooms of Asian grocery shops, herbalists or importers. There are samples of wares lying about carelessly: dried fish, live lobsters in baskets, Cartier-copy watches, table tennis bats, Sampsonite attaché cases, alarm clocks that can be used as telephones and telephones that are also computers, cricket balls, cashmere sweaters, remote-control toy cars and packets of remedies and cures for all of mankind's ills. There is paperwork everywhere, filed in boxes and heaped on desks, and no evidence anywhere of sophisticated office technology, despite many of the products — the latest in high-tech hardware — that pass through the office on their way to buyers.

Dr Ng is a trader. For three decades, working on the principle that if he has a product he has a business, he has traded any commodity that offered him a commission. Not a *decent* commission necessarily, for Kowloon is cut-throat and the man who prowls at the margin is the one who wins the deal.

During the last ten years, Ng has found that the ever-widening doorways, corridors and windows into China have offered him unexpected opportunities and ever-more surprising products to trade. And right now, one of the most surprising products was students. With increasing liberalisation in China since the mid-1980s, growing numbers of high school and university graduates have sought further study opportunities abroad. Liberal times in China meant boom times for agents in Hong Kong and for selected schools in Japan, North America and Australia. And Australia was the most sought-after destination because at the time it had relatively easier entry criteria.

Doctor Ng's first name, the rather unexpected Beam, is supposed to be an Americanisation of his Chinese name and, well, all sorts of names are possible in America. I'm sure that Beams abound in Des Moines, Minneapolis and Atlantic City, but "Dr Beaming" has a special resonance which I doubt is enjoyed by the world's other Beams. (The nearest English pronunciation of Ng is "ing".) Beaming, however, does not accurately describe Ng's countenance, which is alternately blank and agitated in that particular Hong Kong way. He is always edgy and only beams in brief flashes when a deal has been signed and he's won an extra half or three-quarter percentage point.

Where and when Beam Ng became Doctor Ng, I can only guess. He has had a life which took him from his birthplace in Yunnan province in China in 1938 to Hong Kong, then to Vietnam where his father ran businesses in Cholon, Saigon's Chinatown. He grew up there, but as a young adult moved on a wild notion to Accra on Africa's Gold Coast.

This was in about 1958. There he set up shops and import businesses based on somewhat speculative views of how the West African economies would perform when the various countries achieved independence from France and Britain. He even learned French — or a west African *patios* — to assist him in establishing branches in Lomé and Abidjan in the neighbouring colonies, now called Togo and the Ivory Coast. And whilst there he may have acquired the title "Doctor", probably because of the Chinese medical supplies and questionable advice that he retailed throughout the West African colonies.

Now, in 1988, Ng was taking me into China to give a series of seminars to invited audiences about Australia and education in Australia, and specifically to instruct potential students as to what was required for full-fee studies: what they would have to pay, how to enrol, how to apply for a visa, what types of courses were available to them in Australia, and how to prepare themselves for life in Sydney or one of the other cities.

For part of the trip we were to be accompanied by the director of a Japanese college, a Professor Matsuzawa. (Are we Australians unique in not awarding ourselves unearned titles, I wondered.) Professor Matsuzawa would meet us at a designated university in China.

On the day we were to leave Hong Kong, I climbed the stairs to Dr Ng's Tsim Sha Tsui office, past Yip's Barber and Massage Salon, and sat down in the circular waiting room. Around the perimeter of the room was constructed a fish tank — or rather, a number of separate tanks formed into a circle. Some of them contained fish, slippery, patterned carp, or tangles of irritated lobsters, but others were empty or were stacked with wares supposedly on display, receipts and invoices or bits of broken office equipment.

Miss Ho walked through a gap in the tanks and greeted me.

"Laurence. Very sorry, Dr Ng cannot. So . . . we go."

"Who's *we*?"

"Me and Elton."

Now Felicity Ho and Elton Yeung are charming and capable people who work for Ng, along with Stella To and Alice Wan. They can give you figures for the current production runs at the Chun Wah Sports Factory in Tien Tsen and the price of bats that pass through their office — at least on paper — to importers in America or Australia. They can even tell you the price of a Masters degree at a number of Mid-Western universities in the United States or in Toronto, Edmonton, Sydney, Perth or Brisbane, and give you very accurate statements on both the entry requirements for these universities and the commission that their office will derive from an enrolment.

But I felt that for this trip we needed Dr Ng. He was a patient tactician of the sort who could achieve things in China. The denizens of Hong Kong don't look or sound subtle, in fact, they seem the opposite: hurried and quarrelsome people, yelping at one another in staccato bursts, or arguing with a noise like cutlery being sorted. But the best of them at all levels know that by quietly applying pressure at a certain point, months later a satisfactory result will be achieved at a different point. Our forthcoming schedule of seminars was set up in this way — the consequence of nearly a year of political and economic acupuncture applied to people within local and state education authorities. The process had worked and now the seminars had the full support of the bureaucrats in the states which we would visit. In turn, those bureaucrats were now smiling warmly with bared teeth, both at what they had achieved — their own contribution to "opening the door" — and in anticipation of modest junketing when the foreigners arrived.

Beam Ng, diplomatic and secretly baring his own teeth, would let them go on believing that the seminars were their own work, that the idea had originated in their own state offices — in fact, at their own teak desks. In any case, that deal was now done, and Ng was busy finding the pressure points and preparing the needles for another target.

I thought: "Foreign businessmen — even college principals — have gone to prison in China for trying to run their own affairs. I can't go without Beam."

Miss Ho was watching my eyes through her Dior spectacles. She had a round plump face, which always seemed to be smiling and which, I felt, reminded me of something in a yum cha basket. Pork dumplings perhaps, or steamed, stuffed mushrooms.

"No worry, Mr Laurence. No worry. Maybe Beam meet us there. Maybe in Guangzhou."

"Maybe's not good enough. Where is he?"

"Got a problem. Maybe go to Taipei."

"They're so vague when they want to be," I thought. "When they start to say 'maybe', you know that they don't know, or certainly don't want you to know."

"Taipei?" I responded. "Why?"

"Maybe get a good business over that side. But don't worry. Maybe meet Beam tomorrow in China."

Arguing with them was just giving them more bricks for the wall. Elton breezed into the room with a large trolley on to which he had packed our brochures, videos, colour slides, maps and other materials and said that he would send someone to my hotel to collect my bags. We were going to China.

I sat on an aqua-coloured vinyl sofa beneath the circling carp whilst Felicity and Stella made final preparations, shouting at people over the telephone and pulling cash from drawers.

To divert myself, I wished that it was Stella who was coming, as I watched her flitting from desk to fish tank to desk again, her beautiful nails flashing like splintered fire-opals. Beside her Felicity was a plonker: stolid, unyielding and liable to smile at you in a way that had an unbalancing effect.

Stella was suddenly in front of me, her slim fingers curled nicely around a booklet of tickets. They were for the train to Shenzhen, she explained.

The train? Well, that was a relief. One of my other worries was that this afternoon I would be enjoying my first experience of CAAC, China's redoubtable and doubtful airline.

I had been trying to find out which was the first city on our itinerary. If the schedule was as well established as Dr Ng had insisted it was, then surely everyone knew which city we were to visit first. Was it Beijing? Maybe. What about Guangzhou? Maybe. Or Shanghai? Maybe Shanghai.

Had I been able to find out for sure that it was one of these, I would have booked a flight with Cathay Pacific, because you just can't escape CAAC's reputation. In hotels in Hong Kong, the tee-shirts are everywhere. They read:

I SURVIVED CAAC
or
CAAC SURVIVOR
or
CAAC: Chinese Antique Aircraft Club
or
CAAC: Chinese Scarelines

These slogans were surrounded by pictures of aircraft in flames, broken to pieces in paddy-fields or with engines coming adrift in mid-air.

"Great," I said to Stella. "I like travelling by train."

"It's just to Shenzhen," she added. "After that you fry."

Going to China by train from Hong Kong, I found, was less complicated than trying to cross Sydney. Everything in Hong Kong is highly automated and the automation is in working order. However, the automation, the working and the order stop when you reach China.

We walked from the last station on the line across a bridge and into a cavernous customs building at the frontier.

Miss Ho announced that it would be a good idea if I took all the educational material through the various checkpoints.

"Why," I asked, suspiciously.

"Maybe get no problem. For foreigner maybe easy."

Maybe, I thought. But in most countries — except, in my experience, India and Egypt — it's the foreigners who are taken apart at customs whilst the locals pass through unmolested. And, in any case, weren't Hong Kong passport holders foreigners too?

I explained this to Miss Ho, and she just smiled, pointing me and the trolley towards the appropriate queue.

There were other foreign foreigners about: a party of Australians who looked like members of an Australia-China friendship association. They had the faintly shabby, bearded appearance of academics and socialists in their fifties and a hint of pride in their togetherness — they had, after all, survived to see China become the darling of the West. They might have been wearing tee-shirts that read:

I SURVIVED:
  THE LONG MARCH
  MAO ZEDONG
  THE GREAT PROLETARIAN CULTURAL
    REVOLUTION
  THE GREAT LEAP FORWARD
  THE GREAT PURGES
  THE GANG OF FOUR etc., etc.

There were also a few backpackers, anxiously consulting their *Lonely Planet* guides, or, if they were French, their *Guides Routards*, but I was the only person, I felt, who looked like an encyclopedia salesman, pushing a trolley of ill-packed books and papers.

Felicity and Elton passed through an entry point that was for Hong Kong residents and waited for me on the other side.

They made no attempt to hide the fact that they were with

me and that I was pushing a load of material with which they were associated. This seemed to me to undermine whatever sense there was in my taking it through.

At the barrier, the officer took in me, my passport, the trolley and its contents in one slow look, and sent me away to a special room.

The room had low chipboard and glass walls, so that Felicity and Elton were able to lean over the top — on the Chinese side — and chat to me casually as I sweated and awaited questioning, arrest, punishment, banishment or, perhaps, death. Wild thoughts sprang at me. Why had Dr Ng without warning or explanation pulled out? Why had Elton and Felicity been so insistent that I push the trolley, that I take it through customs? *What was in these boxes?* I recalled the advice given to all travellers departing Australia: *don't carry anything through customs for anyone,* and *don't carry any bags or packages that you have not packed yourself.*

I hadn't packed these boxes and I was now responsible for them. At the first murmur of trouble, Felicity and Elton could vanish amongst their billion look-alikes, leaving me to be hectored and bullied . . .

A slow-moving man with a face poking out from beneath his bile-green army cap that reminded me of a reptile — perhaps a turtle — approached and spat something at me. I say "spat" because not only words, but some physical matter came out of his mouth as it opened horizontally.

In my panic I could only think of the Bulgarian exile who was poisoned by spittle (or was it a dart?) in London some years ago. But Elton came to my rescue.

"He wants to know what's in the boxes," he explained, his head and arms hanging loosely over the wall. "Just tell him that's school books in there. Don't tell him something about videos."

This nonchalance astonished me. The officer, getting ready to spit again, shifted his small eyes to Elton, to the trolley, to Felicity and back to me. Surely he understood what was going on here.

"School books," I said.

The turtle mouth opened again and I leaned back a bit for cover. (It *was* poisoned spit that killed the Bulgarian, wasn't it?) Words and spray splattered all over me.

"He says you have to fill in some forms," translated Elton, as I pawed at my exposed skin with a handkerchief. "Over at that bench on the other side."

Here there were rows of stooped and worried people, their brows pinched, trying to decipher the forms and decide what they should write.

I completed the required four copies, and signed a declaration that I was not importing into China hard currency, drugs or pornography. I took the forms to a desk and handed them over. No one read them, but there was a flurry of stamping, with stamps that had too little ink, on to my passport, the forms and pages in other books.

I had declared that my boxes contained "school books" as instructed by Elton. That was only partially true, but seeing the stamps being liberally applied, my anxieties subsided and I began to realise that I would probably be allowed into China.

The atmosphere in this compound, I now thought, was not that of an interrogation centre or torture chamber, but more one of rancid bureaucracy. The turtle pit at a zoo came to mind. You could have written *anything* on those forms — that your boxes contained the Dead Sea Scrolls, or ground-to-air-rockets for the oppressed Tibetans, for example — and nobody would have cared.

Once I was admitted to the other side, Elton congratulated me loudly on having successfully "fooled" the customs officers. The last time he came through, he blustered, showing no shame or prudence, was with a group of Canadian educationalists.

The authorities didn't believe their story about having no videos and, in their own time, silently and viciously pulled apart the Canadians' packages, revealing about fifty video tapes which were then confiscated. The Canadians were fined several hundred American dollars, which had to be paid on the spot (on pain of death by asphixiation or poison spittle, I supposed). Elton added cheerily that the customs men would then have traded the dollars on the black market, because the "fine" was all their own work.

"But no problem," he went on. "The Canadians continued with their lecture tour, and Alice Wan flew in with new tapes next day."

We walked out of the customs hall into a city that was more a building site than buildings. There was something reminiscent of Jakarta here, with a touch of Coolangatta. This was my first view of China and it was Shenzhen, a city that scarcely existed a decade ago.

A taxi took us to the Shenzhen Palace Hotel. It was being built, or finished, or demolished as we arrived — a reminder, perhaps, of Shenzhen's status as one of four Special Economic Zones, and of its success in attracting foreign (meaning Hong Kong and Taiwanese) capital.

The Shenzhen motto is "Time is Money, Efficiency is Life", a perception of life, the universe and everything which was obviously bequeathed to the city by a happy and optimistic Hong Kong benefactor taking the long-term approach.

Were such a motto to be applied to Australia, we might add the words "but stuff it". Applied to China, the missing words could be "where Time and Life are defined by the Thirteenth Party Congress as being periods of no less than 20 000 years". In any case, as I soon learned, Shenzhen is truly a zone, sealed off from the rest of China by barbed wire and security patrols. Only potential employees and those with business plans and Hong Kong or other overseas sources of capital are allowed in.

Hotels in China are huge, like carpeted Forbidden Cities. You follow bell-boys who have just started lesson two in *Streamline English Departures* into elevators that are already beginning to sag, along corridors that resemble tunnels under freeways — with armed guards asleep or lolling at every intersection — to your room which always has a number like 13729, even though at least 12 000 of the rooms are empty.

And if you are part of an official group or invited delegation, or if you have merely arranged to be met, you don't go alone.

So, as Felicity, Elton and I stood waiting for the lift, The Shenzhen Welcome Committee appeared. They had been waiting in the lobby all morning it seemed, and we now had to be warmly greeted and greet warmly in return.

A quick round of handshakes would have done me, but when the lift arrived we all surged in, filling this coffin with smoke and middle-aged and elderly men. Apparently they were representatives from the state educational authority as well as a couple of Dr Ng's local contacts and a senior official from the university where I was to talk that night.

The smoke coming out of them was astonishing and alarming, and I half expected the sprinklers to be activated. But even more alarming was the jollity. Men grabbed my hands and wouldn't let go. Others shook me by the shoulders. This continued as we approached my room. At least I'll be able to disappear in there and rest, I thought.

But when the door was opened the committee rushed in. Some sat on the bed, bouncing as if to test it. Others turned the television on and off and moved the station selector about with abandon. The hotel music system was turned on and up, and the mini-bar ransacked. The last group took up positions in the bathroom, turning on the shower, the taps and the hair-dryer and trying out the toilet. And then they all changed places.

I counted fourteen men, all smoking zestfully, as I stood grinning fixedly and following the path of a migraine as it migrated from behind my eyes to the rest of my head.

Elton put his face in the door to say something happy, but I didn't give him a chance.

"Tell them to fuck off," I said, still grinning.

Elton managed to clear them out — each one shaking hands vigorously with me as he left — and then told me that we'd be meeting them again for dinner at six, before going on to the university for my lecture.

That gave me three hours to rest. The headache was now well established, making me feel as if my head were encased in chunks of rough brick. I realised that I'd had a nascent throb in my head since flying in to Hong Kong a couple of days earlier, and the events of today and the smoke had now brought it to life.

I turned up the air-conditioning and ran a bath. And just as I immersed myself there was a bang on my door.

"Who is it?" I shouted.

There was another clumsy bang.

"Come back later. I'm in the bath!"

Suddenly there was a man coughing quietly in the hallway. One of the guards from the corridors, he had courteously let himself in.

"What the fuck do you want?" I shouted, standing up to grab a towel.

"Pity girl?" he proposed. "Pity girl take a but?"

Girls? Baths? What was he talking about? This was China, after all, where foreigners had been gaoled for doing less than taking hot baths with the locals.

"Hop it," I said waving my hand at the door, "and don't come back."

At 6 o'clock, Elton called to accompany me downstairs to the restaurant. And, as we emerged from the lift, the Welcome Committee rose to meet us, wheezing and coughing their greetings, felicitations and hopes that our lives might be long and that relationships between China and our countries might be fruitful.

The men had spent the afternoon, in fact the entire day, aside from the romp in my room — sitting and smoking in the lobby. "Weed wrecks" is an adequate term to describe these people — their shabby suits, some old-fashioned party tunics, others "Western-style", oozed nicotine, tar, tea and stir-fried shrimps, and each always had a rumpled cigarette cupped in his hand or in his mouth.

Some of them appeared to be wearing two suits at once, as well as each other's shoes. One would have a black canvas slip-on on one foot and a sort of platform sandal on the other. The next man would have the pair of these shoes on his feet. I imagined that to pass the time they had spent the afternoon trying on one another's suits and shoes and some had been caught when the music stopped.

Bursts of clapping and smoke accompanied Elton, Felicity and me as we went to the hotel's over-luxurious restaurant. Here we occupied three large tables, for the fourteen-man committee had attracted others who had some association with any of the organisations represented.

Dinner was a meal of many successive courses. I was not hungry or enthusiastic as I still had a headache and knew that I would soon have to give a talk to about a thousand university students.

The favoured mode of eating was to hold your chopsticks in one hand, cigarette in the other, and sometimes a tea-cup and toothpick as well. All men within chopstick-range of me kept flinging morsels from the serving dishes on to my plate, using their own chopsticks fresh from encounters with their own noodle-coloured gums and tongues.

Elton and Felicity were disgusted by this practice but couldn't show it.

"That's just how they eat their snacks," Felicity confided, "and we have to just put up, isn't it."

After dinner we proceeded to the university in a motorcade of Dong Fengs and Nissan Cedrics.

I sat in the front of one with Elton behind me, thinking: "What am I doing here, in a city that I hadn't heard of until this morning with a carload of men who, if they are not squeezing my shoulders, are pumping my hand with scaly fingers and hiccuping hot hoi-sin sauce all over me?"

Although my arrival was evidently an event — why else so many greeters and why else the motorcade? — and although Dr Ng had assured me that the lectures had been thoroughly planned in advance, when we reached the university it was in total blackness, and no one could find the hall where my talk was to take place.

Ultimately we did locate it, and, incredibly, there were over a thousand eager and talkative students there, crammed into the foyer and on to the court outside. Many had been waiting for hours. Nothing was organised on stage, however, and members of my entourage who had positions within the university immediately began hurrying grumbling caretakers about to set up the video screen, microphones and lights.

"Time is money," laughed Elton.

For the next two hours I showed slides and videos of life in Australia, used overhead projections to explain the structure of our education system and the processes required to obtain the necessary visas, and answered intelligent and penetrating questions.

There was a constant tension between Felicity Ho and a Miss Doris Li as to whose job it was to interpret for me. Miss Li was a member of the university's English faculty and had been chosen in advance of my visit. Miss Ho had assumed that she would undertake the task in each city. The matter was not entirely resolved: Felicity agreed to let Miss Li interpret each of my phrases, but reserved the right to correct her or interrupt as required. Needless to say, she used her right keenly, frequently leaving Miss Li glaring at her with nostrils tightened.

The enthusiasm for Australia was astounding and it gave me an importance that was far from deserved. Australia was a heroic place in their minds (that wasn't deserved either) and I was a celebrity because of it.

After my talk, groups gathered around for closer questioning. People thrust photos at me, and bits of paper with names on them. Did I know Juo Lim, now a student in Sydney, or Quing Din in Adelaide? Only the intervention of my team, the men from the state department, Beam Ng's representatives and Elton and Felicity — some of them breathing roughly in a way that could be heard from deep within their layers of suits and pullovers — saved me from having to carry bags of mail and hastily wrapped gifts to friends and relatives scattered across Australia.

The team bossed its way into the crowd, telling the students to post their letters and that further questions would be answered by Ng's representatives at their offices.

Whilst this was going on, Miss Li busied herself by asking me pointed questions about the standards of English language teaching and speech in Australia. With smartly dictated sentences and observing me with dry, steady eyes, she indicated that she had heard rather *worrying* things about Australian speech. I debated this matter with her in a mechanical sort of way — possibly giving Miss Li further things to worry about — as I waited for our motorcade to reassemble.

Later, as we drove back towards the hotel, I detected that Elton and one of the departmental heads, Mr Wang, were discussing something vigorously on the back seat.

Elton then announced: "Laurence, so now we have another dinner."

I turned to him, wincing. With an uncertain smile he explained. "Mr Wang says we need to celebrate the first lecture. Also men are very hungry."

"Of course," I sighed.

"What a pity," he said, sensing my mood.

Over dinner number two, as my plate was piled high with chunks and portions that I couldn't eat, Elton explained that there would be a lot of eating on this trip. There were three reasons, he went on to explain.

"First, Chinese love to eat."

I knew that.

"Second, because you are a guest in China, they want to satisfy you and be hospitable."

I knew that too.

"And, third, because you are a *foreign* guest, they have an excuse to eat out, maybe at the government's expense. That's why there are so many always crowding in for their share."

I'd noticed that.

"And, fourth," I added with ungenerous mordancy, "despite your third reason, I'm paying for most of the meals."

"Also a reason, isn't it," concluded Elton.

The next morning I was escorted downstairs to breakfast by some men in tight soapy-looking suits. Their hair was matted and I had the impression that they had slept the night in the corridor outside my room. Then I realised that everyone's hair was untidy and matted. (I'm talking about men here — in the places where we went with our group there were very few women.)

Breakfast was all the Cantonese favourites, rather like last night's two dinners in a different order. I sat in a barn of eating, smoking, coughing, snivelling, spitting men and nibbled at bits of rice and fish.

Mr Wang, anxious to please and animate me, ordered two bottles of beer which he forced into me like a roistering Russian at a cocktail party.

Noticing that Felicity was absent, I asked Elton where she was.

"Maybe go to Hong Kong," he explained, reaching for another piece of jellyfish.

Ah, I thought. So now it's just Elton and me.

Then I was farewelled — final toasts of flat beer and bitter tea — and bundled into a car for the trip to Guangzhou. The car was a state-suplied Cedric driven by a state-supplied toad-like figure. My only view of the driver, from the back seat, comprised sudden jets of smoke rising from his head. His state-supplied offsider engaged him in non-stop conversation during the five-hour journey, producing the distressing din of shouting and throat-clearing that talk amongst Chinese anywhere can become.

So Miss Ho had gone to Hong Kong. And why had Elton stayed behind in Shenzhen? And would Dr Ng appear as promised?

I was on the wide plastic-covered rear seat of a sulphurous Nissan Cedric, being driven along hazardous, ruined roads by two men I had never met before, who were carrying on a reckless argument in a language I couldn't understand. The landscape was not one I would have chosen to survey. It consisted of dusty fields, towns made of grey breezeblock and skinny trees with all their branches hacked away. How did education get to be like this, I wondered.

After a couple of hours we pulled into the car park of an enormous opulent restaurant that sat like a Taj Mahal amidst concrete and dust. We coughed and spat for a while and then went inside. The waiters scowled at me, knowing that they would be expected to *hurry* a little with a foreigner around, and busily directed our party to each other's tables.

We sat down and two other men joined us. Who were they?

One was revealed to be an employee of the state education department who had been assigned to prepare a video documentary of my various lectures and journeys.

The other was just a hanger-on, of which there was no shortage in China. In fact I was surprised there were so few at my table — this would be my cheapest meal yet.

During what I took to be lunch, the cameraman filmed us eating from every angle. This had the effect of exciting the diners at nearby tables who concluded that I must be a VIP of at least three-star rating.

We arrived in Guangzhou late in the afternoon still picking our teeth. I was dropped at the megalithic China Hotel ("for the Merchant Prince of Today" is the hotel's slogan), checked in and went up to my room.

And there, just as I was beginning to wonder when I would see anyone I knew, I found . . . The Welcome Committee!

This group, which in all respects resembled that in Shenzhen, had made themselves comfortable earlier in the afternoon and had been smoking tirelessly during the long wait. They clapped as I entered, grabbed my hands and shoulders, and generally had a wonderful time. And then, through the ballooning smoke, I noticed that there *was* something different about this group.

There was a European amongst them.

He came forward and introduced himself as Timothy Freudenberg, a student from Adelaide.

An Australian! All the other men proceeded to slap our backs, offer cigarettes around and raid the mini-bar to celebrate this great occasion.

Freudenberg had been in Guangzhou for five years doing a doctorate in Chinese literature. He was a gangly, scholarly type, still under 30, and certainly out of place amidst all this grubby bonhomie. But he was sufficiently used to it, I sensed, to sit there, unirritated and thinking about other things — perhaps the works of Li Bai or the indirect imagery employed by the Han dynasty poets.

He told me that he had been invited to my lecture the following evening, and would be bringing his fiancee. Indeed, his fiancée, Miss Han Wei, would be my interpreter.

I thanked him for his interest and then told him that I had a dreadful headache and asked him whether he would turf this lot out of my room. Freudenberg spoke to the oldest man present in a very proper accent – he had just the right sound of wind whistling in a narrow cave that characterises Mandarin – and then, translating the man's reply, explained to me that everyone would be delighted to meet me tonight for dinner, since I would surely be hungry. Had I tried Cantonese food, the old man wanted to know.

I told him that I surely had, but I knew that in every Cantonese meal there were surprises. We arranged to meet in the lobby at 8, and they all departed, leaving me with the usual wreck of ashtrays, bottles and soot on the bed.

I lay down and tried to plan how I might avoid dinner. I could, for example, go to the swimming pool for a few hours, or get lost somewhere else in this city-sized hotel.

Towards evening I did go to the pool, which was indoors and part of a health and fitness complex run by an American whose features included a rippling body and redundant head. Sadly the water had a film on it, as if two dozen fatty men coated in massage oil or margarine had recently been cavorting in it. Rather than try to swim through this simmering broth, I retreated to the exercise bikes and was lectured by the American on posture.

Around us were American and European businessmen, today's merchant princes, more or less spiflicated by months of harrowing interrogations and negotiations over a joint-venture for a refrigerator factory or an airport luggage-handling facility. They (and I) were the advance parties for Western countries rushing to achieve something whilst Deng Xiaoping permitted the doors to remain open, and none of us were sure who was included in Deng's warning that "while the open door policy is implemented, decadent things of capitalism will worm their way in."

The colleague of one of these businessmen would certainly have been included. A Belgian, he had been in China a year earlier and had "fallen" for a girl whom he had met at an official reception. Their subsequent liaisons were cut short by a visit from a security official, subtle bullying ("of course, none of this indicates that relations between the People's Republic of China and the people of the Kingdom of Belgium will be anything other than warm, fruitful and co-operative") and deportation. The man went back to Belgium with a stamp in his passport which noted, *inter alia*, that he had polluted a Chinese woman and had offended the masses. He was never to return. Once back in Brussels, the company assigned the man to their West African projects and sent him frequently to Zaire. "We call that the AIDS shuttle," joked his replacement in China, peddling furiously to keep his own libido levels down.

Just as I was settling into the steam of a sauna with my new mates (sharing experiences of hotels, Chinese staff, CAAC and shopping) a hotel employee appeared with a message: a Mr Fang was waiting for me in the lobby so that we could go to dinner.

"They found you," said the American. "They always do."

I went sullenly to my room and dressed. Then, as I entered the lift, the video cameraman appeared and filmed my descent and my arrival on the ground floor where I walked into the Welcome Committee, Mr Fang at its head, and was passed from happy fellow to happy fellow.

In the restaurant, our party of fifteen was joined by Elton and Felicity. I greeted them with the enthusiasm of my own welcome committee, glad that they had reappeared and had not abandoned me to this gang of carnivores.

Elton had been in Guangzhou for the afternoon, too, he explained, but had been busy doing things.

"What sort of things?"

"Ah, maybe some things for Dr Ng. Maybe he make a business here, isn't it."

Elton was not intending to give me any information at all about what he had been doing, and anyway, I didn't really care. Beam Ng had as many business interests as there were *things* in the world, and why should one of his employees waste an afternoon in one of China's largest cities?

Felicity confirmed that she had been back to Hong Kong and had just flown in. Hong Kong! The fabulous harbour city! We were only an hour away from its glittering towers, its solid British institutions, its department stores, its yuppies yapping into their mobile phones, but from here it seemed infinitely remote. I was surrounded by barking, snuffling men, jabbing at me and at things on dishes with their chopsticks, constantly swishing their hands at me (indicating that I should eat this or that) and filling the air with the smell of coal dust. No wonder Hong Kongers were in a state of near hysteria about 1997.

When the deep-fried fish came, Mr Fang made sure that I had all the best parts, growling as he elbowed the others out of the way. At the end, when the fish was just head and bones, I saw where Fang's chopsticks were diving.

"Oh, no, Mr Fang, not the lips," I silently pleaded.

He nimbly darted in and tugged and snicked at these slippery, fat bits and placed them on my plate. He then returned to the corpse having noticed that the *eyes* were still there. In a second or two of gouging he had them out too, and, to my relief, into his own mouth before anyone else had a chance.

Chinese people are always telling you that this or that part of a creature or food type is good for one or another of your organs (one, in particular, it seems). Fish lips are no exception and when Mr Fang had finished with the eyes he waited to see how I would enjoy the lips, explaining and indicating by raising and lowering his index finger that they would help me with the "standing-up straight problem".

Everyone roared at this and watched me intently as I devoured my prize, as if I would get a carnal urge on the spot. For myself, I was less concerned about the standing-up straight problem than my headache and asked Elton to see if Mr Fang had any cures for that.

Our two tables now began to discuss the question, waiters joined in and eventually it was decided that I should see "the American doctor".

That was a better suggestion than whatever culinary treatment Mr Fang might have recommended, and I was permitted to leave the table (Mr Fang obscenely moving his finger again to remind me of the effect of the fish lips) and to go to my room unaccompanied. Felicity said that they would arrange for the American doctor to visit me in the morning.

During the night I had a phone call from a woman who asked me if I wanted a girl sent to my room.

Recalling the unfortunate Belgian, I answered no, and then added that I would be as happy to wait for the American doctor, if that was all right. This obtuse response caused some muffled grumbling between the caller on the other end of the line and someone else. She then said that she couldn't get me a doctor, but inquired whether a nurse would be satisfactory.

Not knowing how I could pursue the conversation, I said goodnight and went back to sleep.

My next disturbance was an untidy clatter at the door. It was 6 o'clock and Miss Ho was there with the American doctor.

American doctor? He was a very elderly Chinese man, but of course, he still might have been an American. His English was excellent — in a learned, correct and non-colloquial way; there was only a vestige of an American accent. It was certainly a while since he had spent any time in the United States.

As I lay on my bed and he felt me all over with hands that were at once soft and vice-like, he told me that he had studied in America and went there "from time to time" to give lectures.

When was the last time he was in America?

"Oh before the . . . about 1937, I think it must have been."

Before the war!

Before the revolution!

Before the Hundred Flowers Movement!

I said, "That was before the Second World War."

He replied, "Oh yes. It was before a lot of things, most of which you wouldn't even have heard about."

Felicity was standing near the window, possibly a bit flustered at seeing me in summer pyjamas, and at this putative display of knowledge.

"See," she put in. "This doctor knows everything, isn't it."

Yes, I thought. More than me, or you . . . especially more than you. At that moment her Hong Kong shallowness was annoying, beside this wise and worldly old Chinese doctor.

His hands brushed and squeezed my flesh for about twenty minutes and then he proceeded to wire me up with hot needles and batteries – from my toes to my head and hands. Then, while he and Felicity conversed in Cantonese, I slipped into what resembled a coma for about three hours.

When I awoke, it was without a headache for the first time in nearly a week. Felicity and the doctor had gone, but . . . what's this that the cat's dragged in? Ah, a man sitting hunched at the end of my bed, watching a turbulent white picture on the television, smoking and lapping at a glass of something from the mini-bar.

He turned, parted his bony-looking teeth at me, and said something to the effect that Mr Fang had sent him up to watch me.

I thanked him, showing my own smile, and ejected him into the corridor.

At about 10 o'clock we assembled downstairs for sightseeing. Elton asked me how I liked the American doctor.

"Fine," I replied. "But he's no more American than you or me or the Nizam of Hyderabad."

Elton translated this for Mr Fang, but ran into bother with the word "Nizam". Luckily Timothy Freudenberg arrived and an animated conversation ensued during which their combined brain-power and languages settled the answer.

"Who's this Nizam of Hyderabad, anyway?" asked Timothy.

"He's an Australian," I replied, telling no more than the truth and leaving it at that.

Timothy was there to check on the arrangements for that evening's lecture and, having done so, he departed.

Mr Fang was carrying the first *brushed* head of hair I had seen in China. It was pushed straight up and back so that it sat like something grey and useful from a hardware shop on the top of his scalp. His eyes glistened as he whispered excitedly to Elton, his forefinger rising suggestively.

"He wants to know about last night," Elton said, obviously embarrassed and not wanting to say the rest.

I knew immediately the source of my midnight phone call.

"Tell him the fish lips didn't work," I replied. "He'll have to think of something stronger."

Hearing that, Mr Fang was unsure whether to guffaw or look crestfallen. Settling somewhere in between, he sucked in a bag full of smoke and said that he would see us for dinner. He then went off to the hard-backed lounges in the lobby where he would sit until nightfall, like so many other Chinese septuagenarians, smoking and sipping bitter tea and dreaming of his days at the Yan'an base camp.

Our tour party was to be myself, Felicity, Elton and two young men from Ng's Guangzhou office.

We went outside and waited for a taxi. After a few minutes, a long, broken-backed and stricken vehicle arrived noisily in front of us. *What the hell's this?* I looked at the markings. It was . . . a . . . a De Soto! I hadn't seen a De Soto since about 1958, and here was one ready to take us on the Ground Tour of Canton!

Felicity, missing the Mercedes-Benz and Honda Legend culture of Hong Kong, looked appalled as we piled in onto the De Soto's screeching seats. Her look didn't leave her as we drove off, riding above clunky, juddering sounds and movements into a dilapidated part of the city.

We were supposedly going to the Guangzhou Cultural Centre, but as we throbbed along, passing one ruined slum after another, I realised that nobody, least of all the driver, had any idea where to find it. Felicity sat in front, a handkerchief pressed to her nose and her cheeks puffed and rigid. Beside her was one of Ng's representatives, apparently our guide. With nothing to point out, and unable to tell the driver anything, he passed the time slyly eyeing Felicity's knees.

The streets along which we passed were crowded, exhausted ash-grey places of urban chaos which went on for mile after mile. My most striking recollections of the drive are of a convoy of men on bicycles, weaving in and out of the traffic carrying jagged sheets of glass, and of a group of women coolly plucking live, gaping ducks as they dangled and flapped from a tree.

But twenty minutes later, when I saw more ducks being plucked, I realised that we were thrashing stupidly along the same streets and had spent two hours tragically lost in a very small area.

"There are at least three people in the car who are inhabitants of this city," I announced testily. "There are at least five who can speak the lingo. Surely we can ask a policeman, or *someone*, where the wretched place is."

We eventually did find the Cultural Centre, or what our driver *claimed* to be the Cultural Centre, as he rocked the De Soto forwards and backwards into the car-park like a great tanker.

What we saw was a very impressive Chinese temple containing glass cabinet displays of pottery, weaving and other crafts from Guangdong province and beyond.

I wandered around, startling the guards, who were seated, either snoring calmly, or reading with acute concentration the smallest items in the smallest print in their minutely-folded newspapers. Every time they were disturbed, the guards would open their mouths wide as if to yawn, before clawing everything up from their throats and chests and spitting wildly in any direction, so startling me in return.

"Did you know," I said to Elton, "that Guangdong and New South Wales are sister-states?" I wasn't sure whether the idea was wonderful or ridiculous, but when you were there, in Guangzhou, it was rather striking.

"Yes," replied Elton, opening his mouth with a genuine

yawn. "I know." I knew he didn't know, and in fact wouldn't have even known what or where New South Wales was.

My Hong Kong and Chinese friends were lagging, obviously now bored with our cultural outing.

"Maybe we go to yum cha, now," suggested Elton. "Maybe you get hungry."

"Maybe not," I replied, not overly excited by the cultural centre myself, but preferring it to another meal.

To keep them interested, I asked questions about the regions of Guangdong, or about a particular piece of pottery, figurine or silk painting.

"Would that be from the seventeenth century?" I'd ask. "Qing dynasty, perhaps?"

"Maybe Qing," Felicity would answer in between yawns. And then, "Maybe we get a snack soon, isn't it."

Finally we went crashing away in our old De Soto to some other village-sized relic of the past. Here there were several temples which local Chinese had only recently been allowed to visit. Most looked as if they didn't value their new privilege all that much and spent their time walking about sullenly and taking pictures of one another draped over statues of temple guardians and gods with the photographic equivalents of Dong Fengs.

"Maybe cut your name on this statue," suggested one of Ng's representatives, pointing to a 1200-year old stone carving that had been well decorated and signed by other visitors.

When I looked shocked he backed away, feeling hurt and muttering about me in a displeased voice.

That evening, I gave a talk to an audience of over 1500 university and senior high school students.

The lecture hall had been well prepared with a video monitor, slide projector and a rostrum where I sat with Felicity, Elton, Timothy Freudenberg and his fiancée, Han Wei, and faculty members of the school of English at the university.

I showed a video — which must have appeared very indistinct to those beyond the first few rows — prepared by the Australian Tourist Commission. It was called *Come and say G'day*.

As it was playing, I noticed Miss Wei feverishly scribbling notes. Everyone else in the hall was immobile, concentrating totally on these views of Paul Hogan loafing on a lilo or hooligans jet-boating on the Derwent River.

When the film ended, Miss Wei announced that she would read the translation that she had prepared — the results of her scribbling. Felicity didn't like this idea and some debate followed between the parties with the dean of English adjudicating.

He decided that Miss Wei's translation should be read and so the video was replayed with Miss Wei gabbling hysterically — demonstrating, if nothing else, that she had a remarkable linguistic ability. This demonstration had Freudenberg smiling the smile of an achiever, whilst Felicity yawned, energetically and visibly showing her contempt.

Then the dean made a long speech during which he kept pointing at me (laughter, clapping), which, when translated by Felicity, turned out to be one of those familiar Chinese rants about cooperation, warm relationships, effort, brotherhood, long life, peaceful understanding and listening to the masses.

Our various prepared talks concluded, Felicity announced that those with particular inquiries could remain whilst the rest should leave.

A few people elbowed their way to the exits; the rest stayed behind and several began to push to the front and gather around the stage. By now the dean was peacefully asleep and the faculty members positioned around him were nodding off too.

With the help of Miss Wei, Felicity and Elton, I began to answer questions. The more we answered, the closer the crowd pressed. Some then began to climb on to the stage — to have a better chance of putting their inquiries. These concerned university programs in Australia, visas, how much a student could earn by working and so on. There were also private queries about the whereabouts of a certain Ling Xiang, last heard of studying at an English college in Melbourne, or a Mr Jian-Ping who went to Australia last June. Photos were thrust into our hands with phone numbers and messages on the back, little parcels appeared with names and addresses on them, and then bigger parcels and then finally chaff-bag sized packages of the sort that Chinese travel with were heaved at our feet.

Elton couldn't believe it. *These turkeys!* What did they think the world was like out there? He started pushing the parcels back at those piling them on us, as I wondered where on earth they had appeared from and how this evening, which had begun as a pleasant, orderly, intelligent interchange, had degenerated into a scene which resembled a day in the life of an Indian post-office (or a Chinese one, for all I knew).

Timothy Freudenberg was aghast. This academic duffer who had wanted to impress me with the Chinese, *his* Chinese, and had wanted so much for me to *like* them, was flailing his long limbs, stiffly trying to get people to stand in line.

Finally Elton and Ng's representatives managed to sneak me out the back door and downstairs to a waiting car. We left the hall, anxious students still hurling their questions and packages at Timothy and Miss Wei, the faculty dreaming gently in the corner of the stage, and fanged back to our hotel.

"Maybe we get hungry now," declared Felicity as we entered. I surprised myself. For the first time since leaving Hong Kong I *was* hungry and happily went with them to the restaurant.

The next morning we were scheduled to fly to the city of Haikou on Hainan Island, the southernmost Chinese region, bordering Vietnam's Gulf of Tonkin.

Travelling to Hainan meant flying and that meant CAAC. I could postpone my encounter no longer.

A convoy of noisy cars took us to the airport, where the Farewell Committee, men with cobwebbed hair and sooty, layered suits, embraced me. A provincial official pushed his way to the front of a squabbling queue with our tickets. Here he argued tirelessly with an equally tireless clerk about securing us seats on an already overbooked plane. This he ultimately achieved and then we stood about waiting for our flight to be called.

Strangely, in the echoing uproar of the terminal, only I heard the announcement, although it wasn't in English. Elton and Felicity joked that it couldn't be our flight, because it was on time, and so we ignored the call and waited, as Haikou-bound passengers rushed past, trampling our feet.

"Felicity, I'm sure that was our flight."

"Cannot."

"How can you be so sure?"

"Can."

Eventually they were persuaded to check and upon being informed by a shouting official that this was indeed the plane to Haikou, entered that panic mode that grips the inhabitants of small or crowded countries in circumstances such as these.

Bags and boxes were dragged and pushed to the exit and passengers for other flights bundled off into corners as we dashed for our plane.

Of course, on arriving at the tarmac, we discovered that there had been no need to rush. Our fellow passengers were standing around the plane mumbling and hawking whilst mechanics whacked and bungled at the undercarriage and engines with wrenches.

CAAC. I had been expecting a frightening-looking aircraft, an Oblomov Turbo, say, something built in Russia, with one wing longer than the other and awkwardly mounted engines. In fact there were such aircraft sitting elsewhere on the tarmac — planes that reminded me for some compelling reason of an Edward Lear rhyme:

> And the Golden Grouse came there
> And the Pobble who hast no toes
> And the small Olympian bear
> And the Dong with a luminous nose
> The Blue Baboon who played the flute
> And the Orient Calf from the Land of Tute . . .

and into which angst-ridden passengers filed, bound for some frozen gulag.

But, surprise, our aircraft was an ordinary Boeing 737, recently purchased secondhand, perhaps, but no lopsided horror from the Land of Tute.

We were permitted, finally, to board, crushing children and small adults as we did so and grabbing any nearby seat. I was positioned beween Elton and an old, blubbering woman.

Two flight attendants appeared, scowled at all of us in turn, and handed out a box of lychee juice and a small gift box to each. A gift from CAAC! That was more than I had expected. The gift in question turned out to be a gold plated pair of wings of a surprisingly attractive design.

That was all the flight attendants were to do; there were no demonstrations of safety procedures, no further presentations of food or drink. The two girls in their austere, dull uniforms sat near the door for the duration of the flight leafing greedily through Hong Kong fashion magazines.

Oil or some other light black liquid — beef soup, perhaps — was dripping from the air-conditioning outlet, and when I turned the little knob to shut it off, the dripping intensified.

I explored the seat pocket in front of me. A Chinese newspaper, a chewed cake of soap, an empty juice box, and ... *something nipping at my fingers.* I withdrew my hand in a rush and mentioned it to Elton.

"Maybe rats," he proposed.

Maybe not rats, I thought and, on peering in, saw a thin stream of ants busy with the remains of some biscuits. *Ants!*

"Ants," I said to Elton.

"Yes, he said without taking much interest. "At least not spiders."

As the aircraft developed full power for take-off, Elton decided to ask me a riddle. Did I know what everyone in Hong Kong said the letters CAAC stood for?

"I give up," I replied, watching the flat, oily grass rush beneath the wings.

"Well, I'll tell you. *China Airlines Always Crashes.* Isn't that quite funny?"

Ha, ha, Elton.

No one had instructed us to fasten seatbelts or ensure that the backs of our seats were upright, so many of the passengers were reclining leisurely as the plane roared towards the clouds, or were leaning forward preparing to vomit. Some seatbelts, I noticed as we climbed, had no buckles at all and would have needed tying around the waist.

For all the imagined horrors, however, the flight was completely uneventful. Descending to Haikou there was a period of what Australian pilots refer to as "weather activity" — as in "there's a bit of weather activity up ahead, so I've switched on the seat belt sign", although here, over the South China Sea, the activity was not accompanied by the same reassuring warning — causing the 737 to hurdle for a while through hot turbulent air. And then we landed.

In the arrival hall we were greeted by the usual Gang of Ten or more, men bundled into two or three suits who had neglected to comb their hair. We grasped one another, exchanged cigarettes and flu germs, and then set off in a convoy of four-wheel drives to our hotel.

Felicity, during this trip, remarked in a disparaging tone that Hainan resembled the Philippines — the worst place that any other place could look like on the Hong Kong mind map. All those coconut palms and irrigation ditches and bamboo huts beside the fields and *animals* pulling ploughs and pedicabs that looked like prams and people in broad hats . . .

Observing those hats, I said, "Look at those hats the women are wearing. I've never seen them before." They were white, wide and flat and made of a silk-like substance.

"Yes," Felicity answered. "All Chinese women wear that hats."

"No they don't. Only here in Hainan."

"Chinese women have to wear hats like that hats. Don't you know about the government?"

"I've never seen such hats, anywhere, in China or elsewhere."

"Isn't it?"

Isn't it?

"Isn't it" is an infuriating device that Hong Kongers, Thais and (would you credit it?) Bengalis use at random and without warning. It's meant to conclude matters by suggesting that the speaker is right, but is leaving open the possibility that a really speculative person might want to come back with another comment. You never do, you just sit there feeling irritable. It has the same effect on me as those porters with limps in Spanish and Italian hotels and Americans who want to show you their shopping in Hong Kong hotel elevators.

That night we had dinner in a vast, crumbling, seaside restaurant. Felicity remarked as we entered, "Look again like Philippines, but maybe delicious."

There were about twenty in our group, so Mr Chen, a local education department official, placed our order. I reflected that the order was rather like God's commands to Noah:

> Of every clean beast thou shalt take to thee sevens, the male and his female; and of beasts that are not clean by two, the male and his female . . . Of fowls also of the air by sevens . . . and of everything that creepeth upon the earth . . .

We ate wildly, pointed our chopsticks at each other, tapped our fingers on the table when we wanted tea (I had to drink bottle after bottle of milky, warm beer, and the occasional glass of orangeade because that is what foreigners always drink), smoked ardently, and discussed the state of the world here in Haikou. At one point, Felicity asked me if I liked snake.

"I've never tried it."

"So you don't like?"

"No . . . I don't *know*. I've never tasted it."

"So we can arrange."

"You don't have to . . . I'm not desperate to try it."

"Don't worry. It's no problem."

"I'm not fussed, one way or the other."

"Isn't it?"

A few courses later a large dish of greenish matter arrived and was placed conspicuously in front of me. Mr Chen and Elton had to prevent other people's chopsticks from clearing it before I was given the best lumps.

"What's this?" I inquired.

Felicity undertook a rapid exchange with a beaming Mr Chen.

"Mushroom and something like that," she said, heaping up my plate.

"Something like *what*?"

Pregnant rats? Monkeys' eardrums? Donkeys' pizzles? The lining from camels' humps? Flying fox lips? Anything was possible in this country, I reflected.

"Something like mouse... you know... but he not borned yet," explained Elton helpfully.

"Ah, something like *that*," I smiled with relief, and grimly moved in on my share, thinking that they had even gone further than Noah in this instance in gathering things that were not yet creeping upon the earth.

The following afternoon I presented a lecture at a teacher training college. Mr Chen and his team were there to organise things for me and to get the clapping going.

The audience was enormous, far too large for the hall, and flowed into the entrance foyer and down the stairs.

It was decided that I would deliver my talk twice, a sensible solution. However, when I had completed the first rendition, and it was time to clear the auditorium for the second sitting, most of those in the first audience would not leave and those on the stairs would not move to allow out those who did cooperate and wanted to leave.

A disturbance of almost sub-continental dimensions erupted during which Mr Chen arranged for me to be whisked through a side door down to a waiting mini-bus. There I sat, in this brand-new Toyota with the air conditioning running, the driver standing at the door to protect me and a crowd swelling around. I felt like Michael Jackson, or Bruce Springsteen with all this crazy attention.

I could hear them hooting at me through the glass, some of them speaking with astonishingly British accents: "I say, Mr Laurence, do you think my diploma would achieve advanced standing for me at Deakin?" or "Where on earth is La Trobe?" or "Would it be acceptable for me to read astrophysics at Melbourne?" or "Is an associate diploma somewhat inferior to a graduate diploma?"... but there was nothing I could do.

My presence in Haikou had triggered a passion for Australia (*read*: somewhere other than China) that the authorities were horrified to see growing to something uncontrollable.

Finally, when Elton, Felicity and Mr Chen came bursting into the car, we took off past the adoring, braying students and rushed back to our hotel.

I told Felicity about the British way a lot of them spoke English.

"Maybe, that's not British," she answered, her smooth flat smile showing that she was miffed. "In Hong Kong we have British English, isn't it."

And that was the end of the matter.

Where was Beam Ng? And Professor Matsuzawa? Until now I had almost forgotten that they were supposed to have joined us *somewhere* on our circuit, but the fright I had had in seeing a crowd more or less out of control and the officials' nervous and angry reaction made me aware that we needed Dr Ng here.

Felicity said that maybe he would meet us in Shanghai where we were scheduled to arrive in two days' time.

Early next morning Ng phoned me. He was in Shanghai and was in quite a flap. There had apparently been serious demonstrations by students outside the Japanese consulate in Shanghai and the municipal authorities had suggested to Ng's representatives that a foreign delegation promoting educational opportunities abroad would "excite" the students further.

The Japanese government had recently discovered that many of the colleges which had been enrolling Chinese students were either bogus ("Sunshine University", "Good Morning Academy" and so on) or were not making any effort to ensure that the students were attending the courses for which they had paid. The traffic in students was revealed to be mostly a labour-recruiting activity, for Japan had now reached that comfortable position of other advanced economies where there were severe shortages of workers at the rough end of the labour market.

Japan's response to this discovery was to refuse to issue any more student visas whilst the situation was investigated.

(Interestingly, the Japanese concern was not so much with the bogus institutions and courses, but with the realisation that there were *foreign* workers in growing numbers in their midst.)

So demonstrations by aggravated students, many of whom had paid their course fees and all of whom were looking forward to several years of relatively well paid work in Japan, resulted.

Dr Ng's idea was that we should capitalise on the Japanese closure and transfer the students to Australia. He wanted my lectures to go ahead and even proposed advertising a couple of extra ones to take advantage of this new opportunity.

His Hong Kong brain was never idle. Not only were there now students to be diverted from Japan, but whilst in Shanghai he was investigating counter-trade opportunities – goods he could buy with the money of those students who would pay in renminbi rather than hard currency. Bolts of raw silk, tonnes of dried fish floss and thousands of remote-control toy cars were looking promising.

We agreed that I should fly to Shanghai as planned and that we would discuss what was to be done once I arrived.

That afternoon we heard that protests had now broken out in Beijing and Chengdu, the remaining cities on my circuit. The authorities there, too, were warning against my visit.

At dinner that night, Felicity said that our hosts had a surprise for me. "That make you very happy, isn't it," she teased.

After a couple of courses and a packet or two of cigarettes, Mr Chen began flapping his hands at a cluster of waiters bearing down upon us with further dishes. They were directed my way.

"Here's your snake!" Felicity announced in triumph.

My snake?

"You say you like snake, isn't it," Elton beamed, as I stared at the little rashers of serpent before me.

My dismay was less directed at the snake than at the appearance of more food, but it had to be eaten, and I think I made a fair job it, while Felicity tantalised me with the hint of further surprises in Shanghai.

The next morning we flew north, with a transit stop in Guangzhou.

Our flight to Shanghai was in a frightfully assembled Ilyushin, the CAAC aircraft of my earlier nightmares. Felicity and I sat next to a man with a parrot on his lap. The bird laughed and muttered fitfully in what I thought was Cantonese, looking at me out of one eye.

I supposed that the bird was to become the man's breakfast — I had no reason to think otherwise as the only partnership that I had observed between man and beast in China was that defined by the chopping board and wok — but Felicity was horrified when I made the suggestion.

"That his friend," she admonished, "who can say poetry."

I asked the man if the parrot could only recite Cantonese poetry.

"Hakka!" the man squawked in a voice not unlike the parrot's.

It was long after dark when we landed at Shanghai's Hongqiao airport.

Beam Ng was there, as well as a crowd of fellows who might have raced up in a convoy of Dong Fengs from Guangzhou, so familiar was their layered clothing and eager friendliness.

But Ng looked worried. The student riots had worsened and these people, amongst them senior education bureaucrats, whilst welcoming me to Shanghai, would not permit me to deliver public lectures about Australia.

Wonderful. I could have been in Hong Kong that afternoon, *by myself* at the Regent having a silent drink at the harbourside bar and gazing at the lights streaming across the water . . .

Instead I had taken a five-hour flight in a mechanical dragon accompanied by parrot abusing me in Hakka.

We went to the Nikko Hotel, conveniently close to the airport in this city of over 12 million, to make our plans.

My party for dinner stretched to three large round tables

— this was the committee which was here simultaneously to welcome me and see me off.

Beam Ng was depressed. His plan to have me interviewed on a radio station in prime time so as to take advantage of the doors to Japan closing was being dashed by these clarty party men brattling and poking at and wolfing down our food with their duelling chopsticks as if rationing were to be introduced the minute we departed.

Ng had even contacted my Canadian counterpart about joining our show in Shanghai to replace the hapless Professor Matsuzawa. Radio interviews, lectures on campuses, perhaps newspaper articles and photographs — the impact would be huge. The Canadian was just now on the other side of the Pacific applying for his visa, preparing his slide show and rolling up his maps of Canada.

But the bureaucrats were adamant. Our food, our beer, our cognac, our English cigarettes made no difference.

The students were a threat to security and our presence and what we had to say would agitate them to an extreme degree. Further, my own safety could not be guaranteed.

That decides it, then, I thought.

"It's very terrible," said Elton sadly. "A very pity." Of course Elton couldn't wait to get back to Hong Kong either. He'd had enough of all these *old* men, these *disgraceful* men, these . . . these *Chinese* men.

Felicity, too, feigned misery. How long had we been away? Six days? A week? Ten days? She couldn't work it out . . . and we had Shanghai, Beijing and Chengdu left. It would be a shame to pull out now, she concluded wistfully, one eye on the grunting men around the table and the other, no doubt, already taking in the shop windows in the New World Centre, Harbour City and Causeway Bay.

So the next day my two scheduled talks were called off. But this didn't stop Ng's local representatives bringing a stream of well-educated and ambitious youngsters to my room to hear my "Next Time, Why Not Choose Australia?" talk.

The city was invisible beneath a dripping fog, which meant that all flights in and out of Shanghai were cancelled.

Over two days, I saw perhaps a hundred disaffected students whose anger with Japan had suddenly been transformed into a romantic fondness for Australia.

On the evening of the second day, a group from a teacher's college visited, with their English teacher who was from Townsville in Queensland. She was a woman of about 45, unmarried I guessed, with messy greying hair that kept falling out of her clips. The clips, in their turn, kept falling to the floor. She had that oddness acquired by people who have lived for too long in a totally alien culture. She was indirect and jumpy, having lost the ability to respond immediately and instinctively to cultural signs.

There was, as well, something ill-assorted about her as if she had spent years concentrating on learning to ride a bicycle slowly or to pluck ducks in her own kitchen.

When this teacher looked at me, I felt she was looking at some point in between my eye and an ear, which made me jumpy, too. But her students thought she was wonderful; she had taught them all about Australia, our sheep, our sweeping sunburnt plains, our wonderful democracy, our lovely homes, and our funny slang ("bewdy bottler", that sort of thing).

She told me all about China. *All* about it. That's something else these people lose track of: when they've said enough. Looking at my ear, or at my nostrils, she told me of the wonderful people she had discovered, the beautiful way they live, the lovely simplicity of it all, the incredible dignity, the amazing intelligence, the lovely slow way they ride their bicycles everywhere . . . (Her students ignored all this as they devoured and debated the literature that I had on Australia.) But then her face and eyes sharpened and she whispered to me with misplaced drama, "But really awful things are going to happen." She nodded, her mouth sealed, and then ushered her class from my room.

When the fog cleared we flew away to Hong Kong and spent over an hour somewhere in the air above Guangdong doing loops around soaring storm heads as the pilot waited for clearance into Kai Tak.

That night I met Beam Ng for a quiet debriefing at the China City nightclub. It was difficult to determine what sort of mood he was in: first he wanted the company of a $200 an hour hostess, then he didn't; next he ordered a Chivas Regal and then decided he wanted a 180-year-old armagnac. He was at one moment expansive and bright and at the next, sombre and philosophical.

"I getta big worry about what happen," he explained. "Not only we lose business, but they all talking about more trouble coming in China."

I wanted to hear more about what people were predicting. What trouble? Until then I had supposed that the student disturbances we had heard about were local and had a specific cause — the refusal of Japan to issue any more visas.

But just as Dr Ng began to expound upon what was worrying him, a man edged his way into our corner and greeted Ng in an explosion of Cantonese. Ng introduced him to me as Eric, a business acquaintance, and invited him to join us. The man sent a waitress to retrieve his glass, bottle of cognac, cuttlefish strips and hostess from another table and then, having apologised to me, the two proceeded to engulf my space with a torrent of language.

I sipped beer and ginseng tea whilst this storm raged, waiting for some hint as to what was the subject of so much agitation.

"Jim getta wonderful business," the man suddenly said, turning to me. (Jim? I hadn't heard anyone refer to Ng by that name before.)

And then they both — "Jim" and "Eric" — explained the idea.

Whilst I was in southern China with Felicity and Elton, it seemed Ng had been shuttling about between Hong Kong, Taipei — as Felicity had admitted — Guangzhou and Shanghai. There had appeared an altogether new and different product for the market: workers for a trade development zone being set up in Darwin in Australia's Northern Territory.

Eric's company had a contract with a couple of state governments in China to supply labour for several overseas projects, an activity that earned foreign exchange for the governments because payment came as a percentage of the workers' wages. Dr Ng had become involved as a rolling stone of a businessman with Australian connections when the opportunities arose in Darwin.

All of this astonished me. I had no knowledge of the "TDZ", as they both called the Darwin project, and was amazed that any Australian government would have agreed to what sounded like a "guest-worker" scheme. But apparently it had, and workers were now being recruited for the Hong Kong-owned companies that would set up factories in the zone.

I also wondered why Hong Kong businesses would go to the trouble of building and operating factories with cheap imported labour in the Northern Territory where they were sure to be harassed by diligent and officious unionists, when they could do the same thing in Hong Kong's own New Territories, or indeed in China itself, without anyone taking the slightest notice.

But I didn't pursue the issue, because what I did know was that people like Beam Ng and this Eric, now working his way towards the bottom of his bottle, saw opportunities for making money where other people saw only an effluvial fog.

Seven months after my return from China, the student revolts that had begun in a small way whilst I was there, and that had grown to world-mesmerising proportions, were savagely crushed by the army. The Great Wall of Iron, the People's Liberation Army that had been so romanticised in the West, was now universally reviled. China, too, tumbled rapidly from favour down to most-detested nation status.

When the Australian embassy in Beijing closed briefly during the panicky exit of foreigners, it was revealed that about 30 000 Chinese students had visa applications there, awaiting processing.

The Australian prime minister, Bob Hawke, responding to the massacre in Tiananmen Square in June with his now familiar tears, proceeded to invite the 20 000 students in Australia to apply for asylum. And the message that was subsequently telegraphed to those still waiting for their visas in China was: once you arrive in Australia you will have the same opportunities.

Well the PM could cry as often and about whatever he wanted. But Belconnen boys don't cry, and the response of the hard hearts in the immigration department was immediate: ways had to be found to drastically reduce the numbers of students eligible to come to Australia to take up this supposed offer of asylum.

Ways were found. The rules were changed and half the people who had applied — and paid fees equal to about a decade's average wages in China — soon learned that they no longer qualified for study in Australia.

Students who had demonstrated against Japan in November and December and against their own government in May and June now found cause to rally outside the Australian missions in Beijing and Shanghai, putting the Australians in the acutely embarrassing position of having to call in for help the very security forces that they had fled from in June.

I suppose that many of the students I spoke to in Shenzhen, Guangzhou, Haikou and Shanghai would have been amongst those 30 000 applicants. About half would have been rejected, and by now would have revised their opinions of Australia. The other half are probably here and almost certainly working to pay off loans drawn on the invisible money lines that span the Pacific from Shanghai to Vancouver, Sydney and Singapore.

Meanwhile, the guest worker scheme has been proved by the tabloids and *60 Minutes* to be a "slave labour scam", and is being put down by the unions. Given that there are now about 40 000 students from China in Australia, it seems to me that the Darwin TDZ people, still short of labour, could do their recruiting in Sydney and Melbourne, so avoiding paybacks to China. But others don't see the synergies (as connections are now known).

Finally, a synergy of another sort. A month ago I received a message from Beam Ng – now running an immigration consultancy which he's called "Australian and Canadian Futures" – that Felicity was to have a baby.

"Please pass on my congratulations," I wrote back, "to Felicity and her husband".

"Thanks," replied Ng.

He's 52 and she's 37. And what I didn't know, until last week, was that they've been married for almost ten years.

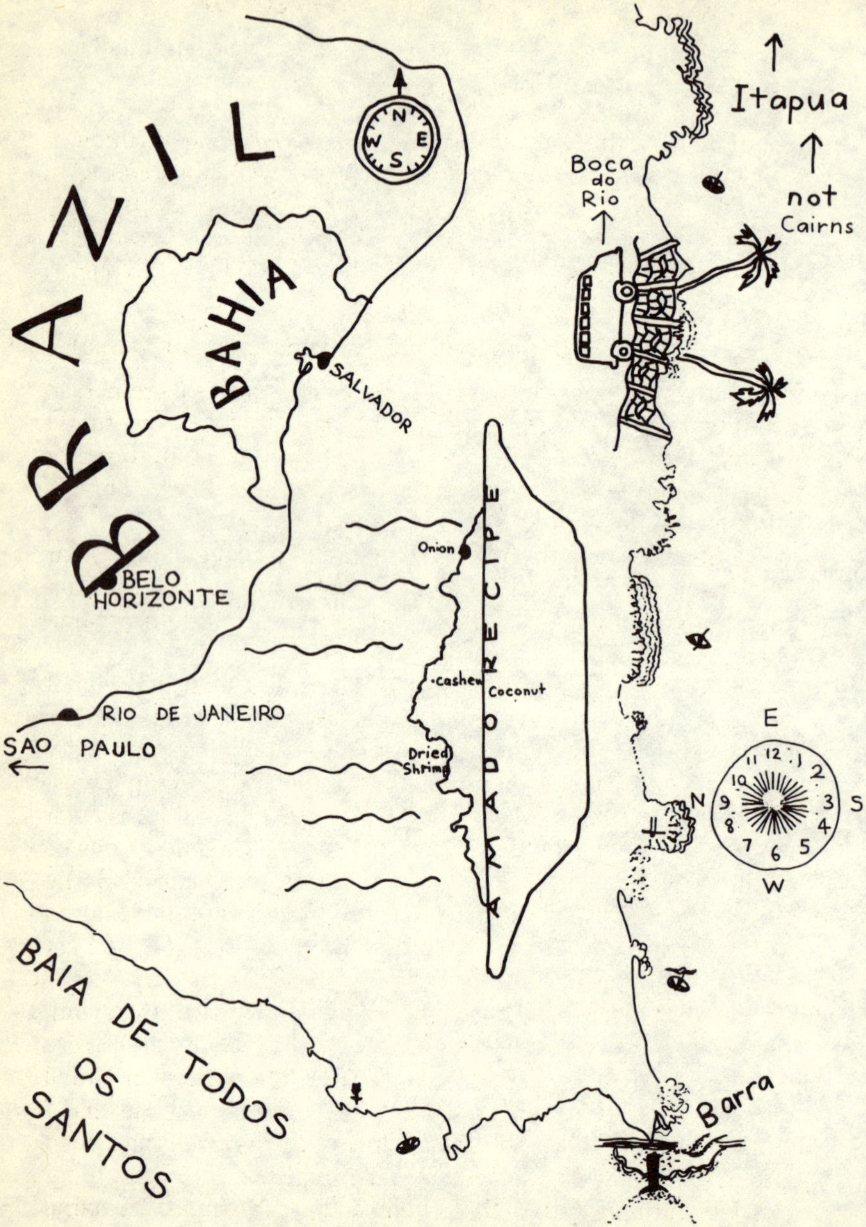
BRAZIL
BAHIA
SALVADOR
BELO HORIZONTE
RIO DE JANEIRO
SAO PAULO
BAIA DE TODOS OS SANTOS
AMADO RECIPE
Onion
cashew
Coconut
Dried Shrim
N
E
S
W
Boca do Rio
Itapua
not Cairns
Barra
12
1
2
3
4
5
6
7
8
9
10
11

Stopover in Salvador

(Salvador, Brazil)

There is a fantastic place in the tropical coastland of Brazil to be visited. A magic and sensual world where you will live and discover friendly, happy people, primitive nature, a rich historical culture. This place is Bahia. A charming and exciting place which Brazilians call The Land of Happiness. *What is* Bahia, *after all?*

(From the Bahiatursa brochure on Bahia)

Exactly. The culture of this "Land of Happiness" seemed so singular and powerful, and yet so hard to focus on, that I wanted to see one of those shows that brought it all together in a ninety-minute diorama – something like "This is Polynesia" in Waikiki, or "Brisbane After Dark".

The hotel receptionist recommended a place called Solar do Unhâo. There, he told me, I would enjoy the best of Bahian cooking and "every night, live music, and the most unique, typical show in Bahia."

The most unique, typical show sounded like just what I wanted. As well, I had been waiting to try some of the famous seafood dishes of this part of Brazil, "a delicious and tasty world", according to the brochure. So Solar do Unhâo it was.

Salvador, the principal city of the state of Bahia, is built upon ridges which descend abruptly to the Baía de Todos os Santos (Bay of All Saints) on the northern side and the beaches of the Atlantic on the west. On my map, the location of Solar do Unhâo didn't seem too far from the hotel, so I set out to walk down the steep, curving streets to the bay.

This, I discovered, was the equivalent of walking from, say, North Head down to Manly, with the difficulty and stress heightened by the fact that it was dark – shows in Brazil never begin before about 10.00 p.m. – and everyone that I had met in Salvador had warned me of the hazards that faced tourists caught wandering around at night.

I eventually found the Avenida do Contôrno – a name

which aptly describes this contour-hugging road – and walked along it beside tumbling *favelas,* shacks of tin, wire and palm fronds jammed on to the verges and slopes between the road and the sea. The footpath here is contained between two high walls, so that you walk along, with not much more light than is provided by the moon, wondering when a loose-jointed Volkswagen is going to over-ride a curve and come exploding over the wall at you. (I could hear them above me, all squealing tyres and worn-out mufflers.) Either that, or some reptile from the slums is going to spring out of the night and do great damage for nothing more than your Westpac Mastercard or a couple of hundred cruzados.

As it was, the *favelados* were not the least interested in me. They sat outside their huts cleaning fish and listening to the radio – each radio at full volume, tuned to a different station.

Finally I made it. The restaurant is part of a cluster of old buildings which were once a church and monastery. Perched just above the bay, and floodlit, it was a dramatic and haunting sight, an evocation of Brazil's colonial era, when Salvador, then called Bahia, eclipsed even Rio de Janeiro and was the country's capital.

I walked down the drive to find the waiting taxis and cars of the more sensible of the restaurant's patrons. In the foyer, elegant men and women – Brazilians – were chatting excitedly in Portuguese. It seemed odd that locals would come in such numbers to a show whose purpose was to present the essence of Brazilian and Bahian folklore to tourists. Perhaps they were from interstate. They were certainly wealthy.

A man introduced himself in German accented English as Maitre Edmundo and showed me to a table. As he did so, I noticed the posters around the walls. They were of scenes and sights in Spain. Curious, I thought.

Then I was presented with the menu. *Bem-vindos a noites da Espanha* (Welcome to Spanish Nights) it was headed. I read further. It was Spanish week in Salvador and, with the help of the Spanish consulate, cultural presentations were taking place throughout the city. Here, at Solar do Unhão, there was a special Spanish menu and several nights of Spanish music and dancing. It was like going to Rooty Hill RSL, expecting to see Kamahl, and being dished up The Platters.

The mansion in which I was seated was so beautiful, however, that I decided to stay. Anyway, it was interesting being amongst a group which appeared to be Salvador's *café-soçaite*, not at all the noisy, energetic black and mulatto crowds of the streets, but people such as you glimpse only behind the tinted windows of their Mercedes and Saabs. And one of them was giving me some very interesting looks.

Dinner was Spanish – paella, prawns, chicken, the usual – and the dancing was Spanish. At first I thought I'd seen better at the Cabaret España in Liverpool Street in Sydney, but once the performers had completed a couple of acts and the rich Salvadorans had loosened and become, well, Brazilians, the current moved both ways and the dancing became charged with tragedy, passion, violence and sensuality – the everyday Spanish characteristics. At those moments I forgot that I was in Brazil, searching for Brazilian culture.

All the while, a young woman seated with her husband and another couple was staring at me. Through the *entremeses*, the soup, the paella, the *flan de naranja* . . . all of which she only played with, she watched me. Several times she walked carefully by me, twice with the other woman, presumably to the bathroom, but made no attempt to communicate.

By now I was twitching – with the flamenco on one side and this very dangerous apparent flirtation on the other. I had been reading Jorge Amado's *Gabriela, Clove and Cinnamon* and had learned that a man who intefered with a married woman should expect the worst, and that the husband would probably escape with a caution. But what about a married woman who interfered with a married man who was only an innocent bystander?

After dinner I wandered out to the courtyard. Within a minute she was beside me.

"*Heitor!*" she breathed. "*Como vai?*" (Heitor, how are you?)
"*O que?*" (What?)
"*Quanto tempo!*" She persisted. "*Talvez uns vinte anos!*" (It's been years . . . perhaps twenty.)

"Só vinte?" I threw in. (Only twenty?)

"Ein!?" (What!?)

"Sorry," I blurted, a bit in Portuguese, a bit in English, "I'm not even . . ."

I didn't have to finish. The woman stared at me in astonishment, muttered a hasty apology, and glided back to the safety of her husband. And I had avoided the fate of the hapless dentist in *Gabriela*.

Later I asked Maitre Edmundo about the Bahian show, this unique, typical event that I had risked my life to attend. It was on every night of the year, he reassured me, but not this week. In consolation he gave me a cigar and a glass of Bahian coffee liqueur and, as the guests filed out to their cars, we sat down with one of the flamenco guitarists and talked about Germany, Spain, Brazil and Australia.

The Spaniard had heard about Australia. Especially about the sticks.

"Ah, estick," he sighed, his eyes closed in wonder. *"Son muy grandes."* And he made a large oval with his hands.

It took the Maitre's Portuguese to divine the object of the guitarist's enchantment.

Steak. Australian steak, it seemed, was known and admired in Spain.

And I still hadn't seen a Bahian show.

"If you'd told me you wanted to go this week, I'd have told you not to", chided the receptionist when I told him about *Noites da Espanha*. "Everyone knows it's Spanish week!"

This man boasted the name of Neil Armstrong Machado. He had pointed it out to me on his badge when I arrived, and revealed that he was born on the same day that man first walked on the moon. A great step for mankind indeed, but a big day for Neil Armstrong Machado as well.

Names of this sort are not uncommon in Brazil. In hotels I've seen a Lyndon Johnson, a John Kennedy and a Martin Luther. I've met a Euclides and a Roosevelt, and in Sydney I know a Brazilian Oscar Wilde.

Neil Armstrong's recommendation for tonight was that I go to SENAC. That was the only place to see a really authentic display of the music and dance of Bahia. And it was cheap, because it was run partly by the state tourist board. But take a taxi, he warned. It was in a very sleazy part of town.

No one could tell me what time the show at SENAC would begin, and they weren't answering the phone. In the event, I turned up at nine, and the show was almost over. In contravention of everything, it had begun at seven.

What I did see was a vigorous dance performed by women wearing the traditional white petticoats and skirts of the region, and men who tumbled around like gymnasts. This was followed by a gentler wedding dance, of a style which I had not expected at all in this region, the coast of which had been populated mainly by Africans, rather than temperate-climate Europeans, whose style of dancing this one closely resembled.

What I had been hoping to see and photograph was *candomblé* and *macumba*. Indeed, the program, in Portuguese, listed *candomblé* as being part of the performance. I had missed it by being late.

Candomblé developed in the north-east of Brazil through slaves brought from the Guinea Coast of Africa. It has since spread throughout the nation as an impenetrable, magical supplement to the more orthodox Catholicism — with which it nicely co-exists — and is one of many examples of the extraordinary influence that African-derived culture has on modern Brazil. But while I could see and hear samba everywhere, *candomblé* and *macumba* kept eluding me. I was always too early or too late or in the wrong place.

Suddenly the compere had us all on our feet following a collection of lithe black performers into another theatre. My program revealed that this was to be a presentation of *Se Castro Alves visse* ("If Castro Alves could see this").

Who was Castro Alves I wondered.

The play was a rippling and rhythmic thirty minutes into which it seemed the entire history of Brazil was compressed. After a while I gathered that it was the *black* history. When "Brazil", a stunning brown woman with green and gold butterfly wings, emerged from a cocoon, there were blacks still cringing in a corner, the legacy of their former enslavement.

This was interesting, as it was the first public comment that I'd seen on the status of blacks in Brazil, a nation that appears to have less racial prejudice and disharmony than any other on earth.

I've since learnt that Antônio de Castro Alves was a poet and the son of a slave. Most of his writings were expressions of anger at the treatment of slaves and it is revealing that his *Voices from Africa* is supposed to be Brazil's most popular poem.

Towards the end of the play, a great battery of samba began and the blacks rose. Black and mulatto women seduced some pathetic looking white men; there was noise and energetic dancing and I was confused.

When the show was over, I went outside to meet some of the cast. Striking blacks, quivering with life, they had many of the preoccupations of young dramatists everywhere — principally their own egos. This at least indicated that not all Brazilian blacks were the underclass. You have to be fairly middle class to have these sorts of preoccupations. But though our limited versions of each other's languages, I was able to discover that Castro Alves is viewed rather as Henry Lawson is in Australia: as an authentic Brazilian writer in an age when art and literature were intensely European in style and outlook.

* * *

> The great indication to people who want to live Bahia with intensity is just one: be at large. The beaches are considered here as a space where each one lives your own happiness . . . The beaches are wonderful and inspired poets, artists, boyfriends . . ."

This is not Neil Armstrong speaking, but my guide to "Bahia: Beaches and Islands". On about my third day, I followed its injunction "to dress your bathing costumes, follow this itinerary and profit the delights of the Bahian Beaches".

And indeed, winding north from Salvador, out of the Bay of All Saints and around the headland of Barra, there begins an undulating line of beaches stretching away to Itapuã, and way beyond to the Equator.

I took a bus as far as Bôca do Rio, the road closely following the coast and separated from the beaches by wide, elegantly patterned ceramic footpaths and thickets of palms. The only place I can think of in Australia where the road follows the curve of the shore in this way is on the Marlin Coast north of Cairns, where there is an equally enchanting run of beaches, and the tropical latitudes are the same.

I descended from the bus at Bôca do Rio because the brochure decreed that: "It's a quite place where you can swim and sun-bathe. This beach is frequented by artists and famous people."

I'm not sure whether the people I saw were artists or famous but once on the beach, I found a place that shapes a way of life — even more so than do the beaches of Australia's east coast.

At the edge there were dozens of little grass and palm huts, each one a bar or restaurant, and as it was Sunday, all were busy. People sat outside, on stools in the sand, and consumed simple snacks of fried fish or prawns and plenty of beer.

Beyond the noisy, total informality of these restaurants there were well-organised games of football — a proper competition seemed to be underway — and a couple of gangs of men with drums and tambourines hammering out the familiar rhythms of samba.

Brazilians seem to use their beaches differently from Australians. Except at a few of the beaches (such as Ipanema) where surfing is well established, they are active on the beach and idle in the water. Look at Australians. We lie around on the sand and burn our energy up in the sea. Another exception in Brazil is what the brochure calls "authentic beauties", the girls stretched out on the sand in heavenly little clusters, or swaying minutely as they stand together watching the football, or gazing to the sea and dreaming of . . . what? Africa perhaps, where some of their ancestors may have come from? America? Tonight? Certainly not of pale gringos.

Marvelling at their bikinis — minimalist creations of brilliantly coloured threads — I succeeded in attracting their attention only by proposing to photograph them.

And so I made my way to Itapuã, perhaps the third most famous beach in Brazil after Copacabana and Ipanema.

Listen to the song *Bahia with H*.

> Let me see with my longing lover's eyes the Bahia of my heart.
> Let me see Baixa do Sapateiro, Charrio, Barroquina Calçada, Itapuã.
> I'm your friend who returns to embrace you, Bahia.
> I'm a poet and I don't want to stay away from your magic . . .

Bahians love their city, their state, but most of all, they love their Itapuã, and it has been celebrated in dozens of songs and poems. (Who has ever celebrated Bondi, except perhaps Lucky Star in *I've Been Everywhere*?)

I established myself at a little restaurant — attracted as much by the carved wooden images of African gods lining the bar as by the three Brazilian goddesses serving behind it — and ate a dish of fish and peppers stewed in palm oil.

Later I read a chapter of Jorge Amado's *Tieta*, in between swims and snatching photos of those around me.

Jorge Amado gives over a whole chapter to a recipe. "We Bahians," he writes, "gross, sensual mulattoes that we are, brought up on yellow palm oil, white coconut milk, and flaming hot peppers, use *maturí* in a rare dish with a distinctive flavour." (*Maturí* are green cashew-nuts.)

I had a friend, a very young academic, who told me once that he had never tasted prosciutto but he had read about it. As a scholar, this was enough to satisfy him. Using this reasoning, I'll present here an abbreviated version of the Amado recipe, which he attributes to Dona Indayá Alves, "illustrious cordon-bleu cook of Bahia".

> *Ingredients:*
> 2 cups of green cashews *(maturí)*
> 4 skewers of dried shrimps
> 1 red pepper
> 1 large coconut
> 7 tablespoons of palm oil
> 3 tomatoes

1 large onion
1 clove of garlic
1 spoonful of tomato paste
6 eggs
salt and coriander to taste.

Cooking instructions:
Boil the green cashews (*maturí*) and season with garlic, salt and tomato paste. Soak the shrimps for some time, then devein and grind in mill with coriander, tomatoes and red pepper.

Brown chopped-up onion in oil in a casserole dish. Add *maturí*, dried shrimp and seasoning. Allow to thicken. Shred half a coconut, bringing the knife towards you (this detail is very important if the mass of grated coconut is to have the consistency of smooth cream) and add to casserole with the milk from the other half, extracted from the fibres and mixed with half a cup of water. Leave on the fire for a while and add the olive oil and three beaten eggs, first the whites, then the yolks. Add a little flour to the eggs. Taste to see if flavour is right.

When everything is cooked, turn into greased baking pan to bake the *maturí* omelet, which is then covered with the three remaining eggs, whites and yolks beaten together, and a sprinkling of flour. Brown in a hot oven. Leave in baking pan until cool.

Amado goes on to comment that the hardest part is finding the green cashews, but suggests that if the reader goes to "Camafeu do Oxossi or Luiz Domingos . . . both of whom own restaurants in the Model Market in Bahia, and asks nicely, one of them might be kind enough to provide a handful or two of those green, tender, virgin cashew nuts".

And if *maturí* are hard to find in Bahia, then sadly for my audience, reading about them will have to do.

On succeeding days I visited Arembepe ("The fame of this beach is due to the passage of Mick Jagger, Janis Joplin and other artists that came here in the sixties"), Pituba ("Here you find beautiful girls on the beach and on the small bares"), the exquisitely named Jardim de Alá ("Don't forget to bring your camera") and Jardim dos Namorados ("Here one can practice soccer and model aeronautics").

And then there were the islands. One morning I took a ferry across the bay to the largest of them, Itaparica. Here is located one of the world's most delightful Clubs Méditerranées, as well as the sleepy old Portuguese town of Cidade de Itaparica and an extraordinarily busy beach, Barra do Gil.

I returned to Salvador in a much smaller, crowded motorboat, and spent the crossing taking pictures of the strong, varied faces of the passengers (I imagined presenting them in a full-page collage, all the races, colours, ages and images of Brazil) and being pestered by a drunken ice-cream vendor.

Sunset over Salvador, seen from the water, was like a rain of flamingoes descending on the Portuguese churches and colonial buildings and bouncing back from the darkening waters. The illumination was sudden, pink and then gone. We chugged on in silence, the ice-cream man slumped stupidly over the stern, his unsold ice-creams dribbling from his box.

* * *

> I came, I came from Bahia to sing, I came from Bahia to tell about so many beautiful things.
> Bahia is my home,
> It's got my soil, my sky, my sea.
> Bahia, which exists to teach us how to live
> Where people don't have enough to eat,
> But from hunger they don't die,
> Because in Bahia there's Mãe Iemanjá,
> And on the other side, Senhor do Bonfim
> Who help the Baianos to live,
> To sing, to samba the real way,
> To die of happiness,
> In the street feasts, in the rounds of samba,
> In the moonlight, in the song of the sea . .

* * *

The focus of the city of Salvador is an extraordinary elevator which connects the Cidade Baixa (lower city) with the upper city. This Elevador Lacerda is the only one that I've ever seen which functions as public transport, two cars attended by waxen-faced black drivers ascending and descending a steep cliff-face night and day. At the top is Praça Tomé de Souza, where crowds gather to view the sunset from the other side — over Itaparica and the Atlantic. And it was here that I first observed a unique local contraption: the trolleys used by drink and cigarette vendors.

These items resemble skateboards, with skateboard-sized wheels and platforms. There is a steering wheel — taken from a car, and the bigger and flasher the better — mounted on a column rising to about a metre at one end. The board is enclosed so that drinks and vacuum flasks can stand up in rows, and at the other end there is usually a radio aerial, some reaching extravagant heights, to which open packets of cigarettes are attached, all the way to the top. Often, too, there is a small transistor radio tied to the aerial.

Driven by noisy boys, these devices clatter around the cobbled streets of Salvador, and up and down the Lacerda elevator, dispensing their goods and creating an effect that is quite eccentric.

Another Salvadoran institution is the women who sell local dishes at street stalls. Mostly plump blacks, these *Baianas* sit under trees dressed in volumes of white skirts and petticoats, white turbans and masses of bright jewellery. Before them are trays of seafood, peppers, nuts and spices, and they'll prepare, on order, dishes whose names — *vatapá, carurú acarajé, mungunzá bobó, moqueca de peixe* — echo tropical West Africa and the Atlantic crossing far more than they do Portugal.

And they *are* an institution. Like street-lamps and flame trees, they are everywhere, often with small daughters growing into the role beside them. Once late at night I saw a couple of *Baianas* packing up to go home. It was a disappointment to see them unravel their skirts and petticoats to reveal jeans and tee-shirts beneath.

> Let me see your balconies, churches, your saints, hills and mountains,
> as in a post-card.
> Let me pray for Senhor do Bonfim.
> Hail sacred, immortal Bahia;
> Bahia of my dreams, I'm glad to know Bahia is Brazil.

You can't escape it. Salvador, Bahia is a very spiritual

place. One song says that there are 365 churches; another says 300. And they are well attended, each with its own special orientation and atmosphere. But if you can't escape them, it's also quite difficult to establish which is which.

The *City Guide* outlines two-, four- and six-day tours to enable you "to profit your stay". But if you wish to allocate three or five days to your sightseeing, the *Guide* suggests that "you should follow, respectively, the first three days of the four-day tour or the first five days of the six-day tour".

So, day one of sightseeing. The first three days of the four-day tour. I begin looking for Igreja (Church) do Senhor Bonfim. By midday, lost, I consult the *Guide* again. "Your first day is still not over," it warns. "If you have less time, you must go quicker."

Still, I did find Pelourinho Square (Pelourinho meaning pillory, a device which was apparently used for torturing slaves), which is surrounded by colonial buildings of great richness and grace, said to be the most outstanding collection of seventeenth- and eighteenth-century architecture in the Americas.

At the Church of Nossa Senhora do Rosário dos Pretos (Our Lady of the Rosary for Blacks) a young "guide" asked me to abandon my written guide — which I was happy to do — and offered to show me around. His name was Ascânio and as we went from church to church he revealed quite detailed knowledge of the history, the architecture and the spiritual significance of each place. Clearly Ascânio was not a real guide, for each time we happened upon a tour party — usually French, Italian or Argentinian — their guides would hiss at him surreptitiously, warning him to get out of their way.

In several glittering churches, Ascânio would introduce me to the priests, who would chat to me briefly before whipping out packets of postcards and stamps and a list of charges for taking various photographs.

The wealth of this area, both in terms of the gold and artefacts contained in the churches and the colonial heritage, is astounding. Somewhere Ascânio pointed out two churches built on top of one another — a bit like those buildings in Bombay which have, say, the Dudley Hotel on the first floor, the Stiffles on the second and the Modern Rest on the third. This extraordinary creation was so ordinary in this city of churches that Ascânio was able to tell me no more about it.

In Praça Quinze de Novembro we came across half a dozen men engaged in *capoeira* — an activity involving cartwheels, kicks and ritualised assaults. It is a martial art, apparently developed by slaves, which is unique to this part of Brazil; you can occasionally see it practised at Bondi beach when local Brazilians are in the mood.

Here in Salvador, the locals were in the mood — but only if I paid them for photographs. Ascânio and I thought this was fair and so I was able to film these martial acrobatics which leave you breathless with worry about your own fitness.

When I was not being ably assisted by Ascânio, I would carry around an assortment of phrasebooks including the Berlitz *Portuguese for Travellers,* the Cortina Method *Brazilian Portuguese: The Easy Method*, Theodolina Salum's *Portuguese Para Quem Fala Ingles* (Portuguese for English-speaking People) and, most perplexing of all, a language disc, two spinning plastic wheels, which had been presented to me at the welcome desk at Rio de Janeiro airport on an earlier visit.

With any combination of these, I was usually able to make myself understood, but of course having your first utterance understood is like being invited to have a swim with your arms tied together: what phrasebooks can't help you with is understanding others. The Berlitz series attempts this with its Quick Reply Features symbolised by a pointing finger. "Just point to a phrase in the Portuguese text and get an answer in English," the introduction confidently instructs. All over the world you see English-speaking tourists blankly stabbing at pages in their Berlitzes, under the gaze of baleful waiters. The belief that all the essential human needs and a few extras can be communicated between two people with this Quick Reply system seems to me to have significance beyond the confines of a tourist phrasebook. There is something here akin to Samuel Beckett's view that only the sounds of breathing and silence mean anything, although he reached that position through pessimism, while Berlitz appears to have done so through optimism.

Each of my books had its quirks and limitations.

The Salum text emphasised the importance of being able to produce sentences such as "I kept on writing the letter" or "When Robert turned twenty years old he liked to play tennis".

Similarly, the Cortina Easy Method assists you to say things such as "It's fine to go out with a gentleman" *("E muito bom sair com um cavalheiro")* or "This cat is ugly" *("Este gato é feio").* But both books lack the Berlitz point-here-for-an-answer feature.

One night I decided to try a restaurant known as Velhos Marinheiros. It was celebrated for its seafood and in particular for its unusual regional dishes.

It was a Friday night and Salvador was alive. I took a taxi and we drove for miles, down steep hills and along the harbour front, past the famous Mercado Modelo (Model Market) and into the docklands. Here we entered a world of dereliction, eventually reaching a dark dead-end surrounded by towering, boarded-up warehouses and silent cranes. The taxi driver said something and pointed at a building. There were no signs, just broken windows, a few dull street-lamps and, beyond, a couple of small, ruined freighters, one of them keeled over on the mud.

I didn't quite know what to say to the driver, nor what to point to in my Berlitz.

A cat provided the answer. It leapt on to the still-stuttering bonnet of the car and stared.

"Este gato é feio," I announced.

The driver agreed, without expressing any surprise, and waited for me to pay and get out. I finally convinced him that I wanted to turn around and go back into town. I wanted to go to a restaurant, I explained, spinning my language disc, one with regional specialities.

We drove back into the lights and stopped outside a vast hall of illumination and noise. There were throngs of people both inside and out, most of whom seemed to be shouting at each other and at people sitting in and on cars in the street.

"Especialidades regionais?" I enquired, just to be sure.

The driver reassured me. I paid and went inside.

As I walked towards a table, numbed by the noise, I had only the slightest sensation that hundreds of people were watching me. I sat down and, as I waited, my senses began to tune again. And the first thing I noticed was that everyone in the restaurant was black.

I was familiar enough with Brazil to know that blacks and whites and everyone in between mix more readily and probably more happily than they do anywhere else. But race relations and a people's perceptions of one another and of outsiders carry nuances that the newcomer cannot hope to comprehend. (Once in Rio I went to a police station to report a theft. In writing her report the officer observed that I was *branco*, white.

"Do you have to note people's colour?" I asked.

"Yes," she replied, "because there are so many."

"So many?"

"So many. Just for the blacks we have about ten descriptive words," she explained.)

So I was not familiar enough with Brazil to know whether there were places where blacks and whites didn't mix and just how you would be received if you trespassed.

But not everyone was black. A waiter appeared from the kitchen — where a brawl seemed to be in progress — and he wasn't even brown. In fact, he was whiter than anyone I'd seen in Brazil — almost Nordic looking. I imagined that he had been a Scandinavian seaman who had left his ship in Bahia, although in his movements and speech he was as Brazilian as any man in the room.

He was tough, too, and this was turning out to be a very tough place. People were drinking heavily — mainly beer — and roaring at women who were circulating from table to table and in and out of rooms at the rear of the restaurant.

I may not have found my seafood restaurant with regional

specialities, but I had certainly found a sailors' restaurant — if that is the word — with a regional ambiance.

I had never been in such a noisy place. The fabulous Cage Bar at Casurina Beach in Darwin or the legendary Quinn's Bar in Papeete came close in savagery, but never reached the decibel levels of this place.

The waiter arrived and asked me what I wanted. Sounding tough, and with a guarded spin of my language wheels, I said that I wanted grilled fish.

"Grilled fish?" the waiter spat. "You can have grilled meat *(churrasco misto)*."

"Sure," I replied. "Grilled meat." And I congratulated myself on an exchange that was as fast as any employing Berlitz's Quick Reply Features.

The meat came to me on metre-long skewers which the waiter stabbed into wooden boards on the table, leaving the skewers quivering in the air.

My main concern now was not to attract any further attention. It was obvious that I was white, but so far only the waiter knew that I was a gringo. In particular, I didn't want the attentions of the prostitutes, a raucous, squabbling collective who, I imagined, would be delighted to shriek at one another about me once they learned that I was a foreigner.

I ate my meal quickly, taking slices of meat from the skewers and aggressively swilling my beer. After a while I began to feel at home and decided that I was probably safer here than in a rough-house pub in Townsville or Mt Isa. Still, it did amaze me that my taxi driver had connected a tourist's wish for a restaurant offering "regional specialities" with this place.

Leaving the restaurant — sauntering now more confidently between the tables — I went to hail a taxi. There were at least a dozen outside, but all were occupied by men and girls frenziedly drinking and smoking.

I started walking, having no idea at all where I was, but supposing that when I came to a main road or intersection I'd have a better chance of finding a cruising cab. And then, around the first corner, I saw a familiar flashing sign. The

Hotel da Bahia, where I was staying, was about 100 metres away.

The next morning I told Neil Armstrong about my night out. He shook his head in sadness.

"Everyone knows not to go to that place," he admonished, as if where I had been was miles across town, and he gazed at me in wonder, suggesting either that he thought me very stupid or that he was amazed to see me alive. Or both.

On my last day in Salvador, I boarded a city-bound bus at Jaguaribe. I had been photographing young people playing soccer on the beach, marvelling at the cool and rhythmic elegance of their play, which I knew my shots would never capture. As I sat in the bus at a set of traffic lights just beyond the bus-stop, I barely noticed a skinny teenage boy clutching an expensive camera. He was running with a friend towards a grass hut on the beach.

As the bus began to move, I found that I had noticed more about the boy. He'd been wearing a torn striped tee-shirt and black shorts, I recalled. And he was a mulatto, aged maybe 14 or 15.

And then the heart of the image came into focus. The camera.

"Odd," I thought, "a boy like that with a camera. Especially that sort of camera. Canon SLR, zoom lens . . ."

On a reflex, I slipped off the little backpack in which I carried my camera and other bits and pieces. It was still neatly zipped up, but almost empty.

We were by now several kilometres away from Jaguaribe, but I just sat there, flattened – and amazed that anyone could have unzipped the bag, removed the camera and then taken the trouble to zip it up again, all without disturbing me.

"You could teach these kids anything," I concluded glumly.

As you would expect, I later discovered that with the camera had gone a couple of rolls of exposed film, the record of my wanderings through Salvador.

Back at the Hotel da Bahia I went to relate the day's events to Neil Armstrong Machado. But then I decided not to. In his mind I was already the most failed tourist to have ever descended upon Salvador.

There was no need to enhance my reputation further.

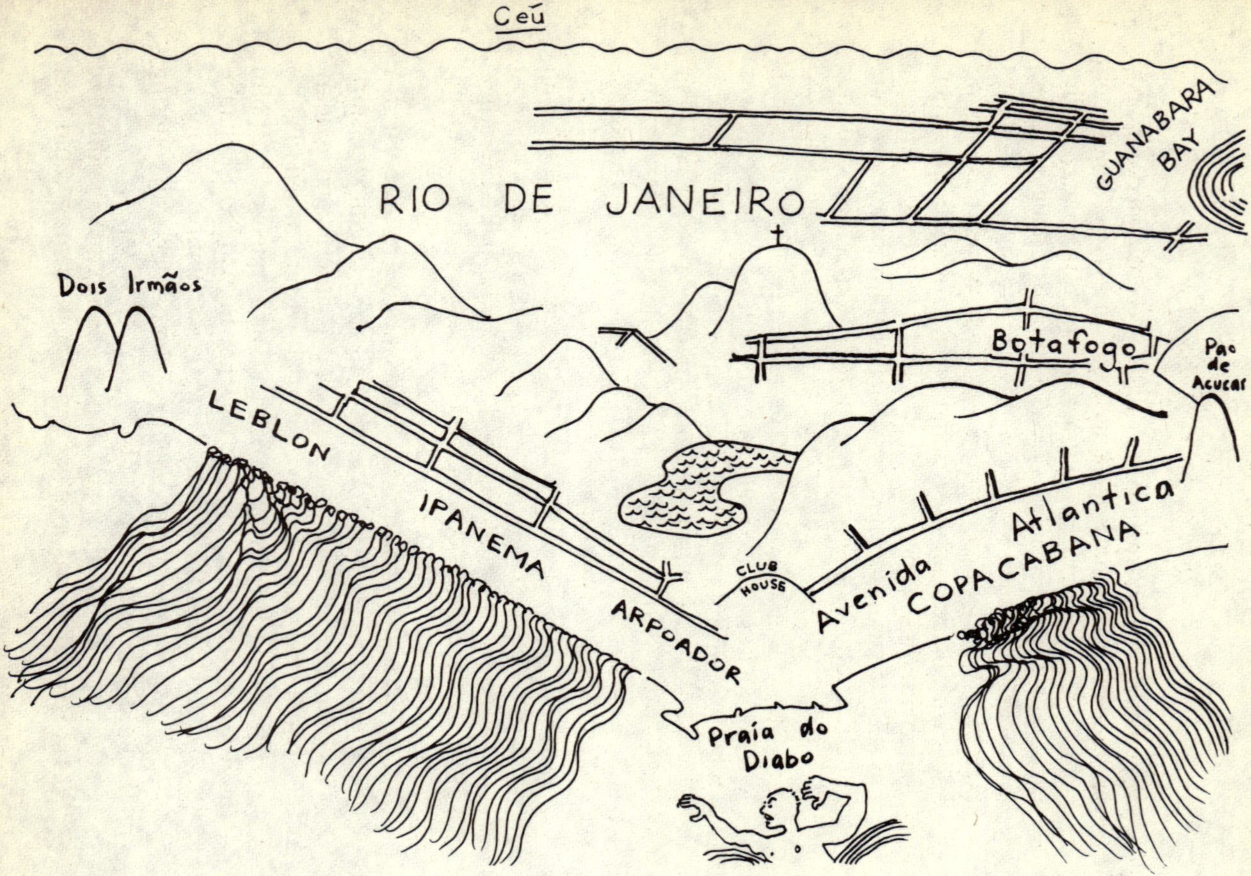
Ceú
RIO DE JANEIRO
GUANABARA BAY
Dois Irmãos
Botafogo
Pao de Acucar
LEBLON
IPANEMA
ARPOADOR
CLUB HOUSE
Avenida Atlantica
COPACABANA
Praia do Diabo

The Accidental Surfer

(Rio de Janeiro, Brazil)

When the inflation rate soars to 3000 per cent, you don't cash bundles of dollars for huge bundles of cruzados. You ration your hard currency because its exchange rate changes daily, if not hourly. As a result, much of your time is spent whispering to hotel doormen or taxi drivers and waiting for their contacts, the parallel-market men — usually dangerous looking spivs with bloodstained eyes and grey, broken teeth — then going with these types into the back of a taxi or some festering alley to complete the transaction. Either that, or you forget the torn, battered local money altogether and use American dollars for everything, as is done in Argentina.

So here I was behind the Othon Palace Hotel, facing a man with a knacker's smile and trying to cash a $50 note. He was abusive, scornful and pleading, urging me to change more, $150 or $200, for which he would give me a better rate. For the $50 it would be forty-five cruzados to the dollar; for the higher amount, fifty. Only a week ago the top rate was thirty-five; why cash more, I reasoned.

As we bantered, one of his spotters appeared, a fat man with a pronounced limp. Moving up the lane he looked like a special effect, shoulders twisting one way, belly the other, good leg forward, belly over, bad leg forward, arms swinging with the roll.

He was followed by his catch, a young tourist in shorts, LA Gear baseball boots, neat white socks and a Mambo tee-shirt.

The money-changer flashed an eye at him and quickly handed me my cash. I counted it, nodded and turned to go.

The tourist was an American and, as I squeezed past him and the spotter, I heard him say that he wanted to change $500. No wonder the spotter's tongue was flapping about.

"Forty," declared the money changer and began counting the notes from a fist-sized roll.

I didn't say anything and kept walking to the end of the alley. Everyone was in it for his own percentage, and that boy's dollars would produce more value before the day was over.

I crossed Avenida Atlântica to Copacabana beach. It was July, the cool season. Rio de Janeiro lies slightly above the Tropic of Capricorn, which it shares with Rockhampton, so its winter is not that of Sydney but of north Queensland. You can swim all year round, but when a south-easterly is blowing the weather swinging in from the Atlantic can be miserable.

Today it was 24 degrees and the beach was alive with tourists, tireless football players and mid-week beach-goers. Almost no one was swimming, although the waves were fair — about a 1 metre swell breaking 50 metres offshore. There was no wind and a lemony sun from the north dabbed at the water, making it spangle and tremble.

I was looking for the site of a body-surfing contest in which an Australian team was to be competing; I knew the team manager, John Sheerin.

And there, not far from where I stepped on to the sand, was a steel and timber stand, still being erected. The one banner which was up read "Rio de Janeiro International Body-Surfing Classic". The logos beneath were those of Coca-Cola and TNT, the Australian transport company.

I walked over and asked a boy who was sitting in the shade of the stand beneath a notice indicating the dates and times of particular events whether he had seen the Australian team.

I had made the approach in Portuguese; he answered in precise American English.

"No, I haven't. I believe those guys haven't turned up yet. Are you from the Aussie team?"

"No, no way. I know a couple of them, that's all."

"Hey, don't you know where they are then?"

"No, that's why I'm here asking."

"We've been expecting them for three or four days but there hasn't been a word. Nothing. Maybe they didn't make it."

That surprised me. I knew that the team had been busy in Sydney arranging sponsorships with airlines and having tee-shirts and jackets made. They certainly would not have missed the opportunity to surf in Brazil.

The boy introduced himself, apologising for not doing so earlier, as Eddy. He explained that he was a university student, not really involved in body-surfing, and had just been hired by the organisers to help run the carnival. He suggested that I return in an hour to talk to Professor Claudio Jacome dos Santos, the president of the Rio de Janeiro Body-Surfing Club and the number one man behind the "meet".

A professor who was also an avid body-surfer would, I thought, be someone of interest, so I told Eddy that I'd definitely be back.

I returned to the Othon to change into my swimming costume. Experience had taught me to take nothing extra to the beach: no money, no camera, no sunglasses, no shoes. Just swimmers, a hotel towel and a shirt that I wouldn't mind losing.

After a swim I went back to the competition stand. There was a man standing talking to Eddy. He was aged about 30, had unruly salty hair and a slim tanned body and was wearing board shorts with an Indian design and surfers' wrap-around sunglasses.

"This is the professor," said Eddy.

This is the professor?

I shook his hand and introduced myself. "What are you a professor of?" I asked.

"Body-surfing."

He explained that he gave body-surfing and lifesaving classes at universities and colleges up and down the coast of Brazil, and this, apparently, permitted him to assume the title "professor".

"But call me Claudio," he added.

He gave me his card, which showed that he had a Masters degree in body surfing from the University of California in La Jolla.

Upon learning that I was also involved in education, he said that we should find time to discuss the body-surfing programs at Australian universities — where they were, during which seasons, what they cost and who the instructors were. He thought that Brazilian students would clamour to study English and body-surfing in Sydney.

I replied that I had no doubt they would, but added that I didn't think that *anyone* taught body-surfing in Australia, least of all the universities.

"Anyway, we'll talk about it later," said Claudio, perhaps seeing an opening for himself here amidst this great lack of body-surfing teachers.

Eddy told Claudio that I was looking for the Australian contestants.

He shrugged. "We had good contact with them until about a month ago. I got a lot of letters, from someone in a place called Tamarama, telling me who was coming and when they'd be here. Five of them were going to be here. And then nothing. We've had no sign of them since, and we need them to make the competition really international."

"What other teams have you got coming?" I asked.

"There's Brazil, Mexico, the States and Peru. So you see why we need the Aussies."

I explained to Claudio that I knew the manager of the team and one of the female contestants and that I was positive they would arrive.

Claudio asked me if I knew where they were supposed to be staying.

I said I didn't, and then remembered that John Sheerin had given me the name and phone number of someone in Rio through whom they could be contacted.

"Who, for chrissake?"

"I don't know. I'll have to go back to the hotel."

I didn't recall whether the person whose name I had been given was associated with the contest or was simply a contact. One of the team members had some work in Brazil, to do with her immigration consultancy, and the name might have had some connection with that.

"Let's go," said Claudio impatiently.

He told Eddy to look after the stand and to watch out for

the scaffolders who were to come and finish it, and we ran across the beach towards the Othon.

Once in my room, I consulted my note book and found the name, Maurício Concalves, and a phone number.

"Maurício," hissed Claudio. "Fuckin' swindler."

"You know him?"

"Sure I do. He used to be the vice president of our club. Last year after the invitations in California he came back and started a rival club. The fucker's stolen the Australians!"

I didn't understand. I couldn't see why Conçalves being the founder of another club would stop the Australians participating in the competition.

"Because Maurício's club is having its own contest, *this week*, in competition with ours. The egotistical bastard couldn't work with us so now he wants to destroy us."

The politics of body-surfing were astounding.

"He's hijacked your team," went on Claudio.

"Why don't we give him a ring?"

"Better we go and see him. Probably the team will be at his place and you can explain what's happened."

I could? I didn't think that in fact I *could* explain this drama adequately, but I agreed to go along with him. I pulled on some shorts and we returned to the beach. The scaffolders were at work, as well as a couple of other club members who were putting up sponsors' banners.

Claudio explained what their traitorous former friend had done and then several of us hopped into a borrowed TNT van and drove northwards towards Botafogo, an exclusive residential area bordering a small beach.

We parked outside a block of apartments and Claudio approached the security guard who told him that Conçalves was not in. He also said that he wasn't aware that he had any foreign visitors.

We headed off in the van back to Copacabana and then on to Leblon, which was the beach where the rival contest was to take place. We walked across the sand, past a volleyball tournament, to a similar scaffold structure.

The signs said "Brazil International Body-Surfing

Classic". The sponsors were Volkswagen and Pepsi-Cola. But there was no one about and no indication as to when the events would begin.

Claudio remarked sourly that the waves looked better for body-surfing here than at Copacabana.

"Just our luck," he muttered. But Brazilians aren't people to remain sour or sombre for long. As we climbed into the van he suggested we go to his clubhouse for a talk and to meet a few of his friends. So here I was, in a VW van, sitting admist flippers, wet-suits, towels and surfing magazines with a group of boys and a zany body-surfing professor. "It's 1965," I felt, "North Avalon, Whale Beach and *The Endless Summer*".

We cruised along Ipanema, dropping several of the boys at the northern end, and turned into the congested residential area at the foot of the wide headland between Ipanema and Copacabana.

Claudio parked the van or, more truthfully, he just left it somewhere, and we set off up the path that climbed the headland. Claudio knew everyone. We exchanged words with two policemen wearing the uniform of the beach-beat — yellow singlet, shorts, running shoes and a gun in a holster — and with a couple of jaunty girls on bikes. I noticed that I was being introduced as *um surfista Australiano*.

Then Claudio bought four bottles of beer from a vendor with a cart behind a bicycle and we continued to the summit of the headland. From here there was a dazzling view over the ocean and southwards to Ipanema and Leblon and to the two granite mountains, the Dois Irmãos (Two Brothers), rising precipitously out of the rocky shoreline. Northwards you could see beyond Copacabana to the Pão do Açucar, pulsating and shimmering through the yellow haze. The view of Copacabana itself was blocked by an old stone fort sitting just beyond Praia do Diabo (Devil's Beach), immediately below us.

And here, open to all of this, was Claudio's clubhouse. It was a small, circular brick building that belonged to the municipal government. Having no immediate need of it, the government had handed it over to the Rio de Janeiro Body-Surfing Club.

We sat on the grass watching the board riders at Devil's Beach and at Arpoador, the next point before Ipanema. A girl wearing board shorts and the minimum legal requirement in bikini tops came out of the clubhouse with glasses and a bottle opener. Claudio poured the drinks.

A boy with the same healthy surfer looks as Claudio appeared, and then another girl.

What a day! What a spot! What great new friends!

We sipped our beers and I answered questions.

Was I in the Aussie team?

Had I been to Bali?

What did I think of the north shore of Hawaii?

Had I been to São Conrado and the beaches further south of Rio?

Not wanting to disappoint anyone too keenly, I said that I wasn't involved in the competition, but that I could surf. Claudio then explained to the others that Maurício Conçalves had hijacked the Australian team and that I was here to help him get them back.

Am I? I started. I didn't think I had a hope of rescuing the team. I'd only heard Claudio's story and for all I knew the arrangements with Conçalves might have been made months ago. Meanwhile the Australians might simply conclude that the confusion was just the usual Brazilian mess.

"Do you like parties?" asked Claudio.

"Sure."

"Tomorrow night, after opening day, we're having a big party, up here and later at my apartment. Please come."

I'm twenty years older than most of these people, I thought. I'm supposedly here on business, with appointments to be kept and deals to be made . . . but . . . one of the girls leaned over and filled my glass. I said, "Thanks, I'd love to come to the party."

Claudio said he was going back to the van to get some flippers so that we could have a surf together.

"Together with who?" I asked.

"You and me."

"Me?"

"Yeh. You want flippers don't you?"

"Er, yes," I replied, thinking that if I was going surfing with a professor of surfing I certainly needed every aid available.

He disappeared with one of the girls. I asked the other if she surfed too or if she just hung around with the body-surfers.

"I don't hang around with anyone," she replied in excellent English. "I ride a boogie. Six months ago I was in Australia at an international body-board contest, at Manly. The Brazilian girls won nearly every event."

This was astonishing. I had accidently wandered into a world of contact between Brazil and Australia that few people knew existed.

She was from Fortaleza, in Brazil's northeast. Fortaleza is like Darwin with surf and the kids grow up there with surfing as their main recreation and knowing little about the world other than what they read in their magazines. California, Hawaii, Australia, Bali . . .

When Claudio returned, we stripped down to our costumes and scrambled down a narrow rocky path to Arpoador. I was quietly relieved that we were not going to Praia do Diabo where there were masses of experienced, aggressive surfers and a big angry looking break that was funnelling past the Arpoador point.

The swell at Arpoador was more lenient, producing 3 or 4 foot evenly rolling and breaking waves. We dived off the point, saving a long swim out from the beach.

For the next thirty minutes I only caught flashing glimpses of Claudio. He looked as if he had a PhD in surfing, so tireless and fast was his performance. He drilled across the breaking walls of these waves like a ballistic missile, pulling out through the collapsing lip seconds before it was too late.

He ignored the boards, thrashing his way on to a wave before they could take off or cutting in above or below them with hair-raising abandon.

I spent a lot of my time swimming out, diving under incoming waves and boards and treading water. But, sensing that my friends from the club were watching from the hill above, I selected a few benign waves (no boards, a clear, even break and likely to give a long slow ride) and surfed with credit, to use an academic term. I managed not to get dumped and at one point, when Claudio was swimming out, cork-screwed across the face of a wave in front of him like a tormented flagellant.

A few more waves and I was exhausted. I picked up a full, slow-moving roller and took it all the way to the beach, until my nose bumped on the sand, a skill picked up as a lifesaver, but rarely used since.

Then I sat on the wet sand, gulping air.

When he finally came in on his last wave, Claudio stood up in the shallows and leapt through the water with his flippers on.

"Hey! Hey!" he shouted. He looked like a man pursued by tiger sharks. "I've got an idea."

"What?" I yelled back.

"You'll do."

"I'll do what?"

"You can be the Aussie team!"

He sat down beside me and took off his flippers.

"Sure. You can handle the surf."

"Handling the surf's not the same as competing against international stars," I replied, my stomach frothing at the thought.

He leaned towards my face, smiling.

"You should see the Peruvians. International stars. Ha. Anyway, how old are you?"

I told him.

"No sweat. The over 35s'll be easy. You'll kill it."

Peruvians and over 35s notwithstanding, I told Claudio that I'd be leaving Rio in two days' time and thought that he'd be better off patching up his differences with Maurício and combining their competitions.

But Claudio couldn't wait to clamber up the hill to the clubhouse to tell everyone his great idea.

After a few more drinks in the clubhouse, I left, saying that I would walk back to my hotel. I had a business appointment later in the afternoon, so I said that I would see him the next day on the beach. He asked me to try to contact the Australians through Maurício that evening.

Once back in the hotel, I asked at the reception whether there were any messages for me.

The clerk said that there were none.

"None?"

"No."

"No? You mean there was one?"

"Yes. There wasn't. Nothing. *Nada.*"

"*Nada?*"

Hearing this exchange, a second receptionist interrupted.

"Are you Mr Murray?"

"Yes . . . well no. But I could be."

"Or Mr Laurence? Right?"

"Right."

"Ah. There was a man here this morning asking for you. I told him that you were not staying here."

"What on earth did you say that for?"

"Well, he asked for a Mr Laurence. We have you registered as Mr Murray. So he just went away."

"Was he an Australian?" I asked.

"I guess. Big shoulder."

I guessed that it was John Sheerin, who knew where I would be staying.

I went to my room and rang Maurício.

A woman answered. When I began the Portuguese phrase, *"Queria falar com . . .,"* she simply handed the phone to a man.

"Maurício speaking," a voice said in American English. I introduced myself and asked whether John Sheerin was there.

"He's out at this moment."

"Are any members of the Australian body-surfing team

there?" They were all out, taking a tour, and Maurício didn't know when they would return.

I left a message for John to phone me and then asked Maurício if he knew that there was another body-surfing contest taking place at Copacabana.

"I don't know nothin' about that," he replied. "The only one's at Leblon."

"You're wrong," I said. "There's one being run by the Rio de Janeiro Body-Surfing Club at Copacabana. I was there today."

"Never heard of it."

"Do you know Claudio..."

"Nope."

I wasn't making much progress, but before saying goodbye, I told Maurício that the other contest also had some Australian participants.

There was silence at Maurício's end.

Two Australian teams in town? he was wondering.

Then he said, "I don't think so," and hung up.

Relations are certainly tense in the once-fraternal world of body-surfing in Rio, I concluded.

I changed and telephoned the person I was to meet in the central part of the city to tell him that I was on my way.

Telephoning in advance is regarded as an eccentric and unnecessary courtesy by Brazilians, as is arriving on time for meetings. In fact, guidebooks for understanding the country always contain warnings such as this one in *Fodor's Brazil*:

> It will save you a lot of aggravation to realize that time does not have the same cultural weight for Brazilians as it does for Americans and Europeans. Punctuality is definitely not a Brazilian strong point. While the business-minded Paulistano can usually be counted on to show up more or less at the appointed hour, the Carioca cannot, and people get slower the farther north you go. In fact, it is common for a Brazilian to appear two or three hours later than planned – if at all – and think that nothing is amiss. You will consider this rude and infuriating; the Brazilians will find it inconsequential and wonder at your compulsiveness. Get used to it. In Brazil, everything is slower and takes longer than you think it's going to, and events often start later than sched-

uled. Free yourself from the constraints of time; leave your watch at home.

This is interesting advice and it is consoling as you sit alone in a waiting room or hotel lobby, but what is needed is further advice as to how we should plan our day if we have three or four meetings in different parts of the city with business people whose penchant for arriving two to three hours late, *if at all*, is considered inconsequential.

Nelson Oliveira was not in when I phoned, but a startled secretary said that I might as well come anyway. Nelson's diary didn't show any appointment at all for the afternoon, but she assumed that he was in Rio – he wasn't in São Paulo, Caracas, Los Angeles, Miami or Milan at any rate, so where else could he be? – and she had a feeling that he would "pass by".

I took a taxi to Centro, to Rua Araújo Porto Alegre. At the place where I alighted, there was a road-block, police cars and fire trucks and a noisy, animated crowd squirming around the building next to the one I was to enter.

It was a bank. Apparently during the (long) lunch break a gang had cut their way into the vault from the floor of the offices above and, incredibly, they had escaped with the loot during the slowly gathering turmoil.

These events were narrated to me in full by Nelson's secretary as I awaited his return from his own lunch.

I waited over an hour, thinking as I've done before when this has happened, "It's no wonder that Brazil has 3000 per cent inflation, a new currency every three or four years, and is the world's biggest debtor..."

Finally, at about 5.30, Nelson arrived. "Oh, Laurence," he shouted, shaking my body. "Welcome to Rio."

He had no excuse and didn't attempt one. But then he said, "I suppose you're thinking, it's no wonder Brazil's got a big mess, no wonder we've got hyperinflation. Right? That's what Americans always tell me." He laughed.

"Silly Americans," I said.

"This is Brazil," he concluded, clapping his hands. "Coffee?" We went outside to a café where we talked about the bank robbery, about football and about a samba show that he wanted to take me to the next night.

I told him that I had met a group of surfers and that they had invited me to a party. Nelson looked astonished. "A *surfers'* party?"

At that point I shared his incredulity. I was sitting here with my briefcase, preparing to discuss commissions, advertising budgets and problems with visas, and feeling rather bemused with the idea that I had been surfing that morning at Arpoador and drinking beer and careering around in a van with 18-year-olds.

I agreed that I'd skip the party and go with Nelson to the samba show.

When I returned to my hotel that evening, I phoned Maurício's number. There was no answer.

The next morning I went for a swim and found Claudio, Eddy, Dalva and Lilly (the two girls from the clubhouse) busy with preparations. The contest was to begin that day.

I told Claudio that I still had not been able to contact the Australians.

He didn't care now, he said. He outlined for me the schedule of events and explained that the over-35 men's contest would take place on Saturday.

"On Saturday I'm going to São Paulo," I remarked.

"Shoot! What for? There's no surf there."

It occurred to me then that Claudio had been so involved in the contest, so concerned about the non-appearance of the Australians and therefore so taken with my appearance that he had not considered for a minute that I was in Brazil for some reason not connected with surfing.

I reminded him that I was there on business — the business of education — and that brought him back to his remark of the previous day that Brazilians would be interested in studying body-surfing in Australia.

We sat down on the sand and discussed the proposition. I promised to explore all the opportunities for such studies in Australia and let him know the details within a month or two.

"So I'm going to São Paulo," I said. "I can't avoid it." I

was quietly pleased that the over-35s were not on until Saturday.

"Anyway," I went on, "you've seen me catch a couple of easy waves. I couldn't go out and compete with real champions."

He began to say something about Peruvians, but at that moment the young American that I had seen changing money in the alley appeared from nowhere and sat down on the sand beside us.

"Claudio!"

"Hey! Marty!"

He was introduced as an American contestant in the under-20s to me, an Australian in the over-35s.

"Fuck," Marty observed generously.

I told him that I'd seen him being stung by the money changers the day before.

"Stung? Why?"

"They gave you forty to the dollar, right? They should've given you fifty or fifty-five for the amount you changed. Five hundred dollars, wasn't it?"

"Fuckin' toy money," Marty replied. And that was all he had to say on the matter.

"Hey, Claudio," Marty said, nodding at Dalva and Lilly.

I was beginning to feel that I was a bit marginal here and that the more competitors who turned up, the more irrelevant I'd be — until the over-35s rolled in. In any case, I had a lunch appointment, and a further meeting in the afternoon.

That evening Nelson Oliveira picked me up at about nine. We went to the Churrascaria do Jardim for a barbecue and later to a samba club near Rio Sul. I forgot completely about the party.

When I returned to my hotel, I found a note to say that John Sheerin had called. The text of his message was confused but he seemed to be saying that the body-surfing contest was in a state of crisis and that I was to phone him at Maurício's.

This I failed to do, either then or early the next morning. The line was constantly engaged.

Saturday morning was wet. Rain gushed and spat in cold torrents, giving Copacabana the forlorn look of holiday resorts in the off-season. A sodden wind tore at the palm trees on the sand and at the TNT and Coca-Cola banners on the contest stand. Sugarloaf was completely encased in low, thick clouds.

Wonderful day for flying. Wonderful day for the Rio de Janeiro International Body-Surfing Classic.

But there was no one on the stands and no one in the surf. It must have been quite a party last night, I reflected, and turned and trudged back across the sludgy sand.

* * *

Side-tracked in Brazil

(Brazil)

From my earliest years I was possessed of the thrilling intimation that this life of mine was destined to coincide with the fulfilment of that promise which for nearly four hundred years had been a dream to which men had given the name Brazil. *Even as a boy when I climbed the hills on my father's farm so that I could look far across the land, what I saw was not the lush pastures where the cattle grazed but a dazzling vision of Brazil, her body langourously stretched out on a glittering river or softly floating away as delicate clouds, luminous and fluid, real and elusive.*

Zulfikar Ghose, *The Beautiful Empire*

Between 1974 and 1976 I lived in Rue Santos-Dumont in Paris. It didn't occur to me then to wonder who Santos-Dumont was — some French general, I supposed. Generals like De Clerc and De Gaulle have given their names to streets in France in much the same way that municipal nobodies like Stan, Eric and Ethel have given theirs to streets in Australia.

So here I was at Rio de Janeiro's city airport, which is called Santos-Dumont. At the entrance is a sculpture dedicated to the man and I read that he was a pioneer aviator, a Brazilian who spent most of his life in France. Alberto Santos-Dumont won a prize in 1901 for the first flight from Saint Cloud to the Eiffel Tower and in 1903 he piloted the first officially observed powered flight in Europe. He committed suicide in 1932 in a flamboyant and futile protest against the use of aircraft in warfare.

Varig and Cruzeiro run a shuttle service between Rio and São Paulo that comprises some fifty flights a day in each direction. The majority of these depart from Santos-Dumont. In the Varig timetable the aircraft type is listed as LOE.

The LOE turned out to be a Lockheed Electra — an aeroplane as stylish today as a Cadillac Sedan de Ville or a Studebaker Lark. It has a neat cigar-shaped elegance and is powered by four throaty props which sound like old backyard factories mounted on the wings.

At take-off, our Electra stood stammering and shaking at the runway's end and then rumbled away on an interminable roll before creeping into the air above the boats on Guanabara Bay. We wheeled in a great arc over the beautiful span of the bridge connecting Rio with the high-rise city of Niteroi, and continued turning through fog until we were parallel with the coast on a southerly track. And there, just beyond my window, it seemed, was the immense statue of Christ the Redeemer standing on the peak of Corcovado, looming like either an omen or a sentinel through a turbulent flurry of thin cloud, whilst hard below, rising suddenly from the black slops of the wind blown Atlantic, was Sugarloaf. Then the plane plunged into a wall of white darkness, emerging forty minutes later on a descent path over a vast territory of high rises, freeways, railway lines and factories, glimpsed through a murkiness broken only by the scattered brilliance of jacaranda flowers.

This was São Paulo, Brazil's largest city, the world's biggest Portuguese-speaking city, the second city of the Americas after Mexico City, the greatest city in the Southern Hemisphere . . . there are a lot of medals for São Paulo, yet comparatively few tourists came here. And at first glance, as my taxi worked its way through quarrelsome traffic to the centre, I could see why.

South America on a Shoestring says that to like São Paulo "you need a skin as thick as a rhino's hide, a gas-mask, cotton wool in your ears and a gallon of eye-drops. Either that or plenty of money and a big black limousine . . ." Such comments attest to the terrific traffic and pollution problems of the city, yet those visitors who do venture to São Paulo – and it is only fifty minutes on the shuttle – will find a city not unlike New York, a place of great history and culture, where theatre – both traditional and avant garde – classical music, opera and modern art more seriously promoted and accepted than they are in Rio.

On my first night in São Paulo I had a meeting with Expedito and Neliane Teixeira, a couple who had lived in Australia for some years while Expedito completed a doctorate in agricultural science. They were now living on the outskirts of the city and both were working on a research farm.

Paulistas really were different from *Cariocas*. Expedito and Neliane had only scorn for those who fooled around in Rio.

"It's like Sydney and Melbourne," Expedito proposed. "In Melbourne, it's an earnest world of ideas, culture and work. In Sydney, it's the beach, *surfing*, frivolity. That's São Paulo and Rio." He said "surfing" with particular derision, I felt.

"Is Melbourne really like that?" I wondered, but I liked the comparison, so I scribbled it down.

"Here's another," announced Neliane, noting me making notes. *Nós damos duro em São Paulo para nos divertirmos no Rio*. That means we work hard in São Paulo so that we can play in Rio."

"That's fine, except we don't play in Rio," added Expedito. "We go to Guarujá or down south to Florianopolis or, maybe, way north to Fortaleza."

"Are you bored with this?" asked Neliane, "because there's another one."

And without waiting for my answer she said, "At the time of Genesis when God made the world, you know what he did? He made Rio so beautiful, with the mountains and the sea, the beaches and water everywhere. What did he give to São Paulo? Just fog. The *Paulistanos* shouted to God that it wasn't fair — that Rio had everything in the world but we had nothing."

"Except fog," interrupted Expedito.

"Yes, except fog."

"And?" I said expectantly.

"So God answered. You know what he said?"

"Sorry, I can't say I do," I replied.

"He said, ha, ha, just wait. You haven't seen the *people* I'm going to fill Rio with yet."

Everyone I met in São Paulo had unexpected origins. They were not the descendants of long-established Portuguese families, or of African slaves, or of a mixture of the two, but the children of Russians, Italians, Poles, Germans, Japanese and what used be called Levantines.

I went to art openings with weeping, melancholy Russians, to avant garde theatre with opinionated Poles, had beer with ranting, foaming Germans, went to football matches with jittery, loquacious Italians and had lunch and went diamond shopping with adventitious Japanese.

The São Paulo region is home to the world's largest overseas Japanese community. More than 300 000 migrated to Brazil in the first half of this century, the original intakes composed of small-scale intensive farmers. The community has long since diversified and is well established in many businesses and professions throughout the states of São Paulo and Paraná.

Amongst all immigrants there remains a sense of being an outsider to a greater or lesser degree, of being a person with a "divided soul". But amongst the Japanese in Brazil this seems to be more pronounced, even in the second and third generations, than amongst other groups, for the Japanese, unlike, say, the Portuguese, Italians or Chinese, have come from a land and society that was traditionally and deliberately sealed, and from which few people have ever emigrated.

One day I went for lunch at the São Paulo Suntory Restaurant with Yassuo Yamada, a business contact. With us was his partner, Paulo Faoud, a Syrian Brazilian. It was an interesting lunch, even from the perspective of the two Suntory Restaurants which I know.

In Sydney the restaurant is staffed by a large majority of Japanese-born waiters, cooks and managers. They are either fairly recently arrived residents of Australia or young travellers on working holidays. And the restaurant clientele is usually about 80 per cent Japanese, attesting to a high level of business activity between Australia and Japan.

In São Paulo very few of the staff were remotely Japanese — of any variety.

Mr Yamada spoke Portuguese to everyone and, except for the food and decor, there was little that was especially Japanese about the restaurant. And this was in the midst of the world's largest overseas Japanese community.

Yamada said that he scarcely spoke Japanese, although his parents had been born in Japan and had come to Brazil as young adults. He presumed that he spoke Japanese as a child, but after he started school, Portuguese quickly became his language.

I asked whether there were any language maintenance programs at school — of the sort run by Australia's community language organisations.

Yamada laughed. "Certainly not when I was young, and I don't think so now. We can't afford that sort of thing in Brazil. Neither of my children speaks Japanese, even though my wife is also Japanese — Brazilian Japanese."

Paulo Faoud apologised for not being able to contribute much to the conversation.

"In spite of my name," he explained, "I'm more familiar with English than Arabic. I don't even know when my ancestors came here from Syria, but I do know they came from a place called Aleppo."

"It's much more recent for us," Yamada went on. "We're still in contact with Japan and, when I go there, I feel very odd. People expect me to be Japanese in every way and are amazed when I can't speak the language and act clumsily. You know all the effort Japanese give to just the right sorts of behaviour."

"The Japanese aren't used to the idea of the melting-pot," he continued. "The fact that someone can be black, brown, yellow or white, but not be from the county or place that they think they *should* be from. They know the world isn't as organised as Japan, but it still shocks them."

I said that this was why I found the Japanese-Brazilian society so interesting, because these cultural and racial beliefs must have made the transformation of Japanese into Brazilians unlike that of other groups.

"Well, here's a new twist," said Mr Yamada. "My company is now involved in sending Japanese-Brazilians *back to Japan!* You see, there are real shortages of workers at all levels over there, and one thing we do have here is an over-supply of labour."

"The Japanese, being Japanese – you know, what we were talking about before – are a bit worried about importing workers from Korea or the Philippines or Thailand or somewhere, so a few of us who go regularly to Japan saw an opportunity."

"So they're happy with the idea of Brazilian workers, as long as they're Japanese," I remarked.

"Yes. It's nonsense really, because after a generation or two in Brazil you don't even *look* Japanese, so they all go over there and everyone is confused."

We all laughed knowingly at this, and Faoud added, "But it's good business. We send them over on two-year contracts and very few seem to stay and become illegal. There's about 50 000 from Brazil and a few thousand from Peru over there right now."

"Funny eh?" observed Yamada. "We came here originally because Japan was too poor and Brazil was rich, or rich enough to provide more opportunities than anywhere else. And now they're importing us as labourers . . ."

"Don't laugh," smiled Faoud. "It's tragic, really."

In the hotel where I was staying there was a small jewellery shop, a branch of H. Stern, a huge Brazilian gemstone and jewellery business. I told the attendant, a well-groomed, scholarly looking Japanese girl, that I wanted to look at necklaces.

She suggested that we go to the main showroom, a couple of blocks away.

She closed the shop and we set off. After my conversation with Yassuo Yamada, I wanted to ask her about being Japanese, but I thought that I shouldn't come right out with the question, so I asked her what other languages she spoke in addition to English.

"Portuguese, of course," she replied, "as well as German and French."

That accounted for most of the tourists.

"Not Japanese?" I asked.

"No," she answered. And then she told me most of the story of her life, to date, as we wove through the waves of humans rolling through the city's pedestrian zones.

Her parents had come to Brazil in 1947, she said, just after the war. They settled in Curitiba, an industrial city to the south of São Paulo, but had then moved north, first to Goiânia, near where Brasília is today, and then on a wild promise to Belém at the mouth of the Amazon.

She was born in Belém, where her father ran a trucking business through the underdeveloped state of Pará and – when the roads began to appear – beyond into Roraima and Amazonas.

Her mother died of a fever when the girl was about 6, so her father sent her and her brother, then aged 9, to São Paulo to live with an "aunt".

The aunt was not, as I supposed, Japanese, but a member of an extraordinary philanthropic family of Russian Jews who had given assistance to the Japanese family when they first arrived in 1947.

So this girl was brought up from the age of 6 with almost no Japanese cultural references and no language.

I remarked that it was hard to imagine her parents coping with the primal, sweltering anarchy of Belém in those days.

"It is hard to think of it, but actually there were a lot of Japanese scattered about – farmers and so on. You find them in some really remote and strange places."

"What happened to your father?" I asked.

"He worked on in Belém and made a lot of money, building a big transport company as the north developed. We didn't see him for about ten years. Then he started to come back here every year, until he finally came back to retire."

"That time – the last time – he arrived with a woman. We were shocked because we'd never heard about her and we'd never imagined him remarrying. She was a mulatta and they'd married years before but had no children."

Her father died a couple of years later, she added, of some tropical plague that was in his blood, and the mulatta stayed for a while in São Paulo, but then drifted back to the tropics where life was more congenial amongst her family and friends.

We entered the jewellery shop and the girl introduced me to the sales staff.

A smooth, classically dressed woman with an icy German accent then proceeded to guide me effortlessly from visions of the torrid port of Belém into the dazzling realms of gold, diamonds and precious stones. I felt that I had to buy *something*, after the delightful company of the Japanese girl who had taken the trouble to close her shop to bring me here, and with this soft garrotting of the German saleswoman, but . . . not what I was being shown.

Each piece was heavy with clusters of diamonds, sapphires and emeralds and was being modelled for me, not on the neck of the saleswoman, but on that of a silky girl in her late teens who seemed to be employed in the shop just for that purpose.

Dazed, I told the woman that I would buy *everything* she was showing me . . . if only I could afford them.

The saleswoman stalled for a moment, gave me a quiet, chilling smile and then shifted subtly to a lesser order of preciousness.

Half an hour later, I had chosen the necklace. I paid, and then the Japanese girl reappeared saying that she would accompany me back to the hotel. I asked where my necklace was. "Don't worry," she replied. "It's taken care of."

This was H. Stern, after all, and so I didn't worry, and assumed that my purchase would be delivered to the hotel later.

We walked back the way we had come. I was relieved that we didn't have the jewellery, as people were always warning me about robberies; even in daylight, I went about São Paulo cautiously.

Once back in the hotel the girl asked me to wait in the shop while she slipped away through a door in the rear. A couple of minutes later she emerged with a little flat velvet pouch. She tipped my necklace out on to her hand.

Stupidly, I speculated that there was some species of pneumatic tube connecting the two shops.

"No silly," she laughed. "I hid it where every woman likes

to put her *joias preciosas* . . . in here," and she shyly patted her own private hiding place.

* * *

In the seventeenth century, southern Brazilians, mostly *Paulistas*, began moving northwards and westwards in a drive to open up the interior of the country. These pioneers became known as *bandeirantes* (because each group carried its own *bandeira*, or flag). They were tough, rapacious, greedy, ignorant, lawless, ruthless, murderous – in other words, men without whose qualities millions upon millions of wild acres could never have been settled. History is always ambivalent about such creatures, but out of the horrors of their lives, and the even greater horrors they dealt their victims, nations of the new world – some whose anthems sing of "boundless plains to share" – have been made.

Paulistas, even today, aren't shy about claiming many of the qualities of the *bandeirantes*. This is what is needed to drive Brazil on into the future, they'll say, not the empty-headed frivolities of Rio. And way beyond São Paulo, the spiritual descendants of the *bandeirantes* are still there, at the limits of whatever is the newest frontier, although today the whole world is against them and wishes that they would go back to their towns to lead orderly lives.

The discovery of gold by the *bandeirantes* in the late seventeenth century in what is now a state known as Minas Gerais, (which means "General Mines": it sounds more poetic in Portuguese, doesn't it?) triggered a gold rush of the sort that would be echoed a century and a half later in California and Australia, a turbulent inundation of desperate, roaring, ungovernable, fortune-seeking men and scandalous sinful women.

Incredibly, out of this rush to Eldorado were created some of the most beautiful towns in all the Americas. To visit them, I went first to Belo Horizonte.

Belo is the capital of Minas Gerais and is an elegant, planned city, circled by the hills of the Serra do Curral del Rey, giving the place its "beautiful horizon".

The city was modelled on Washington D.C. and La Plata in

Argentina, and with its gardens of dense flowering trees, its wide avenues radiating from the city heart and its dramatic, sculptured buildings, it has a classy, sedate feel to it, which is best appreciated from one of the lookouts high in the sierra. Here at sunset you gaze at a city illuminated by fire, as the sun melts into the burnt grasslands to the west of the ranges.

From Belo Horizonte it was easy to travel to Ouro Preto (Black Gold), 100 kilometres away. In the 1700s, Ouro Preto was a super boom town known as Vila Rica (Rich Town) and which preceeded Belo Horizonte as the provincial capital.

When the gold was exhausted, seams of semi-precious stones — topaz, amethyst, aquamarine, tourmaline — as well as industrial minerals, ensured the wealth of Ouro Preto into the twentieth century. Today the cash comes from tourists, for the city has been beautifully preserved as a national monument to both the colonial era and the intoxicating days of gold and gemstones.

The colonial governor's palace is now a mineral museum of great fascination, but the city itself is the real museum, a place of steeply inclined cobbled streets, exquisite public buildings and houses, scented, shaded parks and baroque churches.

The most famous of these are the Church of São Francisco de Assis and the Church of Nossa Senhora do Carmo, which are among the many created by the architect Antônio Francisco Lisbôa, better known in Brazil as Aleijadinho, the Little Cripple.

Aleijadinho's work also appears in the towns of São João del Rei — four hours south of Belo Horizonte — in the form of remarkable religious sculptures, and in Congonhas, whose eighteenth-century buildings are dominated by his statue of the twelve apostles.

Finally, there is Diamantina, whose fame (naturally) derives from diamonds. Seeing Diamantina in Brazil made me curious about Australia's Diamantina River, which flows (on those rare occasions when it has water) for a thousand kilometres through western Queensland and northern South Australia. If you're curious, too, here are the facts: the river was discovered by John McKinley in 1862 and he named it Meuller's Creek after one Ferdinand Von Meuller. Later it was renamed, not after diamonds, but after the splendidly named Diamantina Roma, wife of George Bowen, the first governor of Queensland.

A name is not all that Minas Gerais and Queensland have in common. The landscape to the west of Belo Horizonte bears a remarkable similarity to the western plains of Queensland – a great heartland of grass and clustered shade trees, of low rough hills and barren water-courses shimmering through a red haze of gold dust and heat.

Queenslanders would go to prison rather than mumble words about the primordial truths, unveilable secrets and celestial heights of *their* state. But the *Mineiros* (people from Minas Gerais), being Brazilians and not Queenslanders, are inclined to be more lyrical and, well, sentimental about their land.

Look at this poem, "A Palavra Minas" (The Word Minas) by Carlos Drummond de Andrade:

Minas is not a mountainous word
It's abyssal. Minas is inside and deep
The mountains hide Minas
In the most celestial heights, subterraneous,
is a galley which cuts through iron to
get no one knows where
No one knows Minas. The Stone
the 'buriti' [bird]
the 'carranca' [totem to frighten bad spirit away]
the fog
the lightning
Seal the primordial truth, buried in geological eras
of dreams
Only the mineiros know, and do not revel
even to themselves the unveilable secret called Minas.

I drove back through this geological dreamtime to Belo Horizonte with Pastor Dick Flippin.

Pastor Flippin is a large boisterous Texan whom I met in a church in São João del Rei. As a Baptist he was not at ease with the Catholic excesses of the church, but the excesses and scandals and sins and wild extravagances of the gold rush fascinated him, and as a long-term resident of Belo Horizonte he often journeyed here to immerse himself in the atmosphere of these legendary towns.

In his car I asked him whether he knew that in Australia "flippin'" was an adjective that meant "bloody" or "flaming", as in "you flippin' idiot".

"You mean sumpin' like cotton pickin'?" he asked.

"Yes, just like cotton pickin'," I replied.

The next day Dick Flippin was good enough to assist me with some business at a Brazilian government office. He spoke Portuguese fluently and also knew the right pressures to apply and the right emoluments that, properly handed, would achieve results.

However as we waited in a queue which was more a squabbling tatterdemalion of cotton pickin' bodies and heads, the pastor had a confession to make.

"Sometimes I git so mad!" he revealed. "All this waitin' and waitin'. An' you know what's the hardest part of all? Holdin' on to yer faith in Jesus. You git so mad, but you jes hope that Jesus don' see or hear you."

That evening I found myself in a place where I hoped that Pastor Flippin would not see me. It was a dark and ritzy nightclub, where *tout Belo Horizonte* went to muzzle each other's hair, make-up and earrings and, that night, to flirt with pricey politicians.

During the late afternoon, I had been in an office in an arcade concluding an agreement with a student travel agency. Across the courtyard there was a *really smart* little art gallery into which, I had noticed, baubles of *very smart* people had been entering. My colleagues at the travel agency told me that it was a cocktail party for supporters of Fernando Collor, then a candidate for the presidency of Brazil, and now the nation's president. They were hysterically rude about both Collor and his supporters, saying that he only appealed to the rich and beautiful, an assertion that I could then only accept, given the evidence on the other side of the courtyard.

After my meeting, I wandered across and entered the art

gallery, having told the agency manager, huffily smoking at the door, that I had a journalistic imperative to meet these people.

Once inside, I was amidst the heliotactic glitter of the city's young elite. In minutes I was talking to them — elegant, lively, preppy types who looked as if they were studying law or medicine at the best universities and lived in leafy walled villas in the garden suburbs. And some of them invited me to the reception in the nightclub.

So that evening I mingled with more students and their parents and with journalists and psychiatrists (whose professions seemed to account for most of those in the nightclub who actually worked for a living). We listened to a succession of musicians, ate tiny bits of grilled octopus, sipped (or gulped) our whiskies, and waited for the guest of honour to appear.

Fernando Collor had arrived like a supernova out of nowhere. He had been the governor of an obscure little state called Alagoas in the north, where, I had read, he had attempted little and accomplished even less, although this was energetically disputed by new nightclubbing friends.

His appeal seemed to come mostly from his looks — he was a handsome, young politician, around whom there was a sort of an early Kennedy candescence — and the fact that he was not aligned to any major party or special interest sector, implying that he would have no debts or obligations to meet once he achieved power.

Having no debts seemed to allow Collor to have no manifesto either, except a promise to have a look at the important issues: foreign debt, inflation and the environment. (With hindsight one can now see that this non-aligned vagueness allowed Collor to dream up his inflation shock therapy which he applied within a day of being elected, beginning with an order to lock up the banks on the irrefutable theory that without money there can be no inflation. He left the nation gasping — including, I suspect, the eidetic butterflies gathered that night in Belo Horizonte.)

He came to the club at about 11, entering with a cluster of

minders and cool, translucent women and circulated briefly amongst those who knew or adored him the most, before settling into a dark corner and illuminating it with some of those women.

Well, I thought, that makes one president and one front-running president-to-be that I've almost had contact with in a fortnight. (I had seen the new president of Argentina, Carlos Menem, on the day of his inauguration in Buenos Aires; in fact we had exchanged waves.) That seemed sufficient material for a phone call to the program "Brush with fame" then running on a Sydney radio station.

Waiting in Belo Horizonte's Pampulha airport for a flight to Montes Claros the next afternoon, I read the brochure *Vir Ver BH* (come and see BH) to see what the tourist authorities said about the city I was just leaving.

> It's a pleasure to welcome you!
> Belo Horizone puts at her friend's disposal her biggest treasure – her people, uai! Take note of the way of living, the way of walking, the soft voice, the cross-eyed gaze, get accustomed to it and stay at ease for you're among yours since you arrived and began to act and feel as a Minas Gerais native.
>
> And take care, for this Minas Gerais inhabitants way of being gets hold of you and lets you never loose; within a little while you'll want to have white coffee and to chat a little only to confirm. And so have your time, get to know, love and live this portion of Brazil we are offering you.

I'd missed the cross-eyed gaze, but those Minas Gerais inhabitants, and their little chats and soft voices, *uai!* The appeal did linger.

I read on:

> Here the climate is agreeable, even famous, and we are surrounded by mountains at an altitude of only 2600 ft.
>
> We that live in Belo Horizonte count more than 2,000,000 inhabitants and came from every big and small town in Minas Gerais. That's why Belo Horizonte, being the third biggest city in Brazil, succeeds in sheltering and conciliating different cultures in their most colourful manifestations. The capital of Minas Gerais is linked and communicate with the biggest cities in the country, from which she is almost the same distance apart. The

access is easy and it only isn't made seawise because we (still) haven't got a sea.

Go visit our parks, churches, museums, art and craftsmanship fairs, live with us on the blue days of our baroque towns and in the warm nights of the various places where the young people of Minas Gerais get together.

You have at your disposal excellent hotels, a well mounted touristic structure and a lot of warmth.

– Come, let's begin to resolve the mysteries of Minas in this young capital of the Gerais.

The plane which took me to Montes Claros was a Brazilian-made Bandeirante, so the name lives on and seems apt for this rugged twenty-seater which plies the rough inland routes, tackling the heat and storms and short, stony strips, just as it does in outback Australia.

At Montes Claros, I was met by João Freitas who works in a bank and, on the side, runs an English college.

He spoke English as well as any of the surfers I'd hung around with in Rio de Janeiro, although he'd never been abroad, not even to Miami, where most Brazilians have been if they've been anywhere.

As we drove into town with João's two little children squabbling on the back seat with the glove-puppet wombats and goannas that I'd brought, he asked me, "So, how was Beautiful Horizon?"

"Beautiful what? . . . Oh, you mean Belo? . . . It was great. Met a lot of beautiful *people*."

He had the habit of a certain type of linguistic pedant – particularly those who have not been to the country where the language they've learnt so well is spoken – of translating everything.

He would say, "I went to January River for the Christmas holidays" or "I don't think much of Saint Paul, do you?"

So I said, "Clear Mountains look rather nice, this time of year."

He started momentarily, and then realised. He had never heard anyone translate the name of his own town the way he translated the names of everyone else's.

And then I added, "If you came to Australia and if we were

speaking Portuguese (which I know we wouldn't be, but let's suppose), we wouldn't call, say, New South Wales, Nova Gales do Sul. Or Lightning Ridge . . ."

"Cordilheira do Relâmpago," he said, inserting the phrase swiftly into the conversation.

"Yes, thanks. Or Whale Beach, Praia do . . ."

"Praia *da*, not *do*, Praia da Baleia. Whale Beach."

"And we wouldn't call Broken Hill . . ."

"Morro Quebrado."

"Yes. Perhaps we would, after all," I concluded, watching a teacher's smile of satisfaction spreading smoothly across his face.

João asked me if I would like to come to his college that evening to give a lesson on Australia. The class was an advanced group, composed of about thirty people in their early 20s.

In order to narrow the focus of the talk (where do you begin when asked to talk on "Australia"?) I suggested that the students ask me questions.

As I expected, they knew almost nothing about Australia, and their questions were the equivalent of those that would be asked of a Brazilian in the very unlikely event that he were speaking to a Portuguese class in, say, Charters Towers or Dubbo — inquiries about piranhas and boa constrictors, about the Amazon, about Indians and about beautiful women dancing the lambada.

On those sorts of themes I was asked questions about kangaroos, the desert, Aborigines, boomerangs and sharks.

But a couple of students also asked some quite penetrating questions about race and immigration. The class knew that Australia, like Brazil, was a nation created by immigration, but their view was one constructed in the 1950s and earlier which had stuck. The components of this view were, firstly, that Australia desperately needed workers, secondly, because so many men went there as workers there was an acute shortage of women (the ratio of three men to one woman was thought to apply) and thirdly, that blacks were not welcome.

These were "facts" about Australia that everyone in the class understood to be true.

Living in a country which Brazilians genuinely believed to be harmoniously multi-racial and where racial prejudice was not an issue, my class found this third "fact" quite shocking.

I said that I was pleased to have the chance to bring them up to date, and proceeded to explain that Australia no longer discriminated against non-whites, but only, I regretted, against the poor and poorly educated. Immigration, I went on, was largely determined by skills and professions, wherever people came from.

"So your poor, your tired, your huddled masses, yearning to breathe free, need not bother applying," João Freitas concluded.

"No, I suppose not," I replied, feeling glum and inhuman.

"Then," enthused Freitas to his class, "the only hope is study and application and more study and application."

I quietly doubted that any amount of study and application would give these people the opportunity to visit, let alone migrate to Australia, particularly in the light of what an immigration officer at the Australian embassy in Brasilia had told me.

"Most of the illegal Brazilian immigrants in Australia — prohibited non-citizens in official parlance — and, I believe, in Canada and the US, come from Minas," he revealed. "And as a result we investigate all applications from Minas Gerais with great thoroughness."

The officer asked me if I knew of the city Governador Valadares. I did; it was on the eastern side of the Serra do Espinhaço, and I'd been through it once when I made a short-lived attempt to reach Salvador by road.

Well, Governador Valadares was very much on the hit list. While the statistics weren't to hand, it seemed that a very great percentage of the city's population lived illegally in American and those who didn't kept applying for visas to Australia and Canada.

"They haven't a hope," the officer stated firmly. "If we

see a visa application from Governador Valadares, it's 'no' from the word go. End of story."

"We're not here for the warm and friendly," he added sternly when I looked as if I might be about to put in an appeal for the town and the Mineiros in general.

But while the industrious people of Minas Gerais now find it hard to enter Australia, several industrious Australians have settled in Minas. In Montes Claros, in fact. I met some of them on a couple of occasions at their places of work in the city and at a seminary in the nearby countryside.

Barry Lambert is a 46-year-old missionary who has been in Brazil for nineteen years. It is much more home to him now than Adelaide, where his 86-year-old mother lives and where he began his working life as a painter and decorator.

"We keep strong links with Australia," he said. "My mother writes every week, and, after all, our money comes from an evangelical movement in Sydney. But Brazil – Montes Claros – is home."

Barry's wife Angela is Brazilian and their two children Belinda and Steven are far less fluent in English than they are in Portuguese.

"Belinda was 6 last time we went to Australia," Barry told me. "She talks about it a lot and told us that she would like to study in Australia one day." Both of the children have dual nationality and Barry and Angela are prepared for the possibility that they might decide to settle in Australia in the future.

Barry's main role in Montes Claros is as a counsellor at Tele Vida, a community centre which offers both face-to-face counselling and a phone-in lifeline service. Barry claimed that most of his clients were people with "low-level psychological problems, drug-addicts, alcoholics, people in marital distress and people who have been disturbed by the effects of *macumba* – a ritualistic African spiritism which is widespread in the country."

Brazil has changed dramatically in the years since he first arrived, Barry explained. "Parents who are now 35 or 40 grew up in a very different world. They are often semi-literate, whilst their children are getting a much better education as well as exposure to global culture. Brazil is just moving too fast for them. Drugs are a national calamity — and no one knows what to do about it. It's not so much things like heroin, but the sorts of drugs that you can buy or steal from a chemist shop. The kids here make lethal mixtures — with horrifying results.

"Meanwhile, millions of children are growing up in poverty — and we're seeing the sorts of problems produced in families which just can't cope."

When Barry Lambert first came to Brazil he studied Portuguese for a year in Belo Horizonte and then undertook a six-month apprenticeship under an Australian missionary in the tiny, remote settlement of Manga.

His work then took him to Cachoeira da Prata, João Pessoa and finally to Espinosa, a village in the Espinhaço mountains where he did five years of "church pioneering" — founding and maintaining a new church.

He married Angela in 1974. Steven was born in Espinosa and Belinda in Adelaide when they were there on leave. Since their most recent trip to Australia, in 1980, they have been in Montes Claros.

Barry's identification with Brazil and his enthusiasm for the people are complete. He speaks Portuguese better than English these days — and often when speaking English he slips into Portuguese either unconsciously, or when needing to explain something difficult.

He claimed that Brazilians are always accepting of foreigners, but they have had a particular liking for Australians.

"We're very similar people in many ways. The Brazilians always say that we adapt much better to life here than do others — like Americans or Germans. The Americans find the people just too laid back and the Germans can't cope with the disorder.

"What are the similarities? Well for a start, look at the geography. Brisbane is virtually Belo Horizonte, Adelaide and South Australia are Porto Alegre and Rio Grande do Sul. And then there's Rio and Sydney. Much of what the land produces is the same. Look at the products of Minas, cattle and minerals — it could be Queensland.

"The people are easy-going too, although the Latin and African influences do make a difference. They've even got bushrangers, heroes like Ned Kelly, in the form of the *bandeirantes* who opened up the inland last century."

This image of Brazil as Australia or Australia as Brazil is credible at certain times and places. The red dirt roads that penetrate the dry cattle lands and rolling hills west of Montes Claros, the eucalyptus forests which cover the sub-tropical parts of the country, the incandescent skies and the sensuous beach culture of the eastern seaboard all contribute to the image.

But there is a limit. Brazil — marginally larger than Australia — has a population of 130 million, of whom an amazing 65 per cent are under 30 years of age. There are extremes of wealth and poverty which are alien to this continent and which put Brazil on a par with India, and a political culture which — despite the apparent similarities of a federal system — is remote from Australia's. As well, there is Brazil as an outstanding multiracial society, a nation which was absorbing the descendents of slaves and non-white immigrants into the mainstream a century before Australia had even began dismantling those whites-only immigration policies which João Freitas's class had asked me about.

In terms of how people interact, Barry believes that one of the great differences between Australians and Brazilians is in the use of language. "We — and in talking to you I mean we Australians — are more direct. We say what we want with few words. Brazilians are over-polite. So although they're more . . . what's the word?"

"Informal?"

"Yes, informal. They're more informal than Argentinians, for example, but they'll go round in circles trying to please you or getting out of something. It means you have to be more patient.

"But when I'm in Australia," he added, "it takes time to

get used to how straightforward people are. They tell you what's what and there's nothing left to say."

Barry and Angela both teach part-time at the seminary in the hills just beyond the city. Angela — who is also a counsellor at Tele Vida — teaches a subject called Being a Christian Worker; Barry teaches Counselling and Psychology, Church History, Pastoral and Christian Ethics and Homoletics, which, I learned, is the art of preaching.

The principal of the seminary is Murray Faulkner. I first met him when he collected me in his old pick-up and drove me out of Montes Claros into the red haze of the afternoon. Murray has sandy Scottish-Australian looks and the quiet manners of a well-heeled grazier. We might have been driving to a sheep station in Western Australia — where he and his wife Jenny come from.

The Missionary and Theological Seminary of North Minas has been in its present location for almost six years. Its main objective is to train Brazilians to become cross-cultural missionaries who will later work in pioneering roles in many parts of the world, including Portuguese-speaking Angola and Mozambique.

"A lot of seminaries in Brazil train workers to go only into the big cities," said Murray. "Here we're training them for pioneer work. A graduate should be able to go into the bush or to a remote inland town. There is an emphasis on practical training, in agriculture or plumbing, mechanics or building."

When I remarked that in Montes Claros there seemed to be a very active Protestant community — surprising in a nominally Catholic country — Murray corrected me.

"The community is active, but in fact we're under the Brazilian average. Fifteen per cent of Brazilians are Protestants, most of them active and evangelical. Here in Montes Claros we've got about 10 per cent of the population."

"Of course," Jenny added, not wanting me to have a false impression, "only 15 per cent of Brazilians are *practising* Catholics, so we've got about the same percentages."

As missionaries, Brazilians have the advantage of coming from a "strategic" country — in evangelical terms. It is non-aligned and is identified with the "Third World", so Brazilians have openings in a lot of places. They are working in China, Iraq, Iran, Yugoslavia and India, as well as throughout Africa.

"Many of these people are professionals — doctors, teachers, engineers and agronomists — who are also trained as cross-cultural missionaries," Faulkner explained.

The seminary consists of a number of ochre brick buildings with an unfinished look about them: each is planned to allow for additions in the future. It is set on a hillside of flowering trees and shrubs — poincianas, frangipanis, hibiscus, jacarandas, South African tulips and bougainvillea — and is ringed by thickets of mango trees and gums. Below are the fields where the seminary students subsidise their tuition and accommodation fees. There are abundant fruit and vegetable gardens, and projects for fish farming and cattle raising. At present the seminary provides 70 per cent of its own food needs, as well as producing garlic, coffee and bananas for sale.

"Brazil is an educationally mad country," said Jenny. "We're being pressed to turn the college into a university, so upgrading our three-year diploma in theology to a degree. We're moving towards this, but will need more teachers and a vastly expanded library."

I was curious to know how well an overseas-run institution such as this would be received in Brazil.

"Brazilians tend to think that foreigners are meddling if they're doing something which is not helpful to the country," explained Jenny. "But we've had no opposition — only support. I think it's the fact that our work has such a strong social and practical side to it."

The Faulkners are both the children of missionaries who worked amongst the Aboriginal people in Western Australia.

"I grew up in the Warburton Ranges with the Aborigines," remarked Jenny. "I always knew knew that I'd become a missionary, but I never dreamt that it would be overseas."

It was during training at a Bible college in Tasmania that Jenny and Murray heard "the call" to Brazil. They were present at an address by an Australian who had worked in Brazil for many years, and during the talk, both decided that Brazil was the place they were being drawn to, even though neither spoke to the other about it for some time. The expectation was that they would be returning to their work in Kununurra in the Kimberleys.

They came in 1976. They spent their first year studying language in Belo Horizonte and a further year attached to a Brazilian church, to assist their acculturation. For both of them it was their first-ever visit to an overseas country, and they were here to stay. But adaptation was relatively easy, and both feel quite at home in Brazil. They speak excellent Portuguese — Murray with no accent at all. One of his roles is delivering sermons in various churches in Montes Claros and the surrounding area.

Over coffee in the Faulkners' cool living room, we shared experiences of Brazil and Brazilians. Everyone agreed that the people were happy-go-lucky, warm, musical and sports mad.

"They are also really ingenious," commented Murray. "If they can find a way around things they will — they call it doing a *jeito* or a *jeitinho* . . . a . . . what would you call that?"

"A fiddle," I suggested, "or a scam."

"Yes, but nothing too serious, although it's right through the country, at all levels."

"How reliable are Brazilians?" I asked, recalling a few experiences of my own.

Everyone laughed.

"That's not a word I'd use," commented Jenny, "and it can be very irritating. If someone says 'I'll come over tomorrow', they may or may not come."

"You couldn't say that's unreliable," said Murray, "that's just the way it is. They wouldn't accuse each other of being unreliable for that sort of behaviour."

"Something which you just have to get used to is the bureaucracy," observed Jenny. "At banks, government offices, there is so much paperwork. It drives you mad when you first come to the country — but after a while you don't even notice."

"There's so much bureaucracy here," she continued, "that they've got a federal ministry of 'debureaucratisation'."

"But you know what?" Murray asked. "They're not whingers. No matter how difficult their circumstances they don't complain — they make do."

Jenny commented that during past visits to Australia they had been saddened and disappointed by the way in which people carry on and gripe about supposed hardships which cannot compare with what most Brazilians face.

This was a point made strongly by Barry Lambert during our conversation. Searching for the right word, he had said that in Australia he has been upset by the way in which people *murmur*.

"Murmur?"

"Yes, you know, talking about what they want and what they can't get . . . they're never satisfied."

"You mean they complain a lot?"

"Yes, that's the word, *complain*. Brazilians have got so little and yet they're satisfied. The inflation rate here is something like 150 per cent a month . . . *a month!* How does that compare with Australia?"

A day or two later I met Vicki and Antonio Alkmim. Vicki is from Adelaide and Tony from Belo Horizonte. They have been married since 1981 and have two children, Daniel who is 4 and Michelle who is 7.

The fourteen years that Vicki has been in Brazil have been spent in Belo Horizonte, Espinosa, Rio Piracicaba — where Tony was a pastor — and in Montes Claros, running a Christian bookshop, teaching at the seminary and assisting with Barry Lambert's counselling service.

At the seminary she teaches world religions as well as the crafts of macramé and puppetry. Tony teaches evangelism and music. He is also involved in counselling at Tele Vida, and is a pastor in a church.

When asked why she came to Brazil, Vicki replied, "Once

I understood what Jesus had done for me — dying on the cross — I couldn't keep that love and understanding within me. I asked God 'Do you want me to stay in Australia or go overseas?' He let me know that I was to come to Brazil. I was 24."

"We will stay here indefinitely," she continued. "Montes Claros is our home. When the children are 18 they'll have to decide which nationality they want. I'd like them to know Australia so that they could decide whether to go there or not in the future — perhaps to study, perhaps to live. Being brought up with two cultures gives them a wider view of the world."

Tony was a quietly spoken man whose polite ways immediately suggested to me someone of Middle Eastern — perhaps Lebanese or Syrian — origins. I was right — although his family has been in Brazil for generations.

The Alkmims spent fifteen months in Australia a couple of years ago. How did Tony react to the country?

"The first thing I noticed was that there was no poverty, no dirt. People look well fed, everyone has cars."

"Tony remarked at the time that everything was large," interrupted Vicki, "large cars, large cows, large people."

Tony smiled with embarrassment at being caught saying things like this. I confessed that I agreed with him and he relaxed.

"I also noticed the lack of people," he added, "particularly in Adelaide."

Vicki Alkmim, like the other Australians in Montes Carlos, is fully absorbed in the life of the town and of Brazil. But I leave the last word on the country to Barry Lambert — missionary, pastor and counsellor. We had been talking about the Brazilian "cult of beauty" and its associated psychological problems, which he sometimes sees as a counsellor, and about which he had been reading in academic journals.

"Let's face it," he concluded whimsically, one eye on Angela, "cult of beauty or no cult of beauty, Brazilian girls must be the most beautiful in the world — and you're hearing that from a missionary."

Sitting next to me on the plane when I returned from Montes Claros to Belo Horizonte was a black Brazilian woman and her German husband. She used to work at the Hotel Monterey in Montes Claros and, incredibly, she remembered me from a year earlier when I stayed at that hotel. They now lived in Ecuador, where her husband was working for a European consortium, constructing a water supply system inland from Guayaquil. He reminded me of Wagner, a character in a German novel, *The Snake Tree*, that I'd recently read, and, when I told him that, he declared that before he married he had indeed been a Wagner, working on large-scale commercial ventures, but now would only accept employment on environmentally sensitive development projects.

As the plane cut through the black skies over Minas, the German inquired whether I knew that a couple of the candidates for the Brazilian presidency had raised the subject of Australia in their speeches and had asked why Brazil should not be as well developed or as successful.

"But isn't this just a new version of the old theme of the seventies?" I asked, "With the boom that was going on then, they all said that Brazil would soon overtake Canada."

"No, no," he replied. "This is something deeper . . . a sort of analysis about what went wrong during that crazy period. Those huge, irrational schemes that produced nothing but debt."

I said that I didn't think Australia was much of a model, except maybe in the area of political stability. "What about our foreign debt?" I asked. "Per capita, it's bigger than Brazil's."

"Well, the politicians don't mention that," the German concluded.

Later, as we sped into Belo Horizonte in a shared taxi, the noisy clatter of samba bouncing around the car, the German turned to me with a serious look and shouted, "Let's face it. The difference between Brazil and Australia is explained by the simple historical fact that Australia was colonised by Anglo-Saxons and Brazil by Latins who then imported millions of Africans. What else can you say?" He shrugged and winked at his wife.

At that moment we were all Anglo-Saxons, Saxons and honorary members of the club together.

Then the taxi driver, who had been sitting in his corner in silence, jiggling his head slightly to the music, suddenly broke into our smug cosiness.

"But we got samba," he remarked, turning the radio up.

A couple of mornings later, my flight to Salvador and Recife was delayed by fog in São Paulo. As I waited for hours in Belo Horizonte's extraordinarily futuristic airport, I reflected on the importance of São Paulo as the engine which kept the rest of Brazil moving, and also on the Teixeira's joke that all God had given São Paulo was fog — and exceptional people.

I also had ample time to listen to the arrival and departure announcements — in fact I was listening with special concentration hoping to hear news of my flight. In his book, *Beyond The Silver River*, the British-Irish-Spanish journalist Jimmy Burns observes: "Most airports seem designed to make you want to get out of them as quickly as possible. But Rio's was made to hold you in a sensuous grip. It was not just the smell but also its sounds. The flight information was given over loudspeakers in a soft coaxing voice that seemed to beckon you not so much to fly as to bed."

What Burns heard in Rio is also true of airports in other cities — even never-never places like Manaus and Maceió.

Again and again I heard variations of *passageiros do vôo Varig duzentos e noventa com destino a Goiânia, Brasilia, Teresina e Fortaleza, dirijam-se ao portão dez, para embarque*" spoken by women and men in a languorous purr. The effect was like that sought by some late-night radio announcers, a sort of tranquilised sexuality, but here there was often the added element of two announcers, a male and a female, each trying to out-purr the other. Oddly, until I read Jimmy Burns, I had seen no other comment on this behaviour, even though it was one of the first observations that I, too, made about the country.

It was raining rivers when I finally reached Recife late that evening in a plane that had stopped in Maceió, Ilhéus and Salvador. As I sat in my damp room in a hotel at Boa Viagem beach I wondered what had brought me here. The beaches? Well, with this cyclonic weather, they would not be welcoming. History? Yes, but what I had glimpsed from the taxi — a modern, chaotic city — was not what I had expected.

However, I had a contact, a relative of Nelson Oliveira's whose name was Madre Duarte. The next day when I visited her, at what seemed to be a community centre, I realised "Madre" was not her name, but a title. She was a nun. And what a nun! She was short, almost stocky in her simple habit, with crazy white hair and a warm captivating face. Although in her 60s, she bounded about the college with me, gave me hugs for a relative who lives in Australia and then stuffed me and another nun into her rusty Volkswagen for a tour of Recife and Olinda.

Madre Alvarenga sat in front with Madre Duarte whilst I crouched in the back, hemmed in by heaps of books and papers, huge papier-mâché masks and pieces of puppets — a leg or a head — and looked through the tiny, dripping windows at the 1001 things they were showing me.

They both spoke perfect English and, when not arguing over the exact moment to change gears or whether the gears should have just been changed, they gave me a history lesson that was like peeping into a nest of teeming ants.

"Of course, you know that Recife was once the capital of Dutch Brazil," announced Madre Duarte, one eye on the gearstick and the other on some Dutch building or statue or bridge heading our way.

"Dutch Brazil? I had no idea that . . ."

"Sure. The city was called Mauritzstad," continued Madre Alvarenga. "Here's a statue of . . ."

"It was created in the sixteenth century to trade brazil."

Had I heard that correctly? But before I could pose the question, one Madre or another had posed the answer.

"Brazil's a type of wood. The northeast, here, is where it comes from."

"The Europeans wanted it because of the red coloured dye that it produced. So that's what brought the Dutch in."

"And the Portuguese kicked them out, in the middle of the

seventeenth century. We'll just stop at this church, there are some lovely frescoes . . ."

"So the first Portuguese capital of Brazil was — guess where?"

"Right here. Well, not right here, but on top of that hill where we're going. That's Olinda."

On the road to Olinda we raced through 300 years of history in twenty fevered minutes. It was the Madres' own low-tech sound and light show.

"Now this great wild rich country . . . you know what Charles Darwin said?"

"Charles Darwin was here, too?"

"Of course. Now he said that Brazil's northeast is a great, wild luxuriant hothouse."

"Those were his words. Wild, luxuriant . . ."

"Hothouse. Well, so there was all this wood that was being shipped to Europe and the churches and palaces of Olinda were built with the wealth but . . ."

"As the supply of brazil wood diminished, the centre of the country started to move southwards . . . Oh, this church is Our Lady of Carmo . . ."

"Down towards Bahia and Sergipe. Of course, you've read Jorge Amado. You'll know that it was sugar . . ."

"Sugar was it?" I managed to squeeze in, as the car climbed the steep rise to Olinda. "What was . . ."

"Wood, sugar, gold, coffee, rubber."

"Recife, Bahia, Ouro Preto, São Paulo and Manaus."

"That's Brazilian history," concluded Madre Duarte brightly, the last two statements having speeded up the telling.

Olinda is a UNESCO world heritage site, and much of it is accessible only to pedestrians. We parked and embarked upon a fast walk. The town sits on a hill overlooking Recife and the sea; it is beautifully preserved, another example of the richness of Brazil's colonial architecture.

And Madre Alvarenga gave me an additional reason for the fame of Olinda.

"Of course, you know that the best carnival in all of Brazil takes place here, in Olinda," she explained. "It's much more lively, more real than Rio's."

"And less dangerous," added Madre Duarte.

"You'll come next time at carnival, of course," proposed Madre Alvarenga.

"And we'll take good care of you," promised Madre Duarte.

And I had no doubt at all that these wonderful and charming nuns would.

As we stood on the terrace of a 400-year-old church, the green steaming hills falling away below us to the rippling, slate-coloured Atlantic, the nuns drawing breath softly beside me, it was easy to be seduced by the *richness* of Brazil, this extraordinary, luxuriant, gaudy, multi-racial, exuberant hot-pot . . . It might have been the Anglo-Saxons that started Australia, I thought, but with all this . . .

"But from here, northwards, all the way to Pará and the equator is what we call the great triangle of drought," said Madre Duarte, calmly breaking the reverie.

"There, there's nothing but despair and suffering. It's truly a land that God has forsaken," whispered Madre Alvarenga.

> The man had an incredible voyage throughout the Amazon world. A real periplus, as he said. It made me envious. Not that I ever want to undertake such a mission. I wouldn't wander through those forests if you paid me. Lots of travelling, but nothing clarified; am I right, Nornoha?
>
> Darcy Ribeiro, *Maíra*

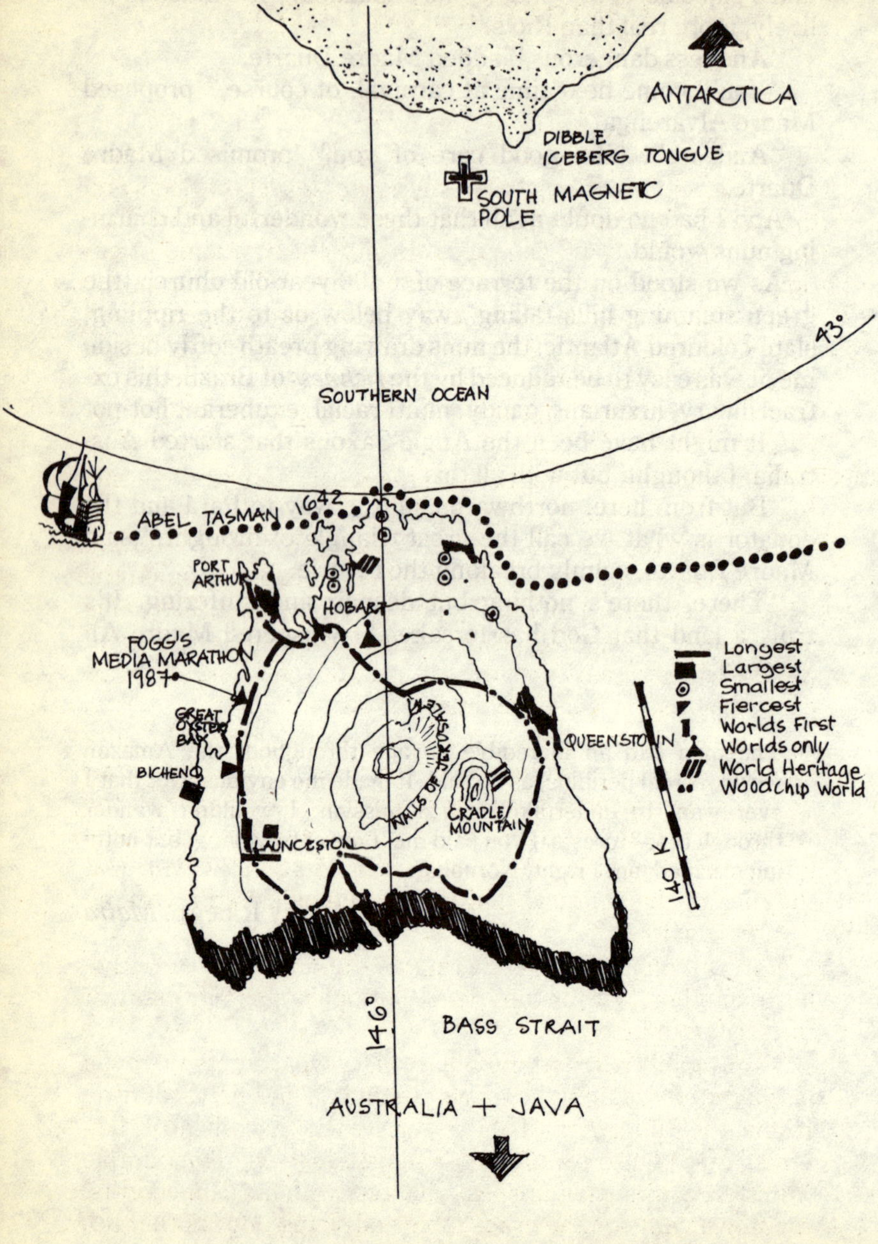
ANTARCTICA
DIBBLE ICEBERG TONGUE
SOUTH MAGNETIC POLE
43°
SOUTHERN OCEAN
ABEL TASMAN 1642
PORT ARTHUR
HOBART
FOGG'S MEDIA MARATHON 1987
GREAT OYSTER BAY
BICHENO
WALLS OF JERUSALEM
CRADLE MOUNTAIN
QUEENSTOWN
LAUNCESTON
Longest
Largest
Smallest
Fiercest
Worlds First
Worlds only
World Heritage
Woodchip World
140 K
146°
BASS STRAIT
AUSTRALIA + JAVA

Tasmania in a hurry

(Tasmania, Australia)

"God bless Evandale, God bless Queen Victoria and God bless the penny farthing." The man with the yellow fangs and top hat is shouting from the midst of a pride of dignitaries assembled on the town hall steps. Beside them, a band of antique musicians, the Jazzmanians, are wheezing away delightfully at the conclusion of an extraordinary spectacle, a penny farthing race, which is apparently the great attraction of Evandale. But who is this man, dressed as an equerry of Queen Victoria, roaring at the empty skies and at us, the gathered hacks and scribes?

And what am I doing here on the receiving end of all this roaring?

Earlier in the afternoon, at the Launceston Hotel and Casino, the Tasmanian minister for Tourism had welcomed the hacks and scribes – all participants in the so-called Tasmania Temptation Media Marathon – to his treasure island, and presented each of us with a "survival kit", which included a canned penis – in case we'd left our own at home.

"There are so many firsts in Tasmania you could fill a book," the minister had warned, and indeed, in the first hour or two of his speech, we discovered that Tasmania had the world's first mall, the oldest hotel in Australia, the oldest telephone exchange, the twelfth largest building in the world (at the turn of the century, that is) and the oldest still-working "water organ".

Forty-five pink organs bolting from their cans was, I believe, another first for the island, but one which left many of the scribes unfazed.

I am rapidly discovering what *real* travel writers do, even if where they're doing it is only Tasmania and not Castaway Island, the Maldives or Tahiti – where they usually do it. Listening – or quite plainly not listening – to the Honourable Minister, committing unspeakable acts with his canned gifts, running a game on the craps table and sizing one another up, all at the same time, are forty-five travel writers from across Australia. Newspapers, airline magazines, lifestyle magazines and radio and television stations are all represented.

Many know one another and recall the last great bash in, well, Castaway, the Maldives or Tahiti. Some, already sodden, brag that they filed their copy before leaving home, piecing it together from their PC memories, media handouts and brochures, and are now settling in for eighty hours of the usual. A few, like me, are nervous about our assignments and our deadlines, are wondering what on earth we will have to write about, and feel a bit startled in the presence of these heavies from the big city dailies and tabloids. My own commitment is to an inflight magazine for business travellers, and already the promised vision of visits to selected highpoints on the Apple Isle is disintegrating amidst uproar over still-working organs and gaming tables awash with booze.

Evandale, where I first saw and heard the thundering man in the top hat, was the group's first stop — highpoint — once our leaders ("Jabbaras", as I think they were being referred to) had told the minister to put a sock in it and dragged us from the roulette wheels and bars to the bus.

By the time our bus party reaches its next destination, the Waverly Woollen Mills, the hacks are bored with firsts and with history. We range through the showroom ("the largest wool showroom in the world"), trying, but not buying, superb jackets and rugs and then traipse absent-mindedly through the mill itself, a beautifully restored, working museum. We learn that the machinery used to prepare and weave wool has not changed much in a century and that "the Japs go ape in the showroom". I spot a sign which reads:

(1) Never let a Child collect Snakes.
(2) If a Child says he has had Contact with a Snake always Believe him.

The man with the top hat and cane now seems to have attached himself to our party and is bellowing a cheery thanks to the mill's proprietor. We board our coach and drive through a silver twilight to the Cataract Gorge, which my map shows to be almost a suburb of Launceston but which might be in the Ben Lomond National Park, such is its utter, wild beauty.

A chairlift ride (yes, the longest single-span chairlift in . . . the world? Tasmania? The Southern Hemisphere?) brings us to a restaurant where the Mayor of Launceston is to be our host. As we dismount from the chair, two young men with the glassy, inhuman appearance of presidential minders usher us through wildflowers and mist to the restaurant. They are also Jabbaras, it is alleged, part of the extraordinarily Jabbara quartet which supposedly devised this increasingly mad cavalcade on behalf of the Tasmanian Tourism Commission.

Over dinner the mayor makes a speech ("Launceston has substantially more sunshine than Melbourne"), while we make a serendipitous discovery of Tasmanian wines, a discovery that soon becomes a journey of plunder as the restaurant's cellars are looted.

The character with the fruity roar declares himself to be the ghost of Jules Verne's Phileas Fogg – Round the World in Eighty Days; Round Tasmanian in Eighty Hours – congratulates everyone in sight, including His Worship, and the *Daily Mirror* man who led the looting, and hurries us all out into the frost and dark.

By the time we reach the casino again, we've staggered along a floodlit path through some remote gorges, ridden small boats through what must have been an hallucinatory dream of still-working gunpowder works, and I've won myself a rare bottle of Heemskerk Cabernet Sauvignon in a quiz invented by the Phileas Fogg fellow. Question: *Which city has Launceston substantially more sunshine than*? I think I was the only member alive enough to answer. Even *Geo* didn't get it.

The prize itself brought forth a song of praise from Les Jabbara. "Rare as hens' dicks (I think that was the phrase) that stuff is," he chimed. "Worth at least a couple of hundred, you bastard."

Friday, 5.30 a.m. Hacks and hackettes stumble about the dark grounds of the Federal Hotel, cursing the Jabbaras and bearing memories of a feverish night of cocktails and keno in ages past. Or perhaps it was only an hour or two ago.

We are hoozled towards a great hot-air balloon and in small groups are sucked into the dawn sky to hover perilously over our colleagues already quaffing champagne on the lawns below. Then Lord Fogg bellows a speech of gratitude to the winds and in moments we are in our coach and on the road to Derby.

Here there is a fascinating museum recalling the tin mining days, a recreated village and the opportunity to pan for tin.

We race through a second breakfast of the local pasties, chips and beer, fail to find any tin, interview local identities who talk of crushed hands and missing fingers and show us the proof as casually as if it were loose teeth we were talking about, and then discover that our coach has broken down.

Coach captain Brian Hinds disappears into its works, Jabbaras I and II get on to their two-way radios, and the media stars wander forlornly about Derby in search of another drink. It's already ten and we should be throwing convict bricks in St Helens by now.

Eventually a Sid James look-alike turns up in an old school bus and we rumble away into the mountains. Somewhere in a swirling fog the "legendary Peter Burns" boards and begins yammering at us about local history, myrtle forests, ant rissoles and the civic problems of St Helens.

This, I realise, is to be the pattern for our marathon. Media I, the advance car driven by Jabbara II, would collect local dignitaries, historians, nizams and nutters and ambush the bus. The personality would be introduced by our master of ceremonies, Phileas Fogg, and would then entertain, confuse and inform the collected scribes as the bus continued on its way.

At some point lost in a haze of morning sunshine and drink we have what is termed in the program Activity With Tasmanian Devil, and an encounter with a hippy family dozing sedately around Tasmania in a bus. In a year they have covered the land between Devonport and St Helens, more or less what the media marathoners have dealt with in a morning.

But back to that devil. The creature concerned, a sports bag-sized lump of hair, black teeth and whiskers, came aboard with a pretty country girl from passing a zoo. Immediately male members appear, popping from cans, whilst hands grope, supposedly patting the bear? possum? ape? ("What the fuck is it?" is the cry from the *West Australian*.)

The sweet girl parts her teeth and warns: "This fella's got enough fangs in them jaws to take any of yers hands off, and them things stickin' outa the tins too."

"What about this one, sweetheart?" sneers a voice from the back of the bus, but the girls from *Follow Me* have got him covered.

Somewhere, too, on that road we intercept our own coach, leaving Sid James gaping after us as we head off into the micro-climate of the east coast.

Bicheno has a "milder climate than Kalgoorlie", the world's largest crabs, mutton bird pâté and superb crays, the last of which we lunch on in quantity at a seafront restaurant.

The Tasman Highway rolls before us as we travel down the coast between a jade sea and a land of round mountain horizons. Everywhere is suffused with a yellow light – which could be the lunchtime Traminer Riesling. Looking at the map I see a world of enchanting names – Scamander, Chain of Lagoons, The Friendly Beaches, Freycinet Peninsula, Schouten Island, Great Oyster Bay, Ile des Phoques, Sleepy Bay, Mistaken Cape and The Hazards – names which beautifully recall this bright, remote seabord.

And then suddenly we are in Paradise Gorge and it's time for Activity With Vicar. The Reverend Hawkins climbs aboard, and is soon up the front, fending off marriage proposals from the *Sunday Observer* and talking of local widows who sleep with shotguns, the better to keep away Tasmanian devils or gallant vicars, I suspect.

At the St John the Baptist Church in Buckland we dash in for a look at the magnificant and famous stained glass windows – many of us still wearing leis presented to us in

Bicheno and looking like junketing politicians or travel writers in Hawaii — and then retreat.

By 6 we have crossed Eaglehawk Neck and descended the Tasman Peninsula to the eerily beautiful ruins at Port Arthur. In Tasmania you cannot avoid the convict past, and here even the hard heads from the big city dailies are impressed as a park ranger shows us around and relates the hopeless dead history of the region. The sun is setting somewhere beyond the wilderness to the west, leaving the peninsular reverberating a soft, cold green as we drive past the empty churches and prisons and graveyards towards Bush Mills.

The Mathesons at Bush Mills have built a prize-winning tourist attraction, a "Living Experience in History", which reveals such activities as sawmilling, shingle-splitting and horseshoe making as they once were. It's a hands-on sort of place, although such is the state of the owners of the hands that the manager decides to keep them from the tools for their own safety and directs us to his very own steam railway.

This is no dinky toy shopping mall ride, but a dinki-di, narrow-gauge steam train that resembles the Darjeeling Mail more than anything else in the world.

It is 11 p.m. Two ugly specimens are in the bus handing out rugby jumpers and who knows what else. Who knows what they're talking about either? They direct us to a waiting launch and we proceed down a darkened, still waterway, drinking champagne, beer and whatever happens to appear on trays before us. There are dignitaries all over the place, His Royal Fogg is hooting at them all and presenting plaques by the dozen. Then someone who might be a mayor is welcoming us to Hobart.

So this is Hobart. Our launch glides across a perfect harbour towards rivers of lights cascading out of mountains and we dock at the Royal Yacht Club of Tasmania.

Our accommodation is to be at the Wrest Point Casino and matters are well organised.

"Your bags in your rooms," Les Jabbara announces.

"What're their names?" cries a wit as we disembark.

That's about all we see of Hobart. At 5 next morning,

Lauren Best Jabbara looks as if she's just stepped from the pages of Vogue as she ushers the shambles that we have become towards the coach.

When dawn breaks and I come to, we are seated for a breakfast of smoked trout and African sausage at the elegant and enchanting Prospect House in Richmond. You wouldn't believe it, but members of the party are uncorking a bottle of Gewurz-Traminer, unable to face the hour between here and the Moorilla Winery.

Set on a gentle curve of the Derwent, Moorilla is producing some of Australia's finest cool-climate wines. Its founder, Claude Alcorso, welcomes our disreputable caravan with a poetic and effortless discourse on wine, Italy, multiculturalism and Tasmania. "I looked at this beautiful landscape," he says, "and saw that something was missing: the grape."

"Yeh, well where's our fuckin' grape?" mutters the *Sunday Telegraph*.

Just in time, Alcorso junior appears with a dozen or two bottles for tasting, whilst in the garden the famous Czech-Australian musician, Jan Sedivka, turns up with some of his pupils and they treat us to an astonishing violin and piano recital.

"We're part of one world after all," sighs Mr Alcorso, as around him even cynical subs go wet at the centre, and Richard Jabbara, his hands jabbing viciously at something in his pockets, suppresses the urge to interrupt and hurry us back to our bus.

The spell of Moorilla lasts just until Peter McKay of Devil Jet Boats comes aboard. He is a noisy, witty sort of character — "gracious, what an appalling ocker you are," Lord Fogg is drawn to observe — and what he has arranged for us is guaranteed to irradiate our hungover synapses.

The Derwent River, which only a few kilometres downstream is wide, serene and tamed, is here, at New Norfolk, infested with rocks, rapids and submerged trees, and this is the stretch chosen by Mr McKay to demonstrate the thrills of white-water jet-boating.

In knots of five we take off and skim at 80 dangerous

kilometres per hour along a watercourse that would worry a trout, our driver leering at us menacingly through a pair of novelty glasses with hideously rotating eyes. His speciality is to rocket you into deep water, pitch the engines into reverse and spin the boat about on nothing, leaving your breakfast surging towards your own hideously rotating eyeballs.

Almost everyone — Jabbaras, minders, PR princesses and journalists, even get-stuffed *Belles* and *Harpers* — is enthralled. Only the *Mirror* scribe, a clapped-out relic of Phuoc Tuy, remains in his corner of the bus, an esky beside him, retelling stories from the war zone to the empty seats.

Later we zoom around Hamilton, marvelling at its convict-built churches, legal opium fields ("the only ones in the developed world", we're told) and the "world's only Roman Catholic church with just one door" (so the felonious Fenians couldn't escape).

In Glen Clyde House there are skilfully crafted souvenirs in wood, leather and ceramics, a lecture reminding us that "there are more craftspersons in Tasmania than in any other state", and delicious Devonshire teas. Halfway through our scones, however, the minders from Media I appear to hustle us all away.

Our coach drifts off into a heartland of oscillated light and shade, of forests of pepper spruce and oak and of poplar-lined highways. Up into the high lakes country where the public relations man from the hydro-electric commission bounds on board to find us all asleep.

No one stirs as he lectures as sternly on hydro-power, the source not only of Tasmania's abundant electricity but also of most of its politics. His lecture hovers like a sombre flame over the dead paparazzi, but soon dissipates into the ambient jug of brandy and nicotine.

After a desultory visit to the Tarraleah Power Station, we collect Mr Jason Garrett, who busies himself at the front of the bus like an eccentric flight attendant, dispensing flies and other fishing paraphernalia from the pockets of his flack jacket.

Mr Garrett is the owner of the London Lakes trout fishing

resort, which is currently occupied by a posse of American fishermen who can't believe the easy abundance of brown trout in the nearby lakes.

Even more they can't believe what this Volvo coach has just delivered. Forty-five men and women, correspondents all from their own private war zones, stumble into the lodge's living room and proceed to savage a couple of tables of food and drink thoughtfully provided by the Garretts.

The Americans just stand there, gulping the air like a catch of brown trout themselves, whilst the Garretts, the Jabbaras, even Fogg himself — now kitted out for fishing like Lord Fogg of the Flies — run around, their hands held high and open, explaining.

They're *journalists*, you see, from the *mainland*.

The Garretts and their fish inhabit a cool wilderness, close to the centre of the island, and the sub-alpine sources of Tasmania's great rivers. "Lunch" over, Mr Garrett escorts a small group of enthusiasts to the lakes where the rivers begin whilst the remainder watch videos and work their way through the lodge's port cellar. One hapless journo, employed by the *Hobart Mercury* and a string of radio stations, has to file four reports a day, so quiet moments such as these find him on the phone dictating stories to some grumbling copytaker whilst the rest of us have already written our one contribution or are still looking for an angle.

Forty minutes later, during our customary pre-departure speeches, Jason Garrett is congratulated on his fine trout, and on the fact that here, for once, we were permitted to sit down for a few moments. However, even as Phileas Fogg roars, Richard Jabbara is sliding his finger across his throat, meaning: wind it up, craphead, Lake St Clair is waiting.

Bounded by Mounts Rufus and Olympus, Lake St Clair broods silently at the eastern edge of a vast national park. Once there, our mad cavalcade boards a boat and we roam about in the clouds for an hour or so, catching glimpses of the awesome ranges lined up to the west.

Back on shore, and in the asylum of our bus, an eager young man from Huon Adventures is raving about rafting on the Franklin. He is to be our guide and guard for a rafting run down to Derwent Bridge, but Les Jabbara, assessing the state of the marathoners, the grisly weather and the time, cuts him short, flicks him a plaque, and deposits him and his wetsuit out into the frost in the midst of a great forest — the Walls of Jerusalem in one direction, Antarctica in another and not even an echo from Phileas Fogg to keep him company, as we grind away into the highlands on the Lyall Highway, headed for Queenstown.

Through the sublime wilderness of the Surprise Valley and down Victoria Pass to an altogether different wilderness — the devastated lands and mountains around Queenstown. We are joined by a Mr Prowse, former mine-worker and now indefatigable tour guide, who embarks upon an eighty-minute marathon of his own — a monologue that accompanies us to pit heads and museums, down valleys scorched grey and red, across hills with the appearance of far-away planets, and into Queenstown itself, a clustered and closed weatherboard settlement with a terrible history, a miserable present and who knows what sort of future.

"Now the grade on both them lines is about one in two hundred," intones Mr Prowse. "Just enough fall to bring the water out, a little bit of assistance for the loco with the loaded rakes . . ."

This most comprehensive retelling of the story of Mount Lyall, Queenstown and the Southern Hemisphere is broken only long enough for Mr Prowse to reveal that he doesn't speak at all at home. "The wife won't have it," he confesses, "so I save it all up for the tours."

"Yeh, well we won't have it either," interrupts some purple grub from the Northern Territory. "Give him the flick."

Fortunately for Mr Prowse, more respectable men and women of the media intervene to save his spiel and . . .

". . . now see them pits just to the left of that great heap of slag, well the grade in them is just over . . ."

Saturday night at the Empire Hotel. Colourful local identities put on a booze-up for colourful media stars. Guests mingle awkwardly and exchange catarrhal looks and words, whilst soaking up beer and listening to a leaden band of troglodytes.

Ducking for cover, I share a drink in a corner with two miners, both in their eighties. One had founded Queenstown's excellent mining museum. The other had been a tour guide for some time.

'Now the grade on both them lines," begins the latter, "is about one in two hundred. Just enough fall to bring the water out . . ." Luckily our travelling panjandrum, in the most extravagant costume ever seen in western Tasmania, embarks upon a booming speech of thanks, and I am spared a trip down the pits again.

It is 4 o'clock on Sunday morning and Shane Jabbara is prowling the motel like some shadowy steppenwolf, driving the slick, stricken animals of the media to their bus.

When we emerge from the wilderness of a brief, tortured sleep in the frozen highlands, it is to find a man dressed like the Gold Stick in Waiting or the Usher of the Black Rod ranting at us from the front of the bus about taxes, kingdoms and royal families descended from God knows where.

Who is he? What is he? *And what the fuck's he on about?*

Even Lord Fogg, partial to a bit of vice-royalty and royal vice himself, finds this self-proclaimed prince, or duke, or ayatollah a bit much and glares at him bodefully, while noting with approval that the hacks in his care are not impressed in the slightest and are beginning to give the ponce a bit of Derryn Hinch.

However, it seems that the prince in question has invited us all to his palace? castle? county seat? suburban house in Strahan? for breakfast and so the rubbishing is cut short. When we arrive, the paparazzi, curtseying furiously, range through the house and gardens, eat his breakfast and give the loony no more time or thought.

Our real excitement in this part of the world is a ride in a high-powered cruiser down Macquarie Harbour – the mouth of the Franklin and Gordon Rivers – to Hell's Gates, the treacherous bars separating the lake from the Southern Ocean. This is an area with a fascinating and violent past and an enchanting present, for it is at the western rim of a unique World Heritage area.

The boffin on board, telling the story of Macquarie Harbour to our party, quotes historian Manning Clark's account of the establishment of the isolated prison settlement on Sarah Island.

"It was hoped," he reads with grim enthusiasm, "that by segregating irreclaimables and worst offenders at penal settlements at Macquarie Harbour where daily labour could be rigorously enforced and where nothing to excite their cupidity could be found, that society could be protected from their violence and their crimes, while they themselves would be saved from further degradation as well as those abominations of men driven by terror and privation into the ways of the beast."

"Heh, heh, heh," is the soft-pedal response from Lord Fogg to this history lesson, as he considers his own abominable band of irreclaimables.

To a bit of natural history now. A grizzled old stump of a man comes forward with a broadboard in one hand and a 10 centimetre bonsai stick in the other.

The reptiles focus hard on him, trying to get the point. But his lesson is appallingly simple. The stick is a baby huon pine. The breadboard, what it might become.

"From this to this," the old piner shouts, waving his materials at us, "takes about a thousand years. Yer huon grows only a coupla feet a century!"

Geo and *Simply Living* are horrified and begin to question the man to establish the priorities he works towards today, whilst the rest turn their attentions to the third of our guests — and one of the few females to whom we've been introduced — a representative of the Huon de Kermadec Historical Society.

So, as our hydrofoil rushes towards the boiling froth at Hell's Gates, Ms A. Bergmann lectures us on aspects of local history, checking our concentration with little barbed tests every few minutes.

As there was now a fair amount of froth inside the boat as

well, I remember little of her talk except the observation that the tragic demise of the Aborigines of Tasmania may have begun in 1772 with the arrival of the French explorer Marion du Fresne. In what could only have been a Gallic display of friendliness, the boating party that went ashore proceeded to kiss the Tasmanians they encountered on both cheeks. This so unsettled the natives — who supposed quite reasonably that the intruders were *tasting* them with a view to eating the tastiest — that fighting ensued and Tasmania's long century of darkness and misunderstanding began.

This is the best explanation for anything that the hacks have ever heard and, in the ensuing pandemonium, even the firm-lipped Ms Bergmann permits Lord Fogg and a few others to taste her own appetising cheeks.

Two hours of oblivion later, we are back in the bus and running through a vastness of sand-dunes and forest towards the now desolate mining and timber town of Zeehan. Here an 88-year-old youngster named George Smith whips us around the finest local history museum that I've ever seen, and then it's three cheers, farewell and on the road again.

The countryside everywhere is so beautiful that the red-eyed gonzos don't bother to look anymore. Our tour is going downhill fast, and there's just time for a final thrill before it disintegrates totally.

At Wynyard airport we board a chartered F.27 — in the company of the charming burghers of Burnie — for a jaunt over the Bass Strait coastal strip and then inland to the Cradle Mountain National Park.

The day is a bright and still 25 degrees, and the flight is superb, the plane skimming at only a few thousand feet over farmlands as pretty as pastels, and then inland to the magnificent and remote temperate rainforests and alpine estates. Only the sound of the Ten Network barking into paper bags behind me breaks the reverie induced by this astonishing panorama.

That night our seedy party is to travel to Melbourne aboard the *Abel Tasman*. Three of us, however, with deadlines in Sydney, are to fly home from Launceston, and so it is with Lord Fogg's panegyric in our honour echoing throughout the city that we depart from Burnie.

*   *   *

In November 1642, Abel Tasman anchored his ships, *Zeehan* and *Heemskerk*, off the south-west coast of the island and proceeded to note in his diary: "This land being the first we have met within the South Sea, and not known to any European nation, we have conferred on it the name of Anthoony van Diemenslandt, in honour of the Hon. Governor General, our illustrious master."

Our own experience of Van Dieman's land had been brief, as Tasman's was, but somewhat noisier. Like Abel Tasman, we had found a place that was little known a few hundred kilometres across Bass Strait, let alone to any European nation.

These sober thoughts preoccupied me as our jet climbed out of Launceston and tracked across the edge of the Tasman Sea towards Sydney. And, finally, I wondered what on earth I would find to write about.